D0899119

Living with Hitler

Front view of the Berghof. On the first floor you can spot Hitler's study, with its three doors leading to the balcony. Situated to the left of the main building are the staff rooms and the dining room. The hall, on the ground floor of the main building, boasted a window of huge proportions offering a breathtaking view to the Untersberg.

Living with Hitler

Accounts of Hitler's Household Staff

Karl Wilhelm Krause, Herbert Döhring
& Anna Plaim

Introduction by Roger Moorhouse

Translation by Eva Burke

Greenhill
Books

Living with Hitler: Accounts of Hitler's Household Staff

This edition published in 2018 by Greenhill Books,
c/o Pen & Swords Books Limited, 47 Church Street,
Barnsley, S. Yorkshire, S70 2AS

www.greenhillbooks.com
contact@greenhillbooks.com

ISBN: 978-1-78438-297-1

Publishing history
The newly revised and corrected edition of *Kammerdiener bei Hitler: Im Schatten der Macht* by Karl Wilhelm Krause was first published in German in 2016; *Hitlers Hausverwalter* by Herbert Döhring was first published in German in 2013; *Bei Hitlers: Zimmermädchen Annas Erinnerungen* by Kurt Kuch was first published in German in 2003

CIP data records for this title are available from the British Library

Typeset in Garamond by Wordsense Ltd, Edinburgh
Printed and bound in England by TJ International Ltd, Padstow

Contents

Illustrations

Introduction

What was it like to work for Adolf Hitler? Not as a minister, or a diplomat or other elevated, esteemed position but as a servant – a housekeeper, a chambermaid or a valet – the silent, the unseen; those who saw Hitler every day, in every mood, in every circumstance; those who brought him his breakfast, made his bed or oversaw the smooth running of his household. Such lowly figures rarely feature in conventional histories. Their memoirs, when published at all, are rarely considered able to compete with those of the 'great and the good' – the presidents, prime ministers and field marshals – for importance or significance. But they too have their place in the narrative; they too have a valid story to tell. This volume makes that point with full force. It is the memories of three of Hitler's closest staff members: his former housekeeper at his Berghof home, Herbert Döhring; one of the Berghof's chambermaids, Anna Plaim; and his former valet Karl Wilhelm Krause.

The first of them, Herbert Döhring, responded to an advert asking for tall men to join a military unit and ended up serving in the *SS-Leibstandarte* – Hitler's bodyguard division – before being appointed in 1936 as housekeeper at the Berghof, which was Hitler's home on the Obersalzberg above Berchtesgaden. There, Döhring acted as a 'major-domo', responsible for the smooth running of the household, even through the extensive remodellings and expansions that were carried out on the building at that time. In this capacity, he developed a very close relationship with his master, so much so that, in later life, he made occasional appearances – jowly and thickly accented – in television documentaries on the Third Reich. He knew Hitler's foibles, knew his security arrangements, knew his favourite colour (green) and knew when he was best avoided – Hitler humming

11

was safe, Hitler whistling was dangerous. Hitler, he said, could be unpredictable, moody, brutal and benevolent, but he was the boss – *der Chef* – and Döhring was doing his duty, just as he would have done, he said, if he had been asked to serve Stalin or Churchill.

Anna Plaim (née Mittlstrasser) was also employed at the Berghof, and worked under Döhring's supervision. Like him, she came into Hitler's service largely by chance. A twenty year old from rural Lower Austria, she was appointed to the staff of the Berghof in 1941, thanks to a cousin who was well-connected with the Nazi Party in Munich. Once there, and once she got over the shock of her appointment, she struck up a close relationship with Eva Braun – Hitler's secret 'mistress' – and, crucially, recorded events in a series of letters home, which survived the war and inform her contemporary recollections. As well as serving as a chambermaid, she also seems to have been unable to resist the temptation to probe a little deeper into the lives – and the wardrobes – of her employers, by trying on Hitler's shoes, and pulling torn-up photographs out of Eva Braun's wastepaper basket.

Her account – covering many aspects of Hitler's household and his entourage, including Rudolf Hess and Heinrich Hoffmann – is gossipy and forthright and is especially interesting for the wealth of insights that it provides about Eva Braun – her personality and the nature of her relationship with Hitler. The Berghof, Plaim says, was Braun's gilded cage – an oasis of plenty amid the madness of war.

The third of the trio is Karl Wilhelm Krause. Originally from the German Navy, Krause was appointed as Hitler's valet in summer 1934, a position he would hold for the next five years. In this role, Krause was perhaps as close to his master as anyone would get: waking him in the morning, serving him breakfast, managing his wardrobe and travelling with him wherever he went. The Hitler he describes is a complex, multilayered personality who could be impatient, exacting and fickle, yet had a good sense of humour and enjoyed a joke. Hitler, he said, was 'like a father' to him.

Hitler's daily routine, Bohemian and dissolute though it was, is now rather well known, but it is nonetheless described in detail by Krause. Hitler, he explains, rose late, ate a cursory breakfast of warm milk and biscuits, and then retired again to read the newspapers or deal with government or party business. After lunch, meetings with his guests or visitors were usually followed by afternoon tea, where Hitler often enjoyed *Stollen* (German fruit cake). The evenings, where they were not taken up with official engagements, habitually ended with a film showing.

Hitler, Krause reminds us, was a keen film buff, who – as well as keeping up with Hollywood's offerings – viewed all of the output of Germany's studios, often passing his critiques onto his Minister for Propaganda, Joseph Goebbels. His favourite film, according to Krause, was the 1935 drama *The Lives of a Bengal Lancer* starring Gary Cooper.

Perhaps more than the other two memoirists, Krause brings the reader closer to an appreciation of the sort of person Hitler was. He gives ample details of their relationship: the lighter moments, the daily difficulties and the squabbles – not least the confrontation that ultimately cost him his job. Importantly, he also outlines Hitler's methods of delegating and giving unspecific orders, emphasising the degree to which his master existed within a bubble that became increasingly remote from the outside world.

These three accounts – brought together here for the first time – were originally published individually, in German, between 2003 and 2013; two were in the form of transcribed interviews, and one was a straightforward narrative. They represent, perhaps, the last wave of publications of the memoirs of Hitler's former staff – a topic that had been given new life by the success of the 2002 memoir of his secretary Traudl Junge, *Bis zur letzten Stunde* (Until the Final Hour). Like Junge – who died in 2002 – all three memoirists survived into the new century; Döhring and Krause both passed away in 2001, while Plaim – remarkably – is a creditable ninety-eight at the time of writing.

The accounts that they give complement one another well, being essentially the recollections of intimate observers; those who were present but uninvolved, forever at one remove from the momentous historical events upon whose fringes they stood. In this respect, they chime with the similar memoirs of Heinz Linge (Hitler's other valet), chauffeur Erich Kempka and secretary Christa Schroeder, all of whom served for many years on Hitler's staff.

Inevitably, the question that many readers will ask is 'what did they know?' It is a fair point. Surely, readers will assume, people who were present at the very heart of the Third Reich must have learnt something – via a whispered exchange, perhaps, or a discarded document – of the heinous crimes then being committed in Germany's name. However, that assumption presupposes that the Third Reich functioned like a normal state, with robust discussions at a governmental level and a verifiable paper trail. But it didn't. As Karl Wilhelm Krause indicates, orders from Hitler were often given verbally and could be astonishingly vague – feeding a rather chaotic bureaucratic system.

So the answer to the question 'what did they know about the Nazis' crimes?' is, frustratingly, 'not very much'. There were a few indications that – in retrospect – hinted at dark deeds, not least Martin Bormann's vindictive, high-handed behaviour, but beyond that little of any substance. We must conclude – paradoxically perhaps – that the gilded cage of the Berghof, or of Hitler's entourage, was not the best vantage point from which to view the true murderous nature of Nazism.

Indeed it was Martin Bormann who – as much as Hitler – played a key role in the lives and careers of the Berghof staff. As Hitler's personal secretary, Bormann assumed responsibility for the day-to-day running of the entire Berghof area, as well as overseeing the building's expansion in 1936. In this capacity, he became known as the 'Lord of the Obersalzberg', and sought to exercise authority over the Berghof staff, and was responsible for the dismissal of Anna Plaim in 1943, considering her unsuitable for service because of her parents' religious faith. Herbert Döhring also got on the wrong side of Bormann, and only earned the latter's respect through his robust self-defence.

For all his machinations, however, Bormann was ultimately not responsible for Döhring and Krause leaving Hitler's service. Döhring requested to be allowed to take up a combat role, and so left the Berghof in 1943, while the circumstances of Krause's dismissal in 1939 are rather more bizarre, involving a missing bottle of mineral water and a white lie.

The three accounts presented here may not have the gravitas of a prime minister's memoir, or the lofty world view of a president's, but they are nonetheless instructive and in their own way revelatory. In different ways, they all demonstrate the capricious nature of life at the epicentre of the Third Reich, where a mistake or a rumour or an allegation could end one's employment forthwith. And yet there were no regrets; all three remembered their employment with a degree of fondness. Krause even met Hitler again after his dismissal and was warmly received by him. All three memoirists were starry-eyed, of course; blinded to some extent – as so many other ordinary Germans were – by their proximity to their Führer, but what is most interesting about their accounts is that very ordinariness. These were very ordinary, normal Germans – cast into extraordinary times.

Roger Moorhouse
January 2018

Translator's Note

Living with Hitler offers us the eyewitness reports of three people, all of whom worked for Hitler's household, and close to the dictator himself. While in their respective roles they obviously had first and foremost to be professionals, and thus not distinguish themselves in any noticeable way through their individual personalities, in my translation I nevertheless endeavoured to convey a flavour of who these people really were, of their family background and their education. All of this is, of course, reflected in their use of language – above all because the book is based on interviews, letters and personal memories.

The two men, Herbert Döhring and Karl Wilhelm Krause, had a solid and strict upbringing, followed by a military education. They came from working-class, traditional homes of the early 1900s, an era when youth was brought up to observe, ask few questions, respond in brief sentences, obey and not indulge in superfluous embellishments. This is reflected in their use of short sentences, their militarily precise language, factual rather than narrative, with little in the way of expansive language or filler words. Anna Plaim (née Mittlstrasser), younger than Krause and Döhring, came from a more comfortable Austrian family, one that was politically aware and close-knit. Anna worked mostly with women, female friends and indeed directly for a woman, which is reflected in a more nuanced use of language. Her accounts reflect more introspection, more observations, more humour and an eye for detail and subtleties.

The stories of both men – one a soldier, the other a sailor – remind us of entries into a logbook: facts, figures, precise timing, dates and a blow-by-blow description of events and conversations exchanged, no self-doubting or questioning. In contrast, Anna's book consists of personal letters; she is telling a story.

The reader will find a mixture of past and present tenses. When our protagonists tell their story, they occasionally get so caught up in the moment that it was as if they relived it in the present.

In Krause's case, he would also often refer to 'we' rather than just 'I'. He seems to have often identified with Hitler, his boss, and it is not surprising that he was called Hitler's *Schatten* – his shadow.

Similar to others at the Berghof, all three were grateful to have found a position in a household in those difficult times of unemployment. This is reflected in my conscious translation of certain phrases, particularly Döhring's use of the German *Chef* to Boss, as opposed to 'Führer' or 'chief'.

Finally, I was keen to convey a sense of the German language as it was used during the Third Reich – thus leaving many expressions, words and titles untranslated. For the most part it is a terminology never before, nor since, used in the German language.

Eva Burke
January 2018

Part 1

The Valet of Hitler:
In the Shadow of Power

Karl Wilhelm Krause

The Valet of Hitler:
In the Shadow of Power

How I Came to Work for Hitler

On 2 July 1934 the Chief of the Naval Flotilla and the then commander of the minesweepers dispatched me to the Naval Department, which was part of the Reich Ministry's Defence Department and located in Berlin, but not without first assuring me of his very good wishes for my future. I was only to report upon my arrival, and then receive further instructions of how to register at the Reich Chancellery. Full of trepidation and with mixed feelings, I travelled from Kiel to Berlin. Though somewhat familiar with the streets of the city, I certainly did find myself having to ask the way to the Reich Chancellery. I was directed to where the Navy Department's Chief of Staff worked, and he, welcoming me with utmost friendliness, went on to present me to several higher-ranked officers, among them the Grand Admiral of the Navy, Dr Erich Raeder and von Blomberg, Commander-in-Chief of the Wehrmacht.[1]

I was asked to answer several questions and was then shown the process of how to register with the Reichskanzler, Adolf Hitler. I was told to contact him the following day. After that I was formally dismissed and ordered to take myself to what had once been a utility building for the Prussian Railway Regiments in von Papen Street.[2]

Today, I can only smile when I think back to that time, with all those feelings of tense expectations and thoughts as to what the next day would bring, rumbling through my head. I was handed an envelope on which was written: 'Report to SS-Oberführer and Adjutant Schaub at 10 o'clock at the Reich Chancellery.'[3]

I got up at 6.45 a.m., cleaned and brushed my uniform, put on the shirt I usually wore for parades and was ready to report by 8 a.m. At half past nine, I turned into the Wilhelmstrasse, waited there for a few minutes, took a deep breath and then resolutely stepped up to the door of the Reich Chancellery. At reception, I stated my purpose and said that I was expected by a 'Herr Schaub' (at the time I had no knowledge about ranks or titles of either of the SS or the SA).[4]

One of the reception staff accompanied me across the small courtyard to Hitler's private apartment, where I was left in the care of the SS officer on duty. This man then led me to the common room of the Begleitkommando and asked me to wait. Two SS men were sitting there, playing chess. At first, they just glanced up and threw me some sceptical looks. Later on, some other men dressed in civilian clothes came in, as well as some SS men. Everyone then briefly introduced themselves.

So much was totally new to me and I slowly had to come to grips with them. Many questions troubled me: what was I doing at the Reich Chancellery and what was my role in the navy? Every time the door opened, I thought that I would be asked to come in. When it slowly became known that I was to become Adolf Hitler's valet, a general discussion broke out, with one person pointing out one thing he thought was relevant, while the next one disagreed and thought a totally different issue needed to be considered. Overall, most of the people there were kind to me and thus were good enough to inform me that Hitler wasn't actually in Berlin at the time, but in East Prussia. He had made this trip to Gut Neudeck[5] in order to brief the Reichspräsident von Hindenburg 'about the whole issue', referring to the Röhm Putsch. From comments made I gathered that his plane would be back in Berlin around three o'clock.

Then followed my first lunch in the dining room of the Begleitkommando. Two orderlies were waiting on tables, serving platters by placing them on the table and then clearing the dirty plates. Everybody had to help themselves to food. For drinks, we were offered beer, orange juice and fizzy water. Everybody could eat as much as they wanted. Since the first excitement and the tension of the past two days had now eased, and because introductions hadn't been delayed, I was actually able to eat my meal properly and did so with a full and hearty appetite. Besides, everyone was now fully apprised of the fact that a marine had joined the group, and as a result they treated me with the utmost friendliness.

After the meal we went off to the common room, where most people seemed to be playing a game of cards, chess or billiards, until the moment when, finally, information filtered through from the airport: 'The plane with the Führer on board has just landed.' Within a split second, life returned to the room and everyone disappeared in an instant, apart from two men. In answer to my question regarding what all these people might be ordered to do, I was told that each one of them had their assigned role and position for when Hitler arrives: firstly, they were to close off the street from the public, and, secondly, they were to open it up for Hitler. Once again, I was overcome with worry as to how all this would pan out. I asked one of those men to show me a spot from which I could observe the Führer's arrival. We were just about to leave the room – I was still standing in the doorway – when Adolf Hitler passed right in front of me at a distance of barely one metre.

I stood to attention. Hitler greeted me with his very deep voice saying 'Heil.' He was followed by a few men from his staff whom I, of course, did not yet know. A few minutes later Dr Goebbels arrived and went to the rooms situated at the far end, where the other men had also gathered. An SS officer had announced me to Oberführer Schaub and returned with the information that the gentlemen wished to eat first, and that thereafter Schaub would appear.

I waited for about three-quarters of an hour until Schaub came back and informed me that the Führer wouldn't have any time today for me. I should report back tomorrow morning, was the message. I decided to remain a little longer in the common room. This gave me an opportunity to get to know nearly everyone attached to the Begleitkommando; as it happened, the future chauffeur Kempka was also part of that group. He made it his business to look after me and also offered to take me back to my accommodation later that day. But first I was encouraged to join them for a walk through Berlin. Initially I made some excuses, but these were soon dispelled by everyone in the room. That evening, we would all gather once again in the Reich Chancellery.

This place seemed to be a mingling opportunity for just about everybody; the entire squadron of the NSKK[6] was there, plus all the members of both Begleitkommandos, as well as others who belonged to quite different ministries.

Occasionally, people belonging to the Begleitkommando would bring along their friends and acquaintances, even those whom they may have met only for the first time that day and even just a few minutes before coming. This probably explained why policemen, who happened to be on duty close to the Reich Chancellery, would also join these gatherings. As far as female guests were concerned, only secretaries would frequent the Chancellery. In answer to my question, do all those people enjoying the meals belong to the Begleitkommandos, or do they work in the offices, I was given to understand that most didn't even belong to staff at all, and that they actually weren't even employed here. 'But they obviously must have known one of the gentlemen, and seeing that they don't have to pay anything, and on top of which they received a very good meal, it just makes sense that they sort of join,' I was told. As mentioned, all it took was a tiny amount of cheek.

This all changed only with the outbreak of war, when food ration cards were introduced. Before that, nearly anybody who was the tiniest bit plucky would come here to eat without any problem at all.

That evening, I did a little tour through Berlin along with Kempka,[7] with whom, it turned out, I was going to spend quite a bit of my off-duty times during the following years. Two other men from the Begleitkommando joined us. Kempka had a small car at his disposal and together we visited a few pubs, calling it a day just as it got to midnight. Based on my request to have an early night, as I had to be fresh the next day, I was dropped off at my barracks. Even though the main events, which I had imagined would happen that same day, turned out to be cancelled, it had been quite a difficult twenty-four hours for me.

I went to the room where I was to spend the night and realised that it was already occupied by another person. He was asleep. By looking at his clothing and his cap ribbon, on which was written *Panzerschiff Deutschland* (Battleship *Deutschland*), I knew that he too was from the navy. Boy was I surprised when I found out the next day that he was in Berlin for the same reason I was. My comrade turned visibly cooler towards me when I told him that I had already been to the Reich Chancellery the day before and had managed to experience quite a bit while there, getting a sense of how things worked. But when I told him that I was actually meant to report formally only today, we became good comrades. We scrubbed up and set off.

We were visibly both deep in thought, weighing up the advantages each one of us had over the other. As far as body height was concerned, I most certainly was a good head taller than him.

What happened then at the Reich Chancellery was pretty much the same as what had occurred the day before. We were scheduled to report to the Reichskanzler but our appointment had been dropped and delayed until the next day. Nor did it take place on the third or fourth day. We were finally called in on the fifth one. What was comforting to both of us, though, was the fact that we had spent several days with these gentlemen at the Reich Chancellery. On some level we no longer took anything much to heart. We also sort of convinced ourselves that we would both be able to stay on in Berlin and also go into service together. Neither of us knew, of course, what shape or form this employment might actually take. But as we were honest-to-god veritable lords of the sea, we knew how to manage each and every situation. We therefore looked forward to everything that was still about to happen and were feeling extremely confident.

On the fifth day, it was already towards evening when SA Gruppenführer Brückner[8] enters the waiting room and asks: 'Where are the two water rats? The Führer is expecting a report.' Brückner arranged my comrade and myself so we walked alongside him, one on his right, the other on his left.

He did this in a very pleasant and humorous way and it really meant a lot to us because initially we had been feeling rather self-conscious. Some years later, Brückner still proved to be the calm oasis amidst this rather intimidating sea of men. You could go to him for advice on anything and at any hour of the day. He seemed to understand everyone and he was always willing to help anyone who needed it. He was the only one with whom one could get along well. He never favoured anybody, he didn't care if someone was an old Party member or not, or whether he even belonged to the Party. He was simply the solid adjutant who didn't mind taking action while fully aware of the risk he would take by doing so. In doing so, he most favourably stood out from many of the others, in fact from most people, who would all too often either just reject everything or else focus exclusively on advancing their own interests and career. Based on this impeccable way of handling himself, Brückner was inevitably going to be shunned and cut off by these particular men. Plots against him were so serious that it actually led to his suspension from duties later on. I will refer to these particular characters who were involved in his fate in due course.

We were taken upstairs to just outside the doors to the private rooms, where Brückner asked us to wait while he disappeared behind one of the doors. We stood there for some ten minutes, but it felt like hours. Then the door opened and Brückner appeared on the threshold, before taking my comrade inside. I was left behind, on my own. Casting my mind back to that moment, I am incapable of reconstructing precisely what thoughts were going through my head during those minutes. After a while Brückner brought my comrade back outside, before going back inside, and so both of us were once again standing in front of the door. I never got answers to the questions I put to my comrade before Brückner emerged and asked that I step inside. He himself did not come with me. The room I had entered was the library. The light was dim. Behind a long table, covered with stacks of books, newspapers and quite a few other documents and lit by a standing lamp which only shone onto a certain spot, was Adolf Hitler, standing with arms folded across his chest. While I was still in the middle of announcing myself, 'Head sailor Karl Wilhelm Krause, from the 1. Räumbootshalbflotille, reporting as ordered', Hitler walks towards me and greets me with a handshake. He then asked me whether I knew the reason for being there. 'Yes', I answered. Some questions then followed about my background, my occupation, my parents and whether I genuinely would look forward to assuming my duties in his service. Asking me whether I was a member of the NSDAP he proceeded to answer the question himself, before I even had so much as a chance to respond with a 'no'. 'Well, quite', he said, 'the Reichswehr, or rather the navy, has taken an oath not to take up political action. And that's how it should be.'[9]

The whole exchange lasted perhaps four to five minutes. I was dismissed with another shake of the hand, told to wait outside and also to send his adjutant back in. The other marine and I were there for a few minutes and then Brückner reappeared and led us downstairs. As per the Führer's orders, he handed each one of us 150 Reichsmark, encouraged us to tour Berlin and return the next day to be notified of the decision. So we strolled through Berlin and ate our meals in the Reich Chancellery. But it was only the following day which would bring us the decision. Early evening, we were called into the large entrance hall. Brückner appeared, saying: 'Who is Krause?' Once I stood to attention and said 'here', he explained that the Führer had decided on myself. He then turned to my comrade and said: 'And you, you can return to service and give our regards to the navy.' Each one of us then received an additional fifty Reichsmark. He then gave me further instructions, ordered me to pick up my stuff from the navy and report to him thereafter. I reported to the Ministry of the Reichswehr and informed them of my acceptance, after which I was handed the official documents to travel to my unit in Kiel. Before my departure, I was warmly congratulated by many high-ranking officers, and then I left Berlin.

My comrades aboard the ship offered me, in turn, their sincere congratulations. I packed my duffel bag, shouldered it and embarked once again on my trip back to Berlin, to my new post. In the meantime, a room had been prepared for me in the Reich Chancellery, which Hitler wished to first inspect personally. Under his watchful eye I had to try out the bed, so he could check whether indeed it could accommodate my height (190 centimetres). I received two light-coloured suits and one black one.

In the afternoon, while Hitler was having coffee with his guests in the garden, I was summoned to see him. He grabbed hold of two garden chairs all on his own. When I tried to take the chairs out of his hands, he waved me away: 'Just let go, man,' he said. 'There will be plenty of opportunities when you will certainly have to do that.' I obeyed him. He then marched up to about the middle of the garden, placed the chairs opposite each other and ordered me to take a seat. I sat directly opposite him. He started off by explaining the duties I was to perform and ended by saying: 'You are a soldier and I won't go to great lengths by demanding an oath from you because I rely on you completely.'[10]

'Whatever you get to hear and see here is nobody's business. You are only responsible to me with respect to my personal matters. While it could happen that you might receive orders, which will come via my adjutant, be aware that they come from me. Otherwise, nobody else may give you any orders.' That was good for me. Later on, when it came to having to deal with the other gentlemen, I wouldn't feel as if I were their subordinate, regardless of who they were.

Hitler dismissed me with a handshake. This was the first time we stood across from each other at eye-level. That same evening I was sent to Munich-Pasing, to a school of hotel management, where I was to complete a training course over the next few weeks. The day it ended, Adjutant Brückner turned up. I was to pack all my belongings within the hour.

We then made the car journey to Berchtesgaden-Obersalzberg. That's when I started my employment at this establishment. I was responsible for Hitler's personal affairs: clothing, laundry, shoes, etc. Later on, my duties would also include meals – not the preparation or cooking of meals, but serving them. In Berlin, at the Reich Chancellery, the kitchen and housekeeping were under the management of Herr Arthur Kannenberg and his wife, and in Munich this department was under a Frau Winter, and on the Obersalzberg Hitler's sister, Frau Raubal, oversaw the management of the house – at least during the first few years. These responsibilities were later handed over to a housekeeper and for several years Frau Raubal fell into disfavour.

In the years of 1936–7, and with the help of Frau Goebbels and the other women, Frau Raubal had wanted to find a wife for Hitler – something that really displeased him. He must have then had a disagreement and a falling out with her. Hitler immediately left the Berghof and went to Munich, and for some time after this incident his sister did not set foot in the Berghof. I never really warmed to Kannenberg.

I certainly learnt a lot at the hotel management school. Frau Kannenberg, who had until then looked after Hitler's private rooms and kept them neat and tidy, showed and explained to me just about everything I needed to know in order to get my bearings. Invariably she supplemented her directions with the words: 'This is the way the Reichskanzler would like to have it.' This actually went on for a while as she insisted on having it her own way in what she considered her domaine. It only shifted when Hitler ordered that it was only myself who was allowed to place purchases and look after his private affairs. Subsequently, quite a bit of tension developed between Frau Kannenberg and myself, and from then on I was pretty much left to my own devices.

VIPs, Women and Diplomats

One evening, just before Hitler retired to bed, he stood right in front of his rooms, which were dedicated for his private use only, and instructed me on the precise time for his wake-up call for the next day: 'At 9.30 a.m. I am to be woken up. At 8 a.m. the reports and newspaper are to be on the stool next to the bedroom. Good night.' This would often be accompanied with a handshake.

During the first years in Berlin his wake-up call was mostly the same. My response was: 'Good night, I wish you a pleasant rest.' Hitler always locked the door behind him. His actual private rooms were situated on the first floor of the old Reich Chancellery and consisted of his study, the library, the bedroom and the bathroom.

During the first years, the reports and the newspapers were always brought upstairs by the SS officer who was posted at the entrance hall and who placed the papers on the said stool. After that it was my duty to do that, which meant that the SS officer on duty brought them all up to me, and that turned out to be my own wake-up call. This, while only a minor adjustment, was a change of procedure nevertheless, and the reason for explaining it is to show that the overall 'newspaper' duties were covered by some ten men alternating with each other. It would sometimes happen that one or other officer of the Begleitkommando accidentally knocked the stool against the bedroom door and thus caused an unpleasant disruption, or that they placed the stool in such an inconvenient spot that it made it awkward for Hitler to actually reach the papers and take them inside. I once made a special point of observing how these papers were brought in: Hitler tended to stretch out only his hand to grab the papers. He did that even without looking. During that process the door remained open, but only by a crack. His hand would always feel for the stool (hence why the latter had to be positioned in the same spot at all times).

Now I come to the wake-up procedure: during the first years there still wasn't any system in place which would have enabled the rooms to be connected to each other by bells. These were installed only later on. Until that time, I always went to the door of his bedroom, knocked and waited for a response. Then I made my report with the words: 'Good morning, mein Führer. It is now (for example) nine-thirty.' After the connecting bell system had been installed, I would press the button three times to make the call. The bell was fastened to the head of his bed. I then waited for his response ring. With the bell button located on his bedside table, he would also press it three times. It was only then that I approached the door, knocked on it and announced the exact time of day. The answer came back as 'Thank you', or more precisely 'Thank you, kindly' or 'Thank you very much', depending on his mood (it often gave me a clue as to what frame of mind he was in). At that point he only rarely asked for anything more. After the wake-up call I went downstairs to the kitchen, prepared the breakfast myself and set it all up. It was only the milk that had to be heated by the kitchen staff on duty. Breakfast always consisted of the following: two cups of lukewarm whole milk, up to ten Leibniz biscuits, and one-third to half a tablet of chopped up, semi-bitter chocolate.[11]

I always kept the milk at a lukewarm temperature and, while bringing it upstairs to his room, kept it under a tea cosy. Practically always to the minute (if he was woken up at 9.30, then at 9.52 or 9.53) he rang. Carrying the breakfast on the tray, I went to the bedroom and from there to the library. The only door Hitler opened by himself was the bedroom door. It was left to me to deal with all the other doors. In those twenty-two to twenty-three minutes I mentioned above, Hitler took a bath, shaved and got dressed. He would press the button just when he put on his jacket. Sometimes he wanted to be woken up at different times: but the time period for washing and dressing himself always lasted a good twenty-two minutes and always remained the same.

Hitler always shaved himself. During my time of serving him between 1934 and Christmas 1943, he never had himself shaved by anyone else, at least not to my knowledge. He did this on his own and apparently did so until his end. He used two razors, one to start off with and one to end up. A new blade was inserted in each razor every day so that Hitler went through two blades a day. The brand of his soap was Steckenpferd-Lilienmilch,[12] the brand of his shaving cream was Peri and the brand of his skin cream was Pfeilring. His hair lotion was called Dralles Birkenwasser. At one point Hitler changed his hair lotion, but then returned to the old brand. He used to put spruce-needle-scented tablets into his bath.

Upon entering with the breakfast, it was me who greeted him first. But it could also often happen that he spoke first. I said: 'Good morning, mein Führer.' or when I was somewhat downcast I would say only 'Morning'. His response also was: 'Good morning' or just *Heil*. To that, I always responded with my own *Heil*, adding nothing further.

He ate his breakfast in the library – not even sitting down. He glanced at the most recent news bulletins, or rather at what were the information documents which at that time were dispatched by the DNB (Deutsches Nachrichtenbüro), and which I had brought up along with the breakfast.[13]

I took that moment as an opportunity to ask him whether he would consider the menu options for lunch. The first menu listed on the card was earmarked for the guests and other people. Then, usually, there were three further vegetarian choices from which he selected one or two, which he then combined into one dish. It could also happen that he said: 'Today, I would like two fried eggs with some green salad.' With respect to the menu of the other diners on that day, he was only concerned with the question: 'Does the dessert actually complement the main dish?' Breakfast lasted some three to five minutes. Then Hitler moved to the official study in the main part of the Reich Chancellery. I went ahead, as there were several rooms we had to cross, the doors of which were locked shut when you entered from the private room. But there was always a key stuck in the keyhole. I opened the doors and left them open until we reached the offices, where the aides were expecting Hitler, and greeted him. I then walked back the exact same route and locked the doors behind me from the inside. Once back in the private wing, I called for the maids. Usually two of the three on duty showed up. They cleaned the rooms, while I looked after only the wardrobe and prepared the razors for the next day.

Meetings, which took place in the Reich Chancellery's official study, usually lasted until one or two o'clock in the afternoon.

My duty during that time slot involved sorting out his personal matters. When the Führer was in the middle of holding his final meeting with some minister or gentleman, one of the officials on duty in the entrance hall used to call me, saying: 'Shadow, the last one is now inside.' (My nickname 'Shadow' goes back to a jocular remark by Herr Werlin, director of the Mercedes-Benz Works, who, while pointing to a photograph, compared me to a shadow.)[14]

After I had hung up, I once again went all the way back, unlocked all the doors and escorted Hitler back to his rooms. That's when he went to the bathroom to freshen up. Then it was off downstairs to the smoking room. All the invited lunch guests and the aides were gathered there. These guests mostly consisted of Gauleiters and acquaintances from Hitler's past, who either were on official business in Berlin or just happened to be there and had got in touch with Hitler's adjutants.[15]

Dr Goebbels was also often part of the lunch party. Hitler greeted them all with a handshake and asked the usual questions: 'How are you?' 'What's new?' etc. I instructed the staff to put the finishing touches to the prepared dishes, and once the food was all set up on the tables I informed Hitler and only him that it was all prepared and ready to be served.

Everyone then followed him to the dining room. Hitler himself always sat in the same spot. He always selected two specific guests to sit at his right and left hand. Dr Goebbels tended to sit opposite him. There was a main table in the dining room and four tables to the side. The main table was set for twelve people, while the tables on the side each seated six. Generally there were some twelve to twenty or so people gathered there for lunch. The meal lasted for approximately thirty to thirty-five minutes. Conversations were always lively, the tone friendly.

Once everyone had finished their meal, Hitler was the first to rise from the table, take one of his guests to the side and walk out together with him to the winter garden. The rest of the gentlemen, guests and adjutants returned to the smoking room for a cup of coffee or a cigarette, and so on. The private conversations between Hitler and the guest invited to walk with him would usually not last long, but then again they could go on for hours. These were usually the times when the SA Leader and Reich Sports Leader Hans von Tschammer und Osten, von Ribbentrop or von Neurath[16] grabbed the opportunity for a formal discussion with the Führer either at or after the meal. Individual Gauleiter who hadn't made an official appointment would also happily seize this moment to have an 'official' word with Hitler.

Diplomats were rarely invited. But of those who were, Hitler highly respected Molotov.[17] After meeting him in autumn 1940 Hitler clapped his hands full of glee and said: 'For once the West can now actually see things as they are ... Krause ... now this has really worked out well.' He also liked the Prince of Wales, the future

King Edward VIII, not least because of the latter's views on hunting. In Hitler's opinion, animals ought to be killed by bow and arrow and not by shooting them from a distance of 400 metres with the help of a telescopic sight. The animal, so he thought, wouldn't even know where the danger was coming from.

The Prince of Wales was accompanied by his future wife, Mrs Wallace Simpson. She was an extremely charming woman, and Hitler once expressed his personal view on her, saying that he could well understand why the king was to abdicate because of her.

There were other foreign guests as well and they found it hard not to be intrigued by Hitler's piercing stare. During the meetings with the British Foreign Secretary, John Simon, in 1934, Anthony Eden (his successor) would usually leave the meeting room before the discussions had finished. Had he stayed longer, according to his comments regarding this at the time, he would have agreed to just about everything.

The well-known racing driver Rudolf Caracciola once said that he would prefer doing the 300-kilometre race any day, rather than having even one meeting with Hitler. That, he said, would indeed make him feel much more tense.[18]

Of his Gauleiters Hitler respected those the most who would not constantly nag him with one or another of their requests. Goebbels was undoubtedly closest to him. Once Goebbels came to Hitler and jokingly reported that Roosevelt had written to him asking him to become his Chief of Propaganda in Washington. Hitler responded with: 'Dear Doctor, it is, of course, for you to decide.' 'No, no, I am certainly staying on here' was the answer.

In 1931 a voters' convention took place in Schwerin. Placards announced Hitler as the speaker: 'Entrance Fee: 60 Pfennig' (in today's currency some €3). As Hitler was detained from attending at the last minute, Goebbels had to step in. The entrance fee was pasted over and reset at twenty-five Pfennig. Hitler, in one of his good moods, would later often say to Goebbels: 'Just be quiet, little doctor, you are worth only half as much as me.'

Rosenberg,[19] while respected, wasn't really much of a presence. Hitler raved about von Ribbentrop, and valued Neurath as a diplomat but not as much else. He never made fun of Göring, or about his obsession for uniforms. He certainly enjoyed listening to jokes, especially political jokes. As long as good jokes are told about somebody, he once said, it is a sign that the person is well liked. He disliked ambiguous jokes. He often praised Sauckel.[20] Some of the other men tended to avoid Sauckel, because he had little formal education and was, in their eyes, a mere plasterer.

At the beginning, Hitler was close to Streicher,[21] but eventually he just dropped him. 'You with your Stürmer', he once said to him, 'just get lost with it'.

Hitler once complained about his Gauleiters, saying that he was minded to send them all back to school so that they would actually learn something, because they were so ignorant about so much, according to him. During one of his car trips he overheard that one of his Gauleiters was suffering from nicotine poisoning. 'One day', he said, 'I might even be pushed to prohibit smoking in all of Germany. But I suspect that, when I issue this order, my old Party comrades will just laugh at me. In ten years, what with the foreign exchange income, I could be saving a huge amount. I would literally be able to buy a new house for each and every German citizen. Those who would become unemployed in the tobacco industry wouldn't have a problem finding a job in a different branch.' At the Berghof, for some time already, smoking was strictly forbidden, because a carpet or a tablecloth had caught fire at some point. Immediately, all ashtrays had to disappear. The only people allowed to smoke in Hitler's proximity were Sepp Dietrich[22] and guests.

Among the ministers, Dr Schacht[23] was held in especially high esteem due to his special expertise and knowledge, but there was no real personal relationship between him and Hitler. 'When it comes to his field, there simply is nobody better qualified than him', Hitler once said, 'but you practically have to tie a person's hands to prevent him from doing something stupid – it's only then that you can safely leave him to remain in his position whether or not your own Party comrades approve of it or not.' Schacht was a man of detail. In the dining carriage of a train where a cup of coffee cost twenty-eight Pfennig, he would pay with thirty Pfennig and accept the two Pfennig change. He would then complain that the coffee was too expensive. There was one meeting I remember, when Hitler had to sign something. While writing, Hitler got some ink stains on his uniform jacket, and so he instructed me to order a new one. While I did not openly disagree, I just left the room and removed the stain with lemon. Schacht, however, was really annoyed at Hitler, saying that one should not be so careless about spending money.

Dr Funk,[24] Schacht's successor, was the total opposite to him. He was much more generous. He would even tip people openly, often right on the street.

Dr Lippert,[25] the then Mayor of Berlin, was to experience first-hand the fact of how easily one could fall out with Hitler. The cause in Dr Lippert's case was that he had planted some trees on the Unter den Linden[26] at Wilhelmplatz. In Hitler's opinion the trees were much too small and he angrily dismissed them as 'tea candles'. 'For that matter', he said, 'one might as well have planted trees which would only mature in five to six years.'

If he was in a particularly bad mood, one of his aides was sent to him to cheer him up, or a funny film was shown, for example *Der Zerbrochene Krug*,[27] which Hitler saw three or four times.

When feeling cheerful, he was very good at making fun of those present at the time or even when they actually weren't there. He did that in a very amusing tone. Nobody was quite able to live up to him. Once his photographer Hoffmann tried it, but wasn't very good at it and gave up.

When feeling tense, Hitler would nervously rub his hand against his upper thigh. Watching one of the ice hockey matches in the 1936 Winter Olympics really drove him crazy. The game ended 1:1. Hitler was so excited that he just couldn't bear watching the game and staying to the end. He left the stadium and asked for somebody to report on the end of the game to him later. His impatience might also explain why he would only rarely listen to an entire programme that was broadcast on radio.

During the first years of my service with Hitler, daily preparations for afternoon coffee would start at four-thirty in the afternoon at the Hotel Kaiserhof.[28] Individual members of the Sicherheitskommando crossed the Wilhelmplatz on foot to get to the Kaiserhof, while Hitler, along with two of his adjutants and myself, drove by car. We would also cross the Wilhelmplatz but then we turned the corner and stopped at the hotel's side entrance, where the hotel manager and an officer of the Begleitkommando stood in attendance before leading us into the hall.

We always had a corner table reserved for us. Goebbels and Göring also joined these coffee gatherings, but rarely at the same time. It was mostly Goebbels on his own. If by chance other people, such as well-known personalities from the film industry, happened to be at the Kaiserhof as well, or Gauleiters or personalities from public life, they too tended to be invited to join his table. Hitler's aides from both Schutzkommandos and myself would be close by, sitting at neighbouring tables. My own seat, whatever the distance, had to be within his field of vision at all times: he wanted me to be within his field of vision, and the other way round as well. At these afternoon gatherings, everyone, above all the members of the Begleitkommando, was dressed in civilian clothes, and even Hitler himself seldom wore his uniform. These were his orders. Coffee hours usually lasted until half past six or seven o'clock, after which he returned to the Reich Chancellery.

There, dinner preparations were well underway. Nearly every evening during the first years, actors and singers from the Opera House were asked to join him for dinner, as well as people from film and theatre. Dinner, too, was an informal affair. During supper I usually gave Hitler a list of films, specifying the titles of some four to six films that were showing during that same period in Germany's public cinemas, as well as abroad. Hitler decided which films would be screened that evening.

Following dinner and straight after a quick cup of coffee in the smoking room, the music room was set up for the film performance (the set-up for the performance was the same as in any other public cinema). We received these films from the Ministry of Propaganda or some film distributor. Up to three films were shown. If one of the them was not exactly to Hitler's taste, it was replaced by a different film. Hitler interrupted the screening with words such as 'Cut. What nonsense. Next one.' Until war broke out, Hitler watched every single film that had been produced at home and abroad and was being screened in Germany. He even got to see films for which the licence board of the Ministry of Propaganda had not yet even reached agreement on whether or not they should be approved for release. Hitler would then make this decision himself.

Then, during the war, Hitler stopped watching films altogether, except for *Deutsche Wochenschau* (German newsreels). These were silent films where one of the adjutants would read out loud the accompanying text with Hitler checking whether the words actually fitted the images. Often he dictated what he thought needed to be corrected. From winter 1942 onwards, Hitler didn't watch the newsreels either.

After the closing credits of the last film had rolled to the end – towards midnight – Hitler returned to the smoking room. Orderlies had coffee all set up in a cosy corner of the room. Everyone got themselves comfortable and it would all turn into a veritable social gathering with guests happily chatting away into the early hours. They spoke about everything and anything – but not about politics. One thing led to another, with even women's fashion being discussed. These chats clearly supported the view that Hitler was a really good and entertaining conversationalist. This, as it happens, was confirmed to me not only by our

German guests but also quite often by visitors from abroad. I, as well, attended most of these late evenings and was privy to most of the goings-on. Mind you, I could only see and hear everything from a distance of one or two metres away from those people who surrounded Hitler. These conversations could often last till late, two o'clock in the morning, or even three o'clock.

After the guests had departed, it was time for the agenda of the following day to be put together with exact timings for the scheduled meetings with ministers, diplomats and Party officials or managers from industry etc. Then in came Lammers[29] and Meissner,[30] who presented Hitler with a separate document listing the private audiences planned. As for me, I submitted the evening editions of the papers and the DNB dispatches, which Hitler would study in depth. While he attended to these documents, I prepared some tea to take to his bedroom (Baldrian tea with a small flask of cognac) which I placed on his *Nachtkastl.*[31]

After he had finished reading the newspapers and the dispatches Hitler retired to his private wing upstairs. Apart from the adjutant on duty, other people only rarely were still around at that time, except for one orderly and myself. During the first years, so until 1937, this was pretty much our daily routine in Berlin, other than Sundays, which until that year had never been spent in that city.

Travelling

Here is how the week was organised: meetings that required the Reich Chancellor's presence in Berlin took place between Tuesday and Friday. Departure from Berlin would always take place on a Friday evening, or Saturday during the day. More often than not, the destination was Munich, and from there we went to Berchtesgaden on the Obersalzberg.

If there was some uncertainty regarding the destination of the trip, the decision was made by the toss of a coin. The question 'should or shouldn't we go to the theatre?' was a case in point. If there was no agreement among them, Hitler would take a Reichsmark coin where the face indicated 'For' and the back indicated 'Against'. He himself would toss the coin into the air and let it drop to the floor. That brought closure.

Once, just at the very beginning of our flight to Munich, an idea suddenly popped into Hitler's head: let's stop off in Nuremberg and visit the theatre there. His plan was to fly or drive by car on to Munich on only the subsequent day, weather permitting. This too was decided by Hitler with the toss of a coin. He never used to go back on these decisions (though whether he also followed the same routine with respect to politically important decisions is something I am not aware of). During these first years, Hitler spent his weekends exclusively in Munich or on the Obersalzberg. He would then return to Berlin, either by plane or by train, on the Monday. Initially, a special carriage was attached to the scheduled D-train,[32] which went from Munich to Berlin, and from Berlin to Munich. Later, a special train only for Hitler and his entourage was put on. The train, as well as the two planes that were at his disposal, always accompanied us.[33] If we took the plane, the special train would also make the trip all the way to the destination point, albeit empty. If we drove by car, the train and the planes always had to follow us. (Hitler's favourite mode of transport was by car. His second most preferred way of travelling was by train, with plane trips coming in at third position – he only used it to save time.).

Travelling, in general, was one of Hitler's favourite pastimes. He hated office meetings with a vengeance, actually he despised anything connected with administrative work. In his own words: 'I cannot imagine anything worse than sitting in an office day and night pouring over files etc., and spending the rest of my life in this miserable way. I am actually frightened of growing older and then only to find out that I am no longer able to travel the way I want to'. This is what he once said while we were driving in a car.

It was always Hitler himself who decided on all the trips – each and every one of them. Nobody was briefed beforehand as to the destination of the trip, or its details. More often than not, he notified us only last minute of where we were heading off to. Having said that, even this was not binding, as we often took quite a different route than had been indicated to us beforehand. While our final destination point was nearly always communicated to us, Hitler would decide which roads the chauffeur was to choose to take us there, and with only a map to help us. This is how it often came about that we ended up driving criss-cross around Germany, travelling along detours to finally reach his desired destination of that day. His convoy mostly consisted of four to six vehicles, with the exception of official journeys, where there were more. The first vehicle was the Führerwagen, then the escort car for the SS, followed by the escort car for the Kripo, the car for the adjutants, and finally came the luggage car.[34]

The convoy consisted only of Mercedes cars as Hitler didn't like it if a car of a different make travelled as part of our cavalcade. Once, for his birthday, Hitler received a Horch[35] as a present. He travelled in this car only once, after which he ordered that it be immediately changed. He gave it to Rudolf Hess, and in return Hess gave Hitler a Mercedes. I once asked Hitler why he only drove Mercedes cars, to which he gave me the very short answer: 'It is the best car.' But then, when I praised other car manufacturers, he gave me a fuller answer: 'Well, the real reason is that during my fighting days, I wanted to own a Maybach.[36] But the manufacturers refused to give me one, as they claimed that I wasn't "prominent" enough for them.' 'There will be no Maybach car for a Hitler' was all they said to me [I still see his smile when I recall him saying these words].

From the Mercedes company as well I received a car but only through using my connections with a director. What persuaded me to choose Mercedes was after my collision with another vehicle en route between Nuremberg and Munich. The other vehicle got totally destroyed, while my car had only minimal damage on the bumper and footboards. That's when I decided that I would drive only Mercedes for the rest of my life. That was the real reason. Barring a few other cars here and there, most of which were for test drives only (Volkswagens[37] in particular), Hitler was a man of principle, and stuck by Mercedes. If, by circumstance, he had to drive another car, he never felt comfortable or safe, and invariably commented: 'No, I certainly prefer my Mercedes.'

There is another anecdote that still sticks in my mind; because I was sitting behind Hitler, in the back seat of the car, it was usually left to me to pull up his collar just before he sat down in his seat. This was because it looked better, when he sat on his coat, that the collar wasn't being pulled down his back. Once, just in the middle of my doing this, Hitler commented: 'If one day you should write your memoirs, don't forget to write that you pulled up Adolf Hitler by his collar.'[38]

The Tie Struggle

One of my main duties was looking after the wardrobe. During my term of being Hitler's valet, he owned a tailcoat,[39] a dinner suit,[40] a cutaway[41] (which he never wore during my time and, according to rumours, only ever wore once, on the Day of Potsdam,[42] 21 March 1933) and a dress suit (which he also never wore). He also had a blue, a brown and a light-coloured suit for everyday wear.

Then there were the uniforms: five jackets (two of them with belts), three pairs of long black trousers and four pairs of breeches. His civilian clothes were so worn out that even a lowly office clerk would not have worn them, unless it was perhaps just for work. Only after I put some pressure on him did he follow the advice of Frau Goebbels, Frau Troost and last but not least of Eva Braun, who all urged him to have a few suits made up, as well as a double-breasted tuxedo and some uniforms.

His uniforms were made in Berlin, the civilian clothes in Munich. Coats were bought in the clothes shop called Herpich, located in Berlin on Leipziger Strasse. Hitler only rarely had a tailor take his measurements, nor did he go to fittings. The tailor nearly always had to work according to what he himself felt would fit Hitler, basing his measurements on some of his old uniforms. How often would I plead with Hitler: 'When can the tailor come? He would love to take some measurements and organise a convenient time for a fitting.' It was usually a somewhat futile task. Throughout my service, which lasted close to ten years, the uniform tailor must have come to the house no more than ten times, either to take measurements or for fittings. But if on the odd occasion I managed to convince Hitler to agree to a fitting, the whole process was still allowed to take only two or three minutes. There was nothing he despised more.

Hitler wore all his clothes loose, sort of hanging around his body. You can well imagine all the criticism I had to listen to. From all sides, even in letters written by ordinary people – they all reproached me. All the complaints came to me. I was blamed for everything. It was, they said, within my remit, and the way Hitler presented himself was a reflection of my work.

I was admonished and requested to make every effort towards having the Führer of Germany present himself to the public in uniforms and suits that fitted to perfection. The fact was that this actually wasn't so easy for me, or rather it was downright impossible when it came to uniforms – quite a few people will still remember the struggle I had.

I often asked the tailor to alter a jacket or a pair of trousers. Once, for example, I requested that the waistline of one of his jackets be taken in a little bit. Then, when I laid out this article ready for Hitler to put on, I myself was also quite curious to find out how this would pan out. But, oh dear. He hadn't even finished buttoning up the jacket when I was summoned. Goodness me, did I get it in the neck. So I just gave up trying to make headway in this particular area. I didn't really feel that it was fair on me to have to engage in such unpleasant dealings. I much rather preferred taking other people's criticism and complaints on the chin. I smiled when I heard them and thought to myself: 'Oh, if only you knew.'

When he was in public, Hitler only very rarely covered his head. His hats, which were velvet, were purchased in the Munich shop called Seidl, while the caps that he wore with the uniforms were bought in Berlin. The way Hitler wore his cap was considered 'impossible'. He had his own peculiar ideas of how these caps should be worn. I often commented to him how 'that really looks like a postman's cap' or 'the engine driver might wear such "lids" on their heads, but certainly nobody else.' He just looked me up and down and said: 'Am I wearing the cap, or are you?' I then told him the stuff people said to me and the objections I had to listen to and made sure to let him know that these came from all corners, but none of this bothered him in the slightest.

Once, at a Party convention, I had removed the wire bow from his cap, and it really looked considerably better. He didn't notice this immediately. Only once we were already on our way, did he realise that the wiring was missing. I was totally convinced that he would throw me out of the car right then and there. Sometimes he would bawl me out. So, while the convention was taking place in the Congress Hall, I drove back to the hotel, picked up the wire bow and inserted it into the cap again. He immediately noticed what I had done and his mood changed instantly, but not before still strictly forbidding me to change anything in his cap ever again.

I do believe, however, that everyone made fun of how he wore his cap. It was the same story with his shoes and boots. He simply couldn't bear parting from his old high boots. He must have bought these well before my time. Moreover, this was the only pair of high boots he even owned. I put in an order for some three pairs of high boots, but he just didn't like the look of them. He always returned to wearing his old ones. Once, when they needed to be re-soled, this had to happen during that same night, so that he could wear them the following morning.

These boots, as well, were the talk of town, what with their unsightly folds. I just totally failed to convince him to wear other boots. It was only shortly before our visit with Mussolini in Italy that he finally agreed to put on another pair. Mind you, the old boots still had to be taken along on every single trip.

I have to admit, though, that these boots, though robust and made out of thick leather, perhaps even sole leather, were incredibly soft and, above all, light as a feather.

As for shoes, Hitler practically wore only patent leather loafers. He owned two simple leather shoes. In cool weather, and when he went for a walk, he put on a pair of lace-up ankle boots with rubber soles, of which he owned just one pair.

He also had a pair of walking boots. To get him to wear shoes of a colour other than black, so that they could go with his light suits, well, that was for many years an impossible option considering how stubborn he was. During the first three years, on principle, he persistently paired his light suits with black silk socks and black patent leather loafers.

Even when it came to his socks, he would grumble constantly as they were always too short, according to him, and apparently always slipped down his calves. 'Can it really not be possible for the Führer of the German people to get a pair of sensible socks?' he exclaimed, and Frau Kannenberg and myself canvassed all the shops in Berlin for some more appropriate socks. The black shoes worn with his light suits were just awful.

But, even in this respect, Hitler only actually came to grips with how it really mattered much later on. I myself had purchased three pairs of brown shoes for him very early on, along with some differently coloured socks, and every time a light-coloured suit was laid out for him I placed some brown shoes next to them. And yet each time he himself would go to the cupboard and take out the black patent leather shoes, while leaving the brown shoes untouched. It was only in 1937, and with Frau Goebbels's help, that I was able to make some progress in this respect. When it came to shoes, my previous efforts and approaches to Frau Professor Troost,[43] on whose taste and sense of colour Hitler relied a lot, remained unsuccessful, as did my requests for Fräulein Braun to intervene.

It was no different with ties. Hitler was just incredibly stubborn when it came to this part of his attire. Even though I was required to prepare two or three ties every time Hitler considered wearing one of his suits, I later realised that he would just go to the cupboard himself and select a different tie to the one I had suggested, and one which, of course, was totally unsuitable. Only on one occasion, when he was visiting the Troosts' design studios, did he put on the tie that had been prepared for him – maybe he was in a rush on that day. Frau Troost complimented him, praising his inspired choice. From then on, he never selected his own tie.

Yes, Frau Troost would often criticise him: 'Mein Führer, what an impossible tie,' she scolded gently, then she threw me a reproachful glance. I could only mutter that the tie that was suitable was still at home. And that was the truth; it was hanging in the small cabinet on a practical clothes hanger that I had designed myself, and which I had purposely ordered with Hitler in mind. Hitler always knotted the ties himself, except for bow ties, which went with his tailcoat or dinner jacket; these I had to tie for him. But this had to happen very quickly, within some twenty-five seconds. Once those few seconds had elapsed, the tie had to be perfect, otherwise Hitler would become disgruntled, shifting from one leg to the other. Nobody is able to do a proper job in such conditions. However, when it came to situations such as these, I was calmness itself, but this would admittedly drive him crazy as well.

Once, he asked me what was actually going through my head when he lashed out at me. 'My work then becomes more interesting and it's no longer so monotonous,' I simply told him. Once, at the table and in front of guests on the Obersalzberg, he said: 'Just take a look at my man Krause – nothing can faze this guy. When I make a fuss, he will only give me one of his ironic smiles, very politely, or just look at me with a totally innocent expression and all the while have his own thoughts, but keeping these to himself. I would love to be as relaxed as he is, even for just five minutes.'

On the second Whitsun[44] day in 1937 I was the cause of great hilarity. Many illustrious German VIPs, including all of the Gau- and Reichsleiters, had gathered for a convention in Munich. At the time, we were staying on the Obersalzberg. Out of the blue, the Führer instructed me to place long-distance calls to each of the participants of the convention and invite them to tour the Führerbau[45] in Munich, the construction of which had not yet been fully completed.

So we then flew to Munich. Nothing was brought along for him. But, just in case, I had packed a light-coloured suit. On our drive from his private quarters on the Prinzregentenplatz, where we stopped first, over to the Führerbau, we passed the Haus der Deutschen Kunst.[46] The sun was shining brightly. Hitler turned to me: 'We should have brought a light-coloured suit along. After the tour I would have then been able to change and we could have had a cup of coffee on the terrace of the Haus der Deutschen Kunst.' I responded that, just to be on the safe side, I had brought along a light-coloured suit. 'Can someone prepare that for me, or do you have to drive to the apartment?' he then asked. And that's when he added, for the first time, 'and have them bring along the brown shoes to go with it'. I assured him that the suit could be prepared by Frau Winter, whom I would call from the Brown House.[47] After having phoned Frau Winter to ask her to prepare the light-coloured suit and to put the brown shoes alongside, the matter – as far as I was concerned – seemed to have been settled. But then Frau Winter called me back to inform me that there were no brown shoes to be found. At first I was in shock, but because until that very day Hitler had always worn black shoes with his light suits I didn't lose my composure. I returned to the group touring the Führerbau, and it had just entered the room which was going to be the Congress Hall. All the gentlemen were assembled in one spot. Hitler wanted to see how the acoustics worked, so he requested one of the invited people to say or sing something. When nobody volunteered, Hitler looked around and spotted me. 'Well, if all of you gentlemen are frightened, one of my people will simply have to take over.' he shouted. So I was told to put myself at the other end of the room and tell them some amusing story of my life.

Everyone sighed with visible relief, having avoided possible disaster. When in proximity to Hitler, most of them were cowards. I myself was still thinking about the shoes that had been forgotten and left behind, and was mulling over how best to impart this news to Hitler, without once again incurring his wrath. Walking to the other side of the room, I still had no idea as to what I was going to shout out. When I arrived at the other corner, I quickly turned around and said with a loud voice: 'May it please the Führer to kindly wear the black shoes tonight, since I have forgotten to bring along the brown ones.'

Well, you wouldn't imagine the laughter these few words gave rise to. Needless to say, it was also a huge relief to me. Hitler then turned to Gauleiter Wagner, to Frau Professor Troost and to the architect Leonhard Gall: 'There, have a look at him. He just removes himself by fifty metres, far enough so that I am unable to slap him across the face.' Years later, Hitler would time and again repeat this episode to entertain others. As for me, I managed just to get away with it by the skin of my teeth. On that day, Hitler didn't change. We went for coffee in uniform and then returned to the Berghof. As mentioned before, the whole issue of dress, and what to wear, became a complicated matter when Hitler travelled.

I never, or only rarely, received any detailed instructions as to what needed to be brought along for a particular journey. Hitler's instructions might be something like 'keep a longer period of time in mind' or 'pack for several days' – other than that, nothing. Only when shorter journeys were ahead of us, he might say: 'You can bring this or that along, I won't be needing anything else.'

If it turned out that something wasn't immediately to hand when he needed it, then you would live to regret it, and that's of course when I would get the blame. That is why I usually started planning carefully well ahead of time and tended to take everything along, things that made sense, but also stupid things, just so that I was equipped and ready at all times and for all eventualities.

Hand on heart, there are few people in the world who packed as much as I did during those years – though as it happens they were a few years only. For each day of the journey – whether it be the hotel or not, and regardless how short the stay was – absolutely everything was packed prior to departure, and unpacked on arrival. In the morning, above all, this all had to happen instantly. Hitler definitely didn't ask me to take my time with anything. All items of clothing, even the tails and the tuxedo, had to be packed in such a way that they could just be taken out of the suitcase and immediately hung up in the cupboard, without any further ironing being necessary.

While Hitler generally led a simple life and while it was quite easy to deal with him when he was surrounded by his close circle of friends – then there was no real etiquette in place – the exact opposite was true when guests were around. He became erratic. And even more so, when ladies were present or due to join.

What a circus. Nothing was good enough. Everyone around him became gripped by a fever. Woe to the orderlies, woe to me, if something went wrong. We were literally petrified, dreading what might befall us if heaven forbid even the slightest thing would go wrong. It was a huge relief everywhere once everything was over and it all had gone more or less according to plan. There were even the rare occasions when one would earn Hitler's praise. But had anything gone awry, you were 'dead', so to speak, at least for that day, and most likely for the next day as well. It was then usually advisable not to show your face, and certainly not if he hadn't expressly called for you. It could also happen that one day he would praise something, and then just as soon reject it the next, or vice versa.

Here is an example: once I had given the instruction that special underpants be made for Hitler, and that they be sewn out of the same fabric as those I knew he usually wore. The seamstress, who was the same woman who had been given the past commissions, cut and sewed these underpants based on the same measurements she had kept from the previous orders. As soon as she delivered the new pairs, I added them to Hitler's old underwear. On one particular morning I enter his room carrying his breakfast, and what do I see? The new underpants were thrown at my feet with the words: 'Remove these things out of my room. They are just totally unbearable.' I took them away at once and added them to the 'stock cupboard' we kept – I myself actually wore them later on. After several weeks, during a longer trip that was ending up in Godesberg, I realised that we had run out of underwear. Fresh underwear, ordered from Berlin and already on its way to us, would not arrive until that evening. What was to be done? I went to have a look in my luggage. There, packed away, I still had three pairs of the said underwear, already worn by me, but washed and entirely clean.

I took them, laid them out for the next morning, and was fully expecting one of his outbreaks. However, seeing that I was fairly certain the laundry courier would arrive from Berlin any minute, I also wasn't overly concerned. I was therefore truly surprised when I realised that he had actually put on these underpants, without me getting an ear full of his complaints. When he had made the fuss some weeks earlier, I therefore assumed that he had just been in one of his bad moods.

One more example: the grey uniform jacket. I had decided to take a risk, make an independent decision and order one jacket 'made-to-measure', since Hitler really stood out – unfavourably so – when he wore his brown jacket during Wehrmacht inspections or manoeuvres. One day, when one of these parades was due to take place, I showed him the grey jacket, and all he said was: 'You can do with that thing whatever you please. As long as I live, I'll only wear my brown jacket.' I was quite surprised when he enquired some six months later, on 1 September 1939 and on the day the war broke out, whether I still had the grey jacket available for him. With some hesitation, I responded with a 'Yes'. He wanted to see it immediately, tried it on right then and there and went ahead ordering several such jackets to be made up for him at once. I remarked: 'Well then, mein Führer. So it's quite fortunate that I still happened to have the grey jacket on hand, ready for when you wanted to wear it.'

Such incidents happened quite frequently, where Hitler would initially reject things, only to then later accept them, realising the advantages they could offer. Hitler changed his underwear as he saw fit. It could happen that he would do so every day, perhaps twice or even three times, or then again there were times when he just wouldn't change for two, maybe three, days. He only wore thin socks, even in his high boots, always put on only short underpants, even during the winter when it was freezing cold, and he never wore an undershirt, only shirts with separate collars, so no casual shirts, and never any coloured shirts, only white ones. His suits were double-breasted, and he only wore a waistcoat when he decided to put on his dinner jacket. He didn't use trouser belts, instead he wore suspenders, and at night he didn't wear pyjamas but rather a nightshirt made out of simple linen.

Butter or Canons

When it comes to the topic of food, all one can actually muster up for the man is pity. He followed a strict vegetarian diet. During some brief periods we were instructed to serve him only raw food. His decision to follow a vegetarian diet goes back to the First World War. After his war injury, his attending physician prescribed a vegetarian diet. And as would often be the case with Hitler, if something agreed with him, he would stick with it thereafter. Once he told us his theory: 'Look here, a lion eats heaps of meat, he then feels sluggish and disappears in some corner and goes to sleep. In contrast, a camel gets a bag of hay and thrives in spite of the desert's hardships. Why wouldn't the same be true for the human being? If he is a vegetarian, wouldn't it then be correct to say that he could be as fit as a camel? So, in other words, why shouldn't he follow a meatless diet as well?'

In Berlin, the kitchen was run exactly like that of a hotel. The actual preparation of meals was under the watch of Herr and Frau Kannenberg. Initially, it was Frau Kannenberg herself who cooked for Hitler. But because the meals had become too monotonous for Hitler's taste, a special cook was then hired to satisfy his particular needs. Right at the start, as always, he was totally enthusiastic about her cooking skills, since she had introduced something new. But his enthusiasm didn't last long, as the meals soon became monotonous once again.

Several cooks were engaged for him, one after the other. One, for example, was hired for just four weeks, to create an exclusively raw-food diet. She was followed by some other cook. By nature, Hitler preferred the Viennese cooks. Some cooks, who really knew their trade, didn't last long because they didn't get on with the Kannenbergs. During the first years it was me alone who would wait on Hitler. I must admit that I couldn't think of anything more boring than his meals. It could well happen that *Semmelknödel*[48] would be served him four or five times in a row, always the same, perhaps with the slightest variation being the way it was prepared – sometimes roasted, fried or boiled etc. In terms of quantity, Hitler ate little. He started eating sardines only in 1941, before that he never even touched fish. He detested any meal that had anything to do with meat, except for *Leberknödel*.[49]

Even the most delicious roast Hitler would define as 'cadaver grub', and us he called 'cadaver gluttons'. This is what his menu looked like: first, there was always soup, followed by the main dish, and dessert to finish. His main dish was often an adaptation of the one that was served to others. For example, when steak was on the menu, he would also get that, but his was made of vegetables. Very often he had only fried eggs. Some slices of bread were added, which had to be baked for him especially – no sourdough. The crust had to be removed beforehand. We had to take this bread everywhere.

Hitler was served a fresh green salad with every meal, mostly dressed with only a bit of lemon juice. An unpeeled apple, sliced into eight, was dessert – later on it was grated apple. One can say that, essentially, Hitler lived on vegetables and fruit alone. All meals, however, were prepared using fine butter; mind you, not during the times when Germany was suffering a butter shortage. During that period, rendered fat was used instead. There was no question in Hitler's mind that his household would be the first to follow the austerity measures. It is true though that Hitler enjoyed eating real caviar with his eggs, but this was extremely rare, and may have happened perhaps only three or four times in a year. When he once enquired how expensive caviar actually was and I told him that one kilo of caviar cost 400 Reichsmark,[50] he immediately issued a strict order that caviar was never to be served again at his table.

He would regularly drink milk, different kinds of tea and hot chocolate. Fachinger[51] was his standard drink. As for alcohol he would have only cognac, which had to be added to his tea when he had a cold. After certain dishes, he also used to drink a *Boonekamp*,[52] which eased digestion. He never drank coffee, not even when it was caffeine-free. He only ate one kind of cake, *Stollen*,[53] which was based on a recipe from the southern part of Germany. This cake was exclusively baked for Hitler by one specific baker in Munich, but he did so without using the recommended amount of fat. Hitler would eat no other cakes.

In Munich, no separate kitchen was kept for Hitler. There, Frau Winter cooked for him, but only once in a while. Otherwise, Hitler mostly ate in public restaurants. Sometimes, when we were invited to Hoffmann, the photographic journalist, we would also have a meal there. On the Obersalzberg, good traditional food was served. Hitler absolutely loved *Eintopf* (a traditional stew). To finish off the topic of meals, I might add that even when it came to large receptions where Hitler himself was in attendance, and when diplomats or VIPs from the Wehrmacht, from the Party or heads of states were visiting, no sumptuous banquets were ever put on. Certainly, the food was fine on such events, and, being catered mostly by Horcher[54] in Berlin, it was most tasty and plentiful.

Hitler actually did not have a favourite dish, except perhaps for Gervais[55] cheese, even though he had a real fondness for all different kinds of cheese.

At the start of the Four-Year Plan[56] in autumn 1936, and in order to make savings, the slogan 'Butter or Cannons' was being promoted. Hitler had the entire household staff of the Reich Chancellery convene, and it was he who gave the strict instruction to no longer use butter in his household but, instead, rendered fat, such as melted lard. 'If all our people economise, then we, my household, have to take the lead in this venture.' We strictly adhered to this. The sandwich platters were sparse, only dry bread was served along with sausages, tomatoes or cucumbers. This prohibition was in force even on the Tag der Nationalen Solidarität, when he had invited the entire group of those artists into the Reich Chancellery, who had signed up to take collections.[57]

Realising that the bread slices served would have no toppings to speak of, I gave in to the pressure of the kitchen staff, approached Hitler and asked him whether they could not, as an exception on this special day, be allowed to spread butter on the bread. He granted the request. Thus, there was meat broth, sandwiches made with buttered bread and potato salad. He would put into each one of the artist's collection box a note of 100 to 1,000 Reichsmark. Later on, the prohibition not to use butter eased off in our household, as well as in the whole of the Reich.

Profession: Reich Chancellor

While Hitler, in his position as the representative of the Reich, was extremely demanding when it came to furnishing the official rooms, the exact opposite was true with respect to his private wing. In Berlin, his private wing consisted of his study, his library, his bedroom and his bathroom. The floors of the study and bedroom were covered in a type of green linoleum. The main piece of furniture in the study was his desk. To its left stood a small table for the phone with all the connection buttons, which Hitler could have pressed himself, but never did. The wall at the back, as well as the side wall, was covered from top to bottom by bookcases which had locked cabinets at the bottom and open shelves at the top. The table for the typewriter, the typewriter itself and a safe completed the study's interior. Hanging on the wall was a portrait of Bismarck, painted by Franz von Lenbach.[58] The size of Hitler's study was some twenty-four square metres.

In the library, every single available wall space was covered by bookshelves. Here there was an open fireplace, in front of which stood a comfortable sofa, four upholstered chairs, a table and a standing lamp. The dominant piece within the room was a huge and heavy oak table placed right in the middle. The room was lit by simple hanging lamps, with some additional standing lamps near the tables. Nobody ever tidied Hitler's desk or the library without first receiving an order to do so. There was a real mess on these tables. Standing between the two large windows was a low table along with two stools.

A very simple but very large iron bed was in the bedroom, covered by a mattress that had a distinctive dip in the middle and was dearly loved by Hitler. He loved soft, moulded mattresses. He very much disliked the modern ones with their firm springiness. All hotels had to take note of that as well. If this particular requirement was neglected, Hitler suffered from backache the following day. A picture of his mother hung above his bed. To its right was an open bedside table. In general, anywhere Hitler would spend the night, the *Nachtkastl* had to be on his right, looking out from where he lay in bed.

Additionally, there were two wardrobes in his bedroom, one of them had three parts to it, with a dresser, above which hung a mirror. A round table was positioned in the middle of the room, along with a chair and a stool. All furniture was made of wood covered by an ivory-coloured varnish. The bathroom was equipped as all normal bathrooms were at the time. All other rooms were public, accessible to anyone, and there was nothing special about them.

Hitler's apartment in Munich was located at Prinzregentenplatz 16. At first, he rented the third-floor apartment and had only one bedroom at his disposal. All other rooms he had to share with the landlord. This particular floor was converted in 1935, after which Hitler also had a library, a dining room, a bedroom, bathroom and a hallway at this address. Not even these now-expanded premises could in all honesty ever be called luxurious. He had only a cupboard, a chest for shoes and a sofa bed in his bedroom. It was so crowded in that room that even two people could barely stand there together. In Munich, Hitler was also registered with the police. You could read the following entry in the official address book: Adolf Hitler, occupation: Reich Chancellor, Apartment: Prinzregentenplatz, 16 and the telephone number. Later editions of the address books[59] mentioned nothing about him.

Later on, Hitler bought up the entire building and only two tenants stayed on. While twelve rooms then became available to him, he actually lived in only those mentioned above. All the rest of the rooms, which were on the other floors, were assigned to the adjutants and his Begleitkommando. Hitler went there a few times to inspect them during the renovation and while they were being furnished.

And what about the Obersalzberg? The house in which Hitler first lived was called Haus Wachenfeld. Everything there was furnished according to local tradition. Being a typical mountain lodge, it did not have any large rooms. When people came for meetings, Hitler's practically permanently visiting in-house guests and those who lived in the neighbouring houses had to disappear out of sight, as there were only two spare rooms available in the house. Adjutants and those listed for a scheduled meeting literally had to stand waiting on the staircase for the meeting rooms to get freed up. One of the rooms was furnished as a winter garden and was only annexed to the main building later on, while the other room served as a dining room, living room and reception room all in one. Hitler's bedroom was but a mere chamber. There was most certainly many a bachelor who lived in greater style. You simply couldn't move in there. One had to take the suitcase out of the room so that you could pack it. There was no room for two chairs.

Once Haus Wachenfeld was converted, some sensibly sized rooms became available. That's when it was called the Berghof. Many, and well-known, photographs documented its interior decoration and grandeur, making a more detailed description in this book unnecessary. When meetings or receptions took place, the Berghof guests were obliged to stay in their rooms and not show their faces, or else they had to leave the Berghof well before. They were allowed to return only once everything was over. The most important receptions at the Berghof were those for the Duke of Windsor, the British prime minister Chamberlain, Lord Rothermere,[60] Mussolini, Schuschnigg, Balbo[61] and Ciano.[62]

Rothermere even spent the night on the Obersalzberg. Additionally, a diplomat, a Russian one to be precise, who had been in Berlin, was summoned to the Obersalzberg so he could officially hand over his letter of accreditation. This diplomat was then ordered to return to Moscow overnight. Nobody ever heard anything more about him. Once, some time later, Hitler commented on this incident, saying: 'The Moscow government was probably upset that their ambassador specifically went to Berchtesgaden to the private residence and was not, as is protocol, received in Berlin.' Hitler had even put a limousine at the man's disposal.

There is more to the story. This ambassador must have left his white gloves behind in Berlin, because, when he checked in his coat and hat in the Berghof's cloakroom, the white gloves were in his coat pocket and still had attached to them the price tag with the Berchtesgaden shop name on it. They were also still fastened together by a clip, so obviously had never even been worn before.

In the apartments, especially in Munich and on the Obersalzberg, some really exquisite paintings decorated the walls, above all Spitzweg, very much loved by Hitler, then Böcklin (I believe it was the *Battle of the Centaurs*). The painting was acquired from Switzerland for some 450,000 Reichsmark in exchange for other paintings: Makert, Rembrandt and others.[63] Hitler also very much appreciated valuable Gobelins.

No Fear of Assassination Attempts

Hitler's security as well as that of his ministers was the remit of the Security Service and thus of the Reichsführer-SS Himmler. Additionally, Hitler himself had two Begleitkommandos, one of them was the Kriminalführung Kommando, which consisted of some twelve men, each and every one of whom was previously a police officer who had then changed over into the service of the criminal police (the Kriminalkommando wore grey SS uniforms). Leader of this commando unit was Johann Rattenhuber,[64] who had been SS-Gruppenführer before that. His deputy was Peter Högl,[65] who then rose up in rank. This Kommando reported exclusively to the SS-Reichs Security Service.

The second commando unit, the Führerbegleitkommando, was recruited from the SS-Adolf Hitler and consisted of fourteen men. The Leibstandarte was a separate unit to the Waffen-SS (which participated in combat later on), and members could rise in its ranks. Led by SS-Sturmbannführer Gesche[66] (his deputy was Sturmbannführer Schädle[67]), it reported to Sepp Dietrich, the Commandant of the Leibstandarte.

There was hardly ever any changeover within the staffing of the Kommandos, which ensured that everyone remained in place and was familiar with everything. Hitler didn't particularly care for any change of faces around him. Both commando units increased to some thirty men in the course of time, but, in terms of guarding Hitler personally and ensuring his security, the same people would always be called on. These were also exactly the same people who looked after the security during journeys and who guarded the respective lodgings.

As for further security measures, say in hotels or public events, these were always decided on by the Reich government in consultation with Rattenhuber. The SS-Begleitkommando was exclusively responsible for the personal and close security of Hitler alone. In the Reich Chancellery, the SS-Kommando was responsible for the private wing and personal matters, such as announcement of guest, but they also had other duties. Two officers of the criminal police stood at the entrance. They had nothing to do with the SS, but simply were on patrol duty on four- or eight-hour shifts. A further six men always had to be on call for any escort duties that would arise.

Guards of the Leibstandarte protected the rest of the area around the Reich Chancellery, the apartment, gardens and hallways, and then there were four pairs of guards who were posted at the four main entrances (four belonging to the Wehrmacht, four to the SS). During the day, their function was purely honorary; it was only during the nights that they were actually on patrol. If we went travelling or drove through cities, special cars followed Hitler's vehicle. SS escort officers were in one car, and in the second one they were from the criminal police. On the occasions where Hitler went on only short unofficial city drives, only three officers of each Kommando would follow us. Then everyone had to wear plain clothes; these drives were secret. The fact was that, if anyone knew ahead of time that Hitler might pass through somewhere, large crowds would gather. When we drove somewhere, wherever that was, and crowds had gathered, Hitler used to say: 'Somebody has opened his big mouth. In the future, I will let no one know where we are going.' He always suspected that at the bottom of the leak were the criminal police officers, who always sent one officer ahead of them. Rattenhuber also tended to send a report either prior or after any outings to his superiors in the police.

At the entrance to his private apartment in Munich, one of the SS-Begleitkommando stood guard. Two policemen and one officer of the Kriminalkommando guarded the front of the house. Initially, during the early years, no security measures whatsoever were taken at the Berghof. Later on, after the conversion, a group of guards arrived, fencing off the immediate and wider surroundings. The actual Berghof itself was, once again, guarded by only two Begleitkommandos. But as more and more extensive construction work was taking place on the Obersalzberg, ever more responsibility was handed to Martin Bormann and increasingly more things were controlled by him. He was, to all intents and purposes, the actual ruler on the Obersalzberg.

It would transpire that none of us any longer felt either comfortable or independent when there, and that was from the minute Bormann decided that posts be positioned everywhere and reports from the head of the guards be gathered daily. Bormann took it even further, having special identity cards issued for the Obersalzberg inhabitants. Without these, it was no longer possible to come near the Berghof. He even managed to have an identity card issued for Adolf Hitler. I was ordered to hand him the said card, but my boss refused it downright and was totally outraged. Paths and footbridges, which had all been open to the public, were now blocked off. Hell would break loose if any guard or patrol from the Begleitkommando would by accident let a civilian pass through, even if it was only the one time and even if that civilian was not even in close vicinity of the Berghof. Once Bormann was informed of such an incident, he immediately had the position filled by another guard. I can safely confirm that every single guard of the protection squad, of both the Kriminalführung Kommando and the Führerbegleitkommando, would quiver in their boots when Bormann was anywhere close to the Obersalzberg, or was staying there. Here he was *Herrscher über alles*.[68]

Hitler didn't much like it when the guards made a fuss of him. Having said that, during our car journeys everyone had to be ready to jump at a moment's notice. If Hitler was recognised driving in the car, the public would just tend to pour out onto the street. Both Kommandos then had to work hard and hold people back from expressing their enthusiasm. It could easily happen that the guards would run alongside the Führer's car, keeping up with its speed, just to be ready to prevent any accidents. Admittedly, the people were really stupid. They would run directly into the middle of the street towards the Führer's car, making it quite difficult for the driver to avoid an accident. But there were no accidents.

The Kriminalführerkommando consisted, apart from one man, of Germans coming from the southern parts of the country, especially from Munich, while the Führerbegleitkommando, other than two men, comprised Germans from the northern parts of the country. Hitler was totally enthralled by his two Kommandos and considered them to be more competent than the entire security service. He himself always carried a pistol. It was the small Walther 6.35, which he kept in his trouser pocket. On his official travels as well as those abroad, he placed in his coat pocket a 7.65 pistol,[69] which was of the Stock brand.

Hitler's order to everyone who drove in his car was to carry a gun and be ready to shoot. Along the inside of the doors in the car itself, some extra pockets had been installed in which eight pistols were kept. I myself carried a 7.65 Walther, which was fastened onto my waist belt. When in plain clothes, I kept it in my coat pocket (and, following Hitler's specific orders, it was kept unlocked and had no bullets in the muzzle.).

As mentioned already, Hitler always bolted himself in his bedroom, even in hotels. There were no other security measures in place. Only after 1943 did he once again keep a trained Alsatian as his side. There were always dogs at the Berghof.

One time, an attack had been planned at the Kaiserhof – two Russian women and one Russian man were behind it. On that particular day Hitler had decided not to attend his regular coffee hour, so it was just coincidence that nothing happened to Hitler that time. After 20 July 1944,[70] things changed. Even the generals had to hand in their weapons before they were to see Hitler, and had to tolerate searches of their briefcases. This was at the behest of the Wehrmacht. Hitler thought that nothing could happen to him. He said that an attacker could, of course, be among the masses greeting him when he was travelling by car, but in his eyes this seemed unlikely to happen in Germany. He was tense, but not cowardly. In the Polish campaign he would certainly stride ahead of everyone, on his own, and without a care in the world.

The Punctual Grossadmiral

The official car routes, such as to the Kroll Opera house or the Sports Palace, had to be test driven by others using a stop watch. Hitler would then ask how long it was until departure. While turning to us with this question, he kept his gold watch, which had a spring cover to it and was always set to run twenty minutes ahead of time, untouched inside his jacket pocket. For him it made no difference having this watch or not, as he didn't use it in any event.

Twenty seconds to half a minute ahead of the scheduled departure time, he got into the car. Hitler could not abide arriving even one second late, but nor could he tolerate arriving a second early. Our timing was thus continuously regulated even during our journey, with the driver accelerating or slowing down as required. One time, we arrived at a performance after having had to drive at full throttle. Usually, before even getting into the car, Hitler would make a point of asking the chauffeur whether he had precisely timed the journey of the route. When he wasn't able to rely on my watch telling him the right time, he was annoyed. This happened once in Weimar. He screamed: 'Get rid of this potato of yours.'

Of all of the decorated dignitaries of the Third Reich, Grossadmiral Raeder always arrived the earliest. There he was, ready on the spot, five minutes early. During the war and due to security reasons, our vehicles were ordered to approach from different directions.

Hitler's Speeches

For a long period of time, people in Germany, and I think abroad as well, doubted that it was Hitler himself who wrote his own speeches. It was even claimed that Dr Goebbels or Minister Hess was behind his speeches. Here is what I can contribute to this, and no one is better placed than myself to make observations pertaining to this matter: nobody ever saw Hitler's speeches beforehand except for an adjutant and the stenotypists who typed up his taped speeches. Furthermore, it is entirely untrue that Wagnerian music inspired Hitler during his speechwriting, or for that matter any music. He dictated his speeches straight into the machine. Before his dictation, he jotted down some key words on small cards, which he used as an aide-memoire, and paced up and down while dictating.

He also made his own corrections to the speeches (an adjutant and a typist then checked over the corrected pages, but really only to clean up any typing mistakes). By the time the final version of the speech was ready, there had been at least three or four previous typed drafts. The big political speeches were handed over to the Foreign Office, or rather the Propaganda Ministry, for translation, but that was done only at the exact moment at which Hitler left the Reich Chancellery, or wherever he was staying, from where he then drove directly to the venue where he was to give the speech. So nobody really ever got to see his speech in full or even a version which was close to the final copy. My remarks earlier also apply to adjutants or typists, since they, for their part, all had shifts of one or two hours and then changed over so they could never actually hear or read Hitler's speeches in their entirety. Additionally, they were sworn to silence.

What did take place, however, is that Hitler would read the speeches of others, especially of those scheduled to speak in the Congress Hall at Party Conventions. He probably did that as a precautionary measure, in order to prevent any unpleasant surprises, which can so easily happen in the course of public political speeches.

Even when he was delivering the actual Reichstag speeches, Hitler was known to deviate from the text and make changes even though he had thoroughly prepared them long beforehand. The Chief of the Reich press would then transfer these amendments immediately onto the carbon copy of the manuscript which would lie in front of him. Hitler – as seen on *Die Deutsche Wochenschau*[71] – always pointed his finger to the respective spot on the manuscript. Afterwards, it was once again Hitler himself who supplied the press with excerpts from his speeches or, if representatives of the press had already sent them for print, he reserved his right to correct those.

Women

Here is a question many people asked themselves: why didn't Hitler get married? What I can state here is that Hitler certainly did not hate women. Proof of this are the many actresses who were invited during the early years to afternoon and evening performances. Often, during our travels, he would suddenly be totally enchanted, exclaiming: 'My God, isn't that a beautiful girl (a beautiful woman).' He then turned around, making me, who was behind him, move to the side so that he had an unrestricted view behind him and could follow the lady with his gaze. If, in any given place, an exceptionally beautiful girl would catch his eye, Brückner more often than not had to find out her address. After that, the lady was invited for coffee, either to Munich, Berlin or on the Obersalzberg, just so that Hitler could have a chat with her. In the earlier years, he also often joined members of the KDDK (Kameradschaft der deutschen Künstler)[72] when they gathered after performances in the theatre and opera houses.

Rumours about Leni Riefenstahl and Frau Winifred Wagner have no substance. He certainly respected Leni Riefenstahl because she was an ambitious woman who, based on remarkable commitment, had put together the films on the Party convention days and the Olympic Games. 'A woman has more sensitivity for this whole thing than a man', said Hitler once, referring to Riefenstahl. And he revered Frau Wagner as the bearer of the Wagnerian legacy, but marriage was never a likely possibility. They certainly were close, however. I was once present during a private conversation between Frau Wagner and Hitler where he mentioned that he was thinking of dissolving the Party. His reason was that for the sake of the unity of the German people no difference should be made between Party and non-Party members, and they should all be on equal footing. Frau Wagner was very surprised to hear this and asked him to consider what his old Party comrades would say to such a decision. This is just an example of their frank relationship.

He was overjoyed when the BDM (Bund Deutscher Mädel)[73] girls came out to openly celebrate him during his trips, and he went out of his way to treat them as being very special. They received gifts of money from him of two to ten Reichsmark per head with the words: 'Why don't you extend your stay for a little bit.' or 'Coffee and cake are on me', and so forth. All that was simply a reflection of his appreciation of beauty. If an especially attractive actress performed in an opera or play on stage (and provided she was also talented), he asked to be introduced to her at the end of the event. Among the film actresses he especially liked were Olga Tschechova and Brigitte Horney.[74]

What Hitler didn't care for was women who got involved in politics. While he conceded that women had achieved big things, he stood firm in his opinion that politics was exclusively to be left to men. This is how he explained his status of remaining unmarried: his principle was that every married partner should lead a decent family life. This was, however, not something he himself could ever offer, considering the colossal amount of work he had to cope with. He would only come home late at nights, and a wife and family would have nothing to gain from him. At most – if he were married with children in real life – they could perhaps have a chat about him. That was his reason to remain unmarried.

Sometimes he made reference to his wartime activities and said that it was a good thing he hadn't been married at the time, as 'the wave of enthusiasm [he] received mostly came from women'. He didn't believe that, had he been married, he would have garnered so much support. 'Just based on instinct alone, females are more inclined to be attracted to (single) men', he said.

I don't want to end this topic without making reference to the alleged diary by Eva Braun. However, let me pre-empt this by saying that, for me, the entire 'diary' is a total lie. While there are some details that correspond to true facts, even those are embellished by wild fantasy.

I knew Eva Braun well. In fact, I knew her from the first day I went into service for Hitler. I don't want to be judgemental in any way, as whatever I say would no doubt be biased. Eva Braun and I didn't get on much better than, as the saying goes, cats and dogs. Once, during the winter of 1935/6, we really gave each other a what for and ever since we had nothing whatsoever to do with each other, except for both of us saying hello and goodbye if our paths crossed.

At the beginning of the war, Eva Braun came to stay in Berlin only twice or three times, and then for no longer than one or two days on each occasion. In the years 1934 –7 she and Hitler were never in Berlin together at the same time. Their relationship became closer only after the war had started. Her parents never came to Berlin, her sisters visited perhaps once or twice. She lived at the Berghof for quite some time and was good friends with Martin Bormann, the actual master of the house, who then hired her as the housekeeper so that she was officially registered at the office for employment.[75]

Eva Braun never came to the headquarters, nor was she called upon for official receptions. At private functions, she came as Hitler's wife, was greeted by him with a kiss of the hand, as with other women as well, and called Evchen, a diminutive of Eva. She herself always addressed Hitler by the familiar *Du*.[76]

There is no doubt that Hitler considered her 'his bride'. But he wasn't the jealous type. After the conversion of the Berghof had been completed, the two bedrooms were linked to each other by a connecting door. Of course, Eva Braun's living expenses were met by Hitler personally. May I add that it fell to Brückner to keep the books. Hitler himself never carried a wallet, but placed his money – up to some 200 Reichsmark – loose in his pocket. Private journeys were always paid for out of Hitler's private funds.

Once, when the entire Hotel Imperial in Vienna was booked out by Party members, the manager of the hotel submitted a bill of 29,000 Reichsmark. This price seemed to be too high in Brückner's eyes, but Hitler just told him: 'Oh, go ahead and pay the bill; maybe the man has very large debts.' When Hitler expressed the wish to own the house in the Prinzregentenstrasse in Munich, he was short of funds. The subsequent release of his book *Mein Kampf* to countries outside Germany then enabled him to purchase the house.

But let's return to the alleged diary. One of the things mentioned there refers to nude dancers performing at the Reich Chancellery. This clearly demonstrates that the diary was false. During spring,[77] a former orderly of Hitler's was called to appear in front of the Spruchkammer.[78] There, he attempted to exonerate himself by asserting that he had been an inmate of a KZ.[79] Responding to the question 'Why?' he stated that he had spread the rumour there had been nude dancers performing at the Reich Chancellery. The orderly had, in truth, been incarcerated in the KZ for entirely different reasons. At the end of every major reception at the Reich Chancellery, it had come to light that several silver items, such as cutlery, cigarette and cigar boxes, had gone missing. The said orderly lived outside the Reich Chancellery and, according to information gathered on him, often entertained female visitors at his home.

After some time, one of these female visitors reported that she had spotted a number of silver items at the orderly's place, which she knew belonged to the Reich Chancellery. This orderly, along with a certain man called Sander, whom he had involved in this affair, was carted off to the KZ as they both belonged to the SS.

The fable about the nude dancers was pure fabrication. What was also invented, just to mention some other examples, was that Hitler drank coffee, which is just not true – and even less true is that he prepared it himself – or that he wanted to learn English. I once asked him whether he spoke any foreign languages and he answered 'No'. 'It would, of course, be beneficial', he added, 'if I knew English. But I won't even start with that, since I know very well that I'll only make a mess of it and that's my reason for not even giving it a try to begin with.'

Other claims made in the 'diary' allegedly reveal that Eva Braun was instructed by some Party bigwigs in how to have sexual relations with Hitler. That's possible, but she hardly had the many opportunities the diary wants us to believe she did. Perhaps on the Obersalzberg, or in Munich, maybe for a few hours. I also never really noticed that Göring ever had a conversation with her, or any talk of some significant length. The claim that she had been his personal guest was denied by Göring's former staff. The relationship between Hitler and Hess described in the diary is pretty much accurate. But Eva Braun was never personally present during any of the discussions between Hitler and Hess. Hitler never stayed up till the early hours of the morning and then went for a walk. And even though he was a great lover of animals, he actually never had a dog near him until the beginning of the Russian Campaign. It was only then that he acquired the Alsatian dog called Blondi. Dogs at the Berghof mostly remained in their kennels and were hardly ever taken on walks.

As for anything related to 'horoscopes' and 'astrology', Hitler didn't pay much attention to this; in fact, he was actually against all these things. Yes, there was the one time when he mentioned that a little old lady once told him in 1922 that he should preferably carry out his activities in the spring time, and never in autumn, as otherwise they would fail. In actual fact this indeed turned out to be true. 'But', he added, 'all this is balderdash. How can anyone see into the future?'

The claim that Hitler only ever had a bath once a month is total nonsense, of course. He bathed every day, indeed, after every speech he took a hot bath and changed into new clothes. But he didn't want to bathe outdoors. He would use dissolving spruce-needle tablets. But it is not true that he soaked his feet in seawater to help him with his foot complaints. Speaking about cosmetic stuff, let me add a word in respect to the 'cosmetic advice for the ladies'. Hitler did in fact like to freely give such advice, above all when he wanted to pull someone's leg. These pieces of information were handed out during light-hearted and social gatherings and were never meant to be taken seriously. Hitler enjoyed making fun of people.

Once, it was already during war time, some ladies bemoaned the fact that it was already quite difficult to get hold of good-quality underwear. Hitler commented: 'Yes, of course, the silk . . . we now require it for other purposes', and then, laughing, he continued: 'You might indeed have to switch to wearing leather underwear, it will surely last you for a long time.' Nobody actually took this comment seriously.

There is as little truth to the claim that Hitler accompanied Eva Braun to the tailor and then drove with her to a water festival at Nymphenburg[80] as there is to the one that the reason for Schuschnigg being treated so badly by Hitler on the Obersalzberg was because Hitler was in a bad mood due to his painful corns. It has to be said, though, that Schuschnigg was treated in a way that does not befit any statesman.[81]

I know nothing about some suicide on the Obersalzberg, nor anything about some 'rival' being liquidated, which seems more like the stuff cheap novels are made of. What seems incomprehensible to me, as well, is that a woman who was capable of following the man on whom she had bestowed her love into death would embarrass him in such an unkind and cold way.

I have no reason to 'whitewash' Hitler. I also believe that everything that happened under the rule of the National Socialists has burdened our people enough not to have to be saddled with untrue stories. But whatever the truth is, it has to remain just that. Towards our future generations and history we are obliged to convey an honest portrayal of who Hitler was and what happened during his time.

Fleet Calendar and Karl May

Hitler possessed a library of several thousand books. It was distributed among three apartments: Berlin, Munich and Obersalzberg. He didn't have an absolute favourite book. His knowledge was acquired by reading a lot. During my service with him, I observed that he read up on topics such as armament and strategy by perusing books by famous military people. On his night table, there regularly lay three books, one of which would be the fleet calendar, which also listed the armament and weaponry of other nations at sea. He himself was mentioned in two editions: the 1932 one and the respective current edition.[82] Most probably Hitler made comparisons. Then there was the *Nauticus* (a Yearbook on Germany's sea interests, published by the High Command of the Kriegsmarine) and a third book, always a different title, but none of them has really stayed in my mind.

Those three books always had to be ready on the table everywhere, with a magnifying glass placed on top, whether Hitler was in Berlin, Munich or on the Obersalzberg, in the train, on a plane, in a hotel, etc. Recently I was asked if Hitler also kept a bible in his library. This actually was the case, but it probably wasn't very important.

Newspapers and reports coming from the DNB were submitted to him on a constant basis. The newspapers were sent in part by the Ministry of Propaganda, and in part by newsagents. We kept all the papers from Berlin, as well as some that came from other parts of the Reich. Smaller provincial papers would be read only when we happened to be there. As for periodicals, magazines, weeklies and monthly publications from all over Germany, these too were collected by us, regardless of where we were, and handed to him, unopened, on a Thursday evening. This was also the case for all foreign magazines while they were being distributed in Germany.

On a Thursday afternoon Hitler would like to remind me by asking: 'Have the newspapers arrived yet?' Often he had already done so on a Wednesday, perhaps thinking it was a Thursday. He absolutely loved to browse through the papers. If he chanced upon an article or image that seemed particularly interesting, he had it translated – never did a word in any foreign language ever cross his lips.

Once the papers had arrived, and if nothing special was scheduled for that evening, Hitler would withdraw to his rooms earlier than usual. He literally devoured the newspapers. Since they were published in Berlin on an hourly basis, the newsagent usually picked them up directly from the publishing houses and had them delivered to us immediately. That was on Hitler's orders, so that there was no delay. If a guest arrived carrying a fresh newspaper, which he had not yet seen, he tended to be upset.

A comment Hitler made about *Der Stürmer* edited by Julius Streicher should be mentioned. He probably didn't read *Der Stürmer* more than ten times seeing that he despised the paper. These were his words: '*Der Stürmer* is no educational tool. Sensible people wouldn't even read it. I can only imagine that it is read by adolescent youths who haven't yet developed – and the only reason that they read the paper is for its articles dealing with sex.' Hitler would often reproach Streicher on this point and, if I remember correctly, even banned *Der Stürmer*[83] in one or two instances. Others would then intervene in order to have the ban lifted. I myself was forbidden to ever present this paper to him.

The moment a new book came out in German, I would usually have it sent to Hitler. I had signed a contract with a large German publishing house in Berlin and they were required to immediately dispatch the books as soon as they had been published. Of course this didn't apply to cheap novels. I regarded it my foremost duty to present Hitler with the new titles in the book industry myself, and not let other people get in there first, so to speak. Hitler returned the books the morning after I had given them to him, or asked them to be kept for his library, properly categorised.

I often doubted him and didn't believe that he could have read the books in such little time – overnight practically. And yet I was proved wrong; once, late at night, I gave him a volume of 356 pages (unfortunately I cannot remember its title). The next morning he returned it to me commenting: 'The book is good. Keep it.' I was totally convinced that he hadn't read it – I remember the number of pages. Some days later Dr Goebbels and an adjutant discussed this book over dinner. Hitler decided to join in. I had to fetch the book, turn to the requested page, was told to read it out loud and then asked to read two further passages. Hitler knew the exact page he wanted to hear. Thus he was able to create some sort of consensus between these two disagreeing men. I realised that Hitler must indeed have read the whole book and, by all accounts, quite thoroughly. Until 1937 Hitler also read the Karl May[84] books. In that year he received as a present a fabulous full edition of these works. He then said: 'These are the best books we have for young people in Germany.'

Religion and the Church

Once, at the dining table, Hitler compared the NSDAP with Christianity. His suggestion was something like this: 'Just like Christianity was fought against 2,000 years ago, but subsequently prevailed, nevertheless so too will the Party prevail.' 'But perish the thought', he continued, 'for anybody to even as much as think about declaring me holy. I will turn over in my grave.'

Hitler maintained there was only one God and that religions are entirely an artefact of man. Christianity, above all, he always considered to be a matter for the Party to deal with. He believed that the NSDAP would represent an absolute power equal to the one the Church holds today, but only once it could look back on a 2,000-year-old tradition. He had no understanding of the fight between religions, none whatsoever. The only thing he would see in this was each respective religious group's thirst for power.

I think it was a minister by the name of Schwerin von Krosigk[85] to whom Hitler, while pointing to the large globe in his study of the new Reich Chancellery, stated that there were no heathens. He basically explained that the black man honoured God, just as much as we do, with the exception that the black man simply stood on a lower intellectual level than us, but was a creature of God, nevertheless.

During the election of the pope,[86] Hitler was quite curious about the candidates. He believed that it was the opportune moment for Germany to sever ties with Rome (similar to what England did under Henry VIII). Then, however, he said: 'No, I won't meddle. I'll leave it to play out by itself. But if he [and he mentioned the name of an American candidate for the Vatican] should be elected, then the Church has been struck by blindness. The Church should look after my spiritual salvation, but should not mix in politics.'

At one of his intimate social gatherings he stated how the whole Church business was costing the state an absolute fortune: 'Each parish who wants a pastor should pay for him out of its own coffers.' And then here is something Goebbels said to Hitler during a conversation over lunch: 'Mein Führer, I have to pay so and so many Reichsmark [he mentioned a very high sum] tax to the Church. I intend to leave the Church. What is your opinion on that?' Hitler responded: 'Dear Doctor, if you don't come up with the money, I will put it down in your name, but stay with the Church. Otherwise I am the only one of my men who is left.'

It was very difficult for Hitler to find an appropriate minister whom he could charge with the Affairs of the Church. Only after having been 'courted' for a long time was Kerrl[87] prepared to act as the *Kirchenfürst* (this is how somebody in this post was called in Hitler's circles). Nobody else among Hitler's Party comrades volunteered to take this on.

Hitler, who repeatedly stipulated that 'everyone should be happy in his *façon*',[88] categorically refused to get involved with Church matters, and wanted to be left alone and not be forced to intervene in any way or at any time.

During the early years, Hitler was not prepared to even set eyes on a Christmas tree in his apartment. I once asked him why he didn't organise a Christmas party, and in actual fact he never even went to one, except for the one organised by the Alte Kämpfer.[89] This is the response I received: 'One Christmas evening some years ago my mother died – it was right underneath the Christmas tree.'[90]

Towards Christmas several men were ordered to look around the shops all over the city and purchase items listed on a piece of paper, which they then deposited both in the Reich Chancellery and in the Munich apartment. There, Hitler himself would inspect the paintings, busts, statues, porcelain sets, watches, fountain pens etc. and decide which object should go to whom as a present (all items made of gold were always first engraved with his initials).

The presents for Göring, Dr Goebbels and some families he knew well from previous years would generally be presented by Hitler in person. His immediate entourage and the personnel of the Reich Chancellery received a cash gift. All others, as well as the families of the SS-Leibstandarte Adolf Hitler, family friends from the war, acquaintances who were not well off, etc., usually got a Christmas parcel containing the following: a goose, a bottle of rum or cognac, half a case of cigars, or tins of meat (rice with chicken, for example), a Christmas *Stollen* and biscuits.

Once all the presents were distributed in Berlin, off went the rest, transported by an extra train to Munich. En route, the train personnel also received presents. The train driver and the conductor got their respective present as well and, if there was a changeover on that route, the new shift got their presents during the changeover. Then in Munich presents were wrapped once more. Wrapping presents by himself was probably one of Hitler's favourite pastimes. 'It is a real pity that I couldn't browse the shops myself and select this or that for somebody or another', he would say. When all presents had been wrapped and delivered by the truck drivers, it was usually late, perhaps 9 or 9.30 in the evening. Hitler then retired to his bedroom, where he stayed until the second day of Christmas (26 December). Breakfast, lunch and dinner, as well as newspapers and news reports, were left on a stool at the bedroom door, and along with a knock an announcement was made: 'Breakfast [or whatever meal it was] is ready.'

Hitler emerged only on the second day of Christmas. That's how it was in 1934, 1935 and 1936. But once, on Christmas Eve in 1937, he really took me by surprise. I myself had been invited to a family celebration and really longed for the moment that Hitler would at last retire, which would have allowed me to take my leave.

But then he suddenly entered the room where the remainder of the presents were being kept: those that hadn't been distributed and which would need to be returned to the shops after the festivities were over. He picked one present. We both wrapped it while spread out on the floor. Just when I was tying the knot and he was holding the string down with his right hand, I sort of got his thumb caught in the string and, laughing, he jokingly hit me in the neck. He ordered me to personally deliver this particular present, but first to prepare his tuxedo. In response to my incredulous look, he just said: 'Yes, I mean it, prepare the tuxedo.' I also had to order a taxi. It was supposed to wait for him in a side street, off the Prinzregentenplatz. I carried out Hitler's order by driving the last available of our cars, and then immediately returned and, seeing that these staff wanted to celebrate as well, discharged the driver. This then left nobody at the apartment, with the exception of the Begleitkommando on the lower floor and the two Munich policemen in front of the entrance.

I was instructed by Hitler that the Kommando was not to give him a guard and only one policeman was to stand in front of the entrance, the other one could go home. After I returned from the errand I followed up on this order. When I assured myself that all had been carried out as commanded, I went upstairs. There, who should come towards me but Hitler, wearing his dress shirt, his tuxedo trousers, but still in socks and without shoes, holding the two ends of his bow tie in his hands: 'I just wasn't able to tie the bow.'[91] Oh dear, he had made such a mess of the bow and his collar that I needed to get two new ones for him out of the cupboard.

When he had finished getting dressed, and after I had informed him that there no longer were any cars available, that nobody of the Begleitkommando had been previously informed of any likely outings and that it would take a while for the cars to arrive from where they were parked in the garage, Hitler said: 'For God's sake, didn't you let anyone know that I still wanted to go out?' 'No', I answered, and had no idea what all of this was supposed to mean. I was instructed to enquire one more time if the Begleitkommando indeed was already at his Christmas celebration, which was taking place in the house, along with punch bowls etc., and that nobody was standing on guard at the entrance, as was usually the case, and whether it was really the case that only one policeman was on duty.

We then very quietly tiptoed downstairs, whooshed like thieves through the house and out to the waiting taxi. Nobody had noticed us, and Hitler was visibly relieved. I wanted to take the seat next to the chauffeur, but Hitler grabbed me by my arm and pulled me onto the backseat of the car. So I sat on his right-hand side. He then whispered some Munich address into my ear, which I relayed to the driver. He did this several times and thus we travelled through Munich, from one place to another, with constantly changing destinations. His last command was 'Luitpold Café'.[92]

I was rather surprised at his behaviour and wondered what he could possibly want at the Luitpold Café. And you can image the surprise of the cab driver, even though he had no idea who was sitting behind him in the car. But he was definitely relieved when we got off at the Luitpold Café and I had paid him. The minute he held the money in his hand, he shifted gears and sped off. He probably thought we were a pair of mad men, and maybe he wasn't far off the truth, as I myself felt that this entire venture was very strange. Without even going inside, we then went on foot to the Königlicher Platz.[93]

Seeing as I felt responsible for Hitler's security, I kept turning my head back to check, but he simply said: 'Just walk alongside me, and don't worry on my account, since nobody will actually believe that Adolf Hitler would take a walk by himself through Munich.' When somebody passed us, he just lowered his head or looked sideways. Unrecognised by anybody, we finally arrived at the apartment on the Prinzregentenplatz. Suddenly an icy rain surprised us, forcing Hitler to first lean on my shoulder and then, for the last bit, to walk arm-in-arm with me, since he was concerned about his new pair of patent-leather shoes. But somebody must obviously have noticed us, since Himmler and Rattenhuber, who were in charge of the Kriminalkommando, asked me the following morning, full of reproach, why I hadn't notified anybody well beforehand with respect to this escapade. Himmler then gave me strict orders that in the future I was always and unfailingly to report to the Kriminalkommando, even in those instances when Hitler forbade me to do so. I never heeded this command.

The following day we drove to the Berghof and, ever since that time, we spent Christmas at the Berghof. On New Year's Day we would return to Berlin, because Hitler had to personally be in the city to receive the diplomats conveying their governments' New Year's wishes.

His query to the nuncio whether the New Year's reception could possibly be scheduled on a different date was warmly received by all diplomats, since nearly all of them wanted to spend their Christmas break back in their home country, and usually had to cut their holiday short only because of this courtesy visit. As the new Reich Chancellery had now been completed, the reception was thus confirmed thereafter to take place on 10 January.[94]

What Was Dr Morell's Position and Role?

Even though Hitler was rarely sick, he was never fully in good health either. He was constantly surrounded by various doctors attending him. His first actual personal physician, or rather accompanying physician, was Dr Karl Brandt.[95] He was a surgeon, and was only really kept on in case something might happen to us during one of our many travels. Thus no internal specialist was part of our team. Since Hitler continually suffered from intestinal pains and gastric bloating, Dr Grawitz[96] was consulted in 1935 (at the time, he was Head of Medicine at the Berlin-Westend hospital). He prescribed a special medication for Hitler: rubber pills filled with some liquid. At first, these pills worked. But after a while the old pains returned and were more severe than before.

One day, when Hitler complained about them, his photographer journalist, 'Professor' Hoffmann, advised him to perhaps consult a Dr Morell and enquire about what treatment he might be able to offer. It was Hoffmann who introduced this physician. He examined Hitler during the course of several days. He, of course, excluded Dr Grawitz from his investigations. He mentioned that the pills Dr Grawitz had prescribed were actually harmful, if taken over long periods of time. Dr Morell then prescribed different cures for the stomach and bowel conditions, and Hitler followed these to the letter. He actually did feel that his condition improved to some extent. It goes without saying that from then on Dr Morell came to be a permanent visitor to the house.

It didn't take very long after that for Morell to join the inner entourage, and even be given the title of 'professor'. He thus was an integral member of staff and much to everybody's annoyance, especially of the adjutants, he became a virtual fixture. At first we nearly had to hire a minder for him, as he constantly went missing, was fooling around somewhere and, overall, it was just very difficult to get him to arrive on time. He thought he was God-knows-who and could work wonders; he gossiped with Hitler, faffed around and sometimes acted as if he couldn't count up to three. After performances or outings, Hitler would often ask him how he enjoyed this or that. Morell then started to whinge and complain: 'Nobody ever bothers looking after me. I could hardly keep up. I had to sit in the luggage wagon,' and so forth. Hitler would then explode, and the adjutants had to tolerate a huge telling off. Later on, special attention was bestowed on Morell.

Medical care for Hitler (with the exception of dental care, an operation on his vocal chords and one treatment for earache in 1944–5) was entirely put into the hands of Dr Morell. The operation on Hitler's vocal chords was performed by Professor von Eicken[97] at the Reich Chancellery, and no efforts were spared. Had the operation failed, Hitler would have lost his voice. This fact was known only within his closest circle. For his dental care an entire and specially equipped permanent dental surgery was set up, both in Berlin and on the Obersalzberg. Dr Blaschke,[98] or his locum Dr Richter, attended.

Hitler's ear troubles in 1944–5 were as a result of the 20 July 1944 assassination attempt, in which both his eardrums burst. He was treated by Dr Giesler, a Wehrmacht doctor and student of Professor von Eicken. Hitler's recovery went well, but there was one day when he remained in bed saying that he was ill, which incidentally was the first time in many years that this happened. The doctor waited to be admitted, reflected on what might have been the cause and, still deep in thought, passed a cupboard in which were kept a lot of Hitler's medications and many different tablets. Being a doctor, he of course was interested as to what these drugs were, and came across a packet bearing the words: 'Anti-gas tablets'. He immediately established that it was these tablets that had caused Hitler's health to be so poor. In his opinion these drugs contained a high dosage of strychnine.[99] By drawing Hitler's attention to this fact and informing him that these pills were actually poisonous, the doctor nearly brought about Dr Morell's dismissal.

But, with the help of Reichsleiter Bormann, Dr Morell succeeded in presenting this whole event as a harmless incident. Misrepresenting the facts towards Hitler, these two men claimed that the other physicians were intent on wanting to take Dr Morell out of the team that had been entrusted with Hitler's medical care. They then proceeded to sideline the doctor who had treated Hitler's ear problems, as well as all the other doctors, such as Brandt, Hasselbach and Haase and even Dr Stumpfegger[100] the surgeon.

Thus, Hitler's health was entirely and throughout all these years in Dr Morell's hands. I might even go so far as to maintain that he was a guinea pig for Morell because Morell prescribed God-knows-what. Just about anybody would have been worn out by the many injections Morell gave Hitler nearly every day. When I once asked Morell how he had actually decided on this particular injection treatment, he responded: 'I was a marine surgeon and specifically assigned to control epidemics. In my opinion, this treatment proved to be the best.' Whatever ailment one would present to Dr Morell – toothache, headache, back problems, a cold – he always administered an injection. The pain subsided, or even disappeared totally. The effect of these injections lasted for many hours or even days. After a while, you actually felt something was missing, something was not sitting quite right, unless you had this injection. The same thing was true for Hitler. During the last years, he virtually lived on this treatment.[101]

Hitler consumed pills in bulk. Throughout my service to him he never went to bed without having taken sleeping pills. He usually had two pills, either Evipan, Phanodorm or Tempodorm. After each meal he swallowed, as prescribed, a teaspoon of sodium bicarbonate dissolved in water. Hitler's skin was very sensitive to the sun. Just the slightest bit of sunshine was enough for his cheeks to turn pink or even red, very easily allowing the conclusion that he surely must be wearing make-up. Some people who had no idea about the sensitivity of his skin really did believe that he wore make-up.

Hitler would always suck on eucalyptus sweets and carbonated tablets. On every desk there would be one box of each, and I myself also had to keep them in my pockets, so that I could hand him a tablet if he requested it, above all during car journeys. He took masses of other pills; any drug the doctor prescribed him, and, if he hadn't specified the daily quantity or the times at which they should be taken, Hitler would simply take one after the other, from morning to night. He was really frightened to catch anything contagious, above all colds and catarrh. If someone in his inner circle ever had even the slightest hint of a cold, he was, under all circumstances, to avoid coming anywhere near Hitler

If someone suffering from any kind of medical ailment did happen to get near him, totally by accident, you could be certain that the very next day Hitler would have contracted the same disease. This is exactly what happened when anyone had a cold in his vicinity. If he became aware that one of his staff was suffering from the flu, Morell immediately had to fall into action and take counter measures – as usual with injections.

I myself once suffered from catarrh, and therefore didn't want to be on call, but Hitler urgently required my services. He said: 'Go to Morell and get injected.' I answered: 'I will not be injected and won't go to Morell – otherwise I'll be going to him forever.' I said this out loud, in front of several guests, among whom was von Blomberg, who responded: 'So, in view of this, let me give you the official order right here and now to do as instructed.' And here is what I said: 'And I will disobey the official order.' Many, among them Himmler, turned to me and asked: 'What's got into you to respond to the Führer in this way?' I simply said: 'I will do exactly what I want with my own health.' I am putting this in writing here, just to prove that one could contradict Hitler.

The Change in Hitler

Until 1938–9 I would say that Hitler was a second father to me, as until then he took care of everything that concerned the staff who were working for him, even with regards to small personal matters. He enquired of housekeeping staff how their respective parents were, he wanted to know their personal wishes and so on. Staff, for their part too, put their full confidence in him and would turn to him, via Brückner, with their own requests and concerns. When he had put something in place for somebody, such as financial support, Hitler would enquire afterwards whether his instructions had been followed. If a close friend was ill, he had flowers sent to him. Thus there was hardly what one might call a 'partition wall' between him and us. If someone from his staff wanted to get married, they simply went to Hitler. He would be sure to be most generous to people, and present them with a significant gift.[102] Here are some examples.

Once someone whose livelihood depended on Hitler suddenly found himself unemployed. Overnight this person came into work. It was obviously thanks to Hitler's intervention. And another example – at the daily cinema screenings both at the Berghof and in Berlin, Hitler, generous in sharing his leisure time, expressly wished for the entire house staff to be present and watch the films along with him.

The following episode further underlines how considerate he was towards others: on 9 November Hitler stayed at a place that he had frequented in the past. This particular inn had always been a simple hotel. When Hitler drew the curtains shut in his room, one of them fell to the ground. He quickly shut the door so that the owner wouldn't notice anything. Together we then fixed it.

During the war, once the Wehrmacht adjutants had reported that they no longer expected any flights to arrive that night and that the enemy planes were departing, Hitler would say: 'I can only go to bed after the last plane has left Germany, and after the last of the people has emerged from their air-raid shelters. I won't rest easy until such time that I know this has happened.'

Another comment made by Hitler, which I overheard at the Berghof, also supports my opinion that he only reluctantly agreed to put aside other matters, in order to refocus and concentrate on military matters: 'Believe me, I much prefer constructing buildings, such as we now have in Munich, than constructing destroyers. This building costs me two million, for a destroyer I pay twelve. I could put six such buildings up and they would, one day, be testimony of our era; but a destroyer, within no time at all, will be nothing but a piece of scrap.'

This kind of personal and direct connection by Hitler with others, and which I described here only in very broad terms, changed during the years 1938–9. Just before the annexation of Austria, he turned visibly more formal. He was so consumed by the affairs of the Wehrmacht that, unlike before, people simply lost their nerve to come up to him with anything that weighed on their mind.

His adjutants, above all Martin Bormann, would also keep much away from Hitler, which resulted in him in the end not being informed about so many issues. Even as far as I was concerned, I, who practically was in hourly contact with him, was barely able to have a conversation, let alone consult him about anything that troubled me personally. It was as if all communication had been cut off. A high firewall had gone up.

This conscious, or unconscious, isolation of Hitler vis-à-vis the outside world intensified considerably after Stalingrad. I was never a witness to any discussion involving Stalingrad. Just once Hitler mentioned that, if the front at Zaporizhia came to a halt, he'll just have to fly there himself and make things happen. He actually did fly there. General Field Marshal von Manstein was there to receive him. Theirs was a cool exchange of greetings. Troops, on the other hand, welcomed him, as well as Field Marshal von Richthofen (who arrived a bit later), with wild enthusiasm.[103]

Following the briefing, architect Bruckmann, who was also present, enquired as to why the front was continuously retreating in spite of weekly arrivals of fifty-two goods trains compared to just the one train during the previous year. It was true that the front had in fact come to a brief halt just outside of Zaporizhia. But then, suddenly, sixty Soviet panzers broke through. That was February 1943. I still remember Hitler criticising the fact that all airports had been built to the east of the Dnieper and not to the west.

If something went wrong on the military front, it was usually Keitel's[104] turn to appear on the scene. Their arguments were loud and fierce. Hitler became so agitated that his lower jaw swelled up. He repeatedly reproached the generals and yelled that everything always went wrong unless he himself was there on the spot. When the front continued retreating, nobody was to be found who would willingly stand at Hitler's side and address the generals. When there were talks about setting up a new army, the suggestion was for Himmler to head it up. Hitler refused. 'Might he perhaps also want to head up the Air Force?' was his curt retort. In the past he would take his meals with the general, but after this he completely withdrew. One got the impression that he wanted to evade questions, which would invariably be put to him by his entourage. After the assassination attempt on 20 July 1944, he was totally isolated (I can vouch for this based on my visits to Berlin. Since my family still lived in the Reich Chancellery I would invariably come in close contact with him during these times).[105]

Nobody exploited this isolation and loneliness of Hitler more than Martin Bormann, who exercised unbelievable influence on Hitler. In my opinion many instructions to the Party and to its divisions were henceforth coming directly from Bormann, without him ever having prior discussions with Hitler on such matters. He totally excluded anything and anybody who wanted to get near Hitler, and he even had himself made part of the military briefings with the Wehrmacht.

How I Fell Out of Grace

The first serious altercation between Hitler and myself happened at the beginning of the invasion of Poland.[106] That was the point when I decided to return to the navy. At the time the headquarters were in the Sonderzug, which was then stationed in Pommern (Gross-Born), from where daily trips to the front were undertaken.[107] As the first of these trips was a very brief one, nothing had been packed for Hitler. However, there was a standing order in place which specified that a few bottles of Fachinger must be taken along on every journey as it was incredibly hot during the first days of the invasion.

I had given instructions to that end to the orderlies who always accompanied us on these trips. They thus knew to bring along two to three bottles of Fachinger in a bucket filled with ice. (These orderlies followed our convoy by car and carried with them picnic cutlery and anything else that would be needed.) This all went according to plan with respect to two trips we had made. Then there was one day when we weren't travelling to the front. On the following day we departed very early from headquarters to travel a bit further than usual, right up to the very front line. It was hot. Lunch was prepared at a country inn. On the menu was peas with bacon.

Hitler ordered me to enquire whether there was any place for him to eat. The general in charge of this particular section of the front said to me: 'Everything is ready for lunch. Just make your own personal arrangements for the Führer's meal. Everything will be organised.' But since peas and bacon was on the menu, i.e. a one-pot dish, and because I knew that Hitler wouldn't make any special demands in this case (the only option would have been, seeing as he is vegetarian, to pick every single piece of bacon out of the dish) I no longer worried about it. When lunchtime came along, everything was set up on tables arranged in a large circle. It was all supervised by a Wehrmacht lieutenant. I communicated with him by eye contact and just stayed close by in case I was needed.

The only drink these gentlemen had was water, as everyone wanted to make a particular point of abstaining from alcohol in the presence of the Führer. During the meal I had to attend to Hitler. He asked me whether the glass in front of him contained Fachinger water. In the event, I was actually only able to verify this after having explored the issue with the lieutenant in charge of the meal. I then informed Hitler that the water was clear spring water, that the doctors had analysed it and that the troops had been drinking it for three days already (Hitler would often drink clear spring water when on the Obersalzberg). He asked me once again whether I had brought along any Fachinger water. I responded, *'Jawohl*, mein Führer, Fachinger must be available. I will ensure that it is served immediately. Maybe it just hasn't been put on the table because it is so hot outside.' He answered: 'I'd rather drink warm Fachinger than this water here.' I responded: 'I will have it brought to you immediately.'

I searched for an orderly and also checked myself in the car that transported all the smaller items, and realised that there there was no Fachinger. The orderly in charge informed me that, on that morning, he had not added any fresh bottles and that the driver of the car had taken the bucket containing the rest of the bottles out of the boot before departure. I felt like I'd been hit over the head; I could hardly believe it, and asked each of the other truck drivers whom I knew, and whom I had given some Fachinger bottles in the past, if perhaps anyone of them had a bottle of Fachinger on him. But it was as if the whole thing was jinxed. On that day, absolutely nobody had a bottle of Fachinger on him. I was just about to return to the dining room, where the group was eating, and report to Hitler that there indeed was no Fachinger available (I was prepared to be thoroughly bawled out), when Hitler came down the stairs, together with the other gentlemen, and approached me.

When he saw me, he tersely ordered me to report to him later that evening. When I told him that there was no Fachinger available and that the orderlies had forgotten to bring it along, all he said was: 'You can spare me your stories, you knew fully well that there was no Fachinger, and you were just putting me off with the other water.' His demeanour and tone left me in no doubt that, this time round, he was serious. To make things worse, more mishaps had occurred on that day, which certainly didn't exactly help put Hitler in a better mood.

Originally we had wanted to be back at headquarters by five o'clock in the afternoon. A lieutenant had gone ahead in an armoured reconnaissance vehicle, but got lost and didn't drive along the prescribed route. At the end we were on enemy territory. That certainly didn't bode well for my forthcoming report.

We arrived late that day at our destination, which was where the Sonderzug was stationed. Hitler himself headed the convoy, with the stars guiding us so that we were able to at least be sure that we were heading in the overall correct direction. When I reported to him, he took me into his compartment and, addressing me in a serious voice, said: 'What on earth went through your head? Do you actually think you can do with me what you want? Today you have kept me waiting and you have deceived me. I do not want to set eyes on you again.' He then opened the door himself for me to pass through. After so many years in his service, I thought I knew him well enough for me to not have to take this matter all too seriously.

Only later did I come to understand why Hitler's reaction to this petty and minor matter was so disproportionately aggressive. He was in a bad mood because – and I only later found this out – he had received the news that, during an attack by his Leibstandarte, twenty-five of their men had been found massacred in a fruit orchard. Their eyes had been gouged out and their genitals cut off. I could thus, in retrospect, better understand his behaviour.[108]

The next morning, while I was serving him breakfast, Hitler asked: 'What is it you are still wanting around here?' I gave him a short answer: 'I just want to clarify what happened yesterday.' He responded sharply with: 'You can leave. I don't want to see you any more.' Because I stood still, his eyes, with an awful expression in them, measured me from top to bottom, after which he got up from his breakfast and returned to his compartment, where he bolted himself in. I knew that this was it and decided to immediately return to my old unit, which was with the navy. I went to Obergruppenführer Brückner and reported the entire incident to him. Brückner agreed and said: 'You know the Boss even better than I do. Go to Berlin for a few days. I'm sure everything will blow over.' I replied: 'This time, that will not be the case. Please, I beg you, put in a word for me so that I can go back to my old unit, which as you know is with the navy.'

A few hours later Brückner had a word with Hitler. I remained in the corridor. The door was left open. It was in the train. I was able to listen in on everything. Brückner asked: 'What should happen with Krause?' Hitler responded: 'He should go to Berlin, report to Kannenberg and work as an orderly at the Reich Chancellery.' I heard this and said, in a loud voice so that Hitler could hear it: 'I am from the navy, I was a valet and I will not work as an orderly for some Herr Kannenberg. I request to please get permission to report immediately to the navy.'

As it turned out, Hitler did not give me permission to do that, but instead ordered me to go to Berlin. My salary would remain the same, he said, and other than that he couldn't tell me anything more. So I turned to General Bodenschatz,[109] who was the representative of the Luftwaffe, and enquired whether there was a flight to Berlin. It turned out that within one hour a plane was leaving Oppeln airport (during the night the headquarters had been moved close to Oppeln) for Berlin. I asked that a seat be held for me, packed my suitcase, flew with the Flieger Storch[110] to the airport and travelled to Berlin. After some time in Berlin, I drove to Munich where I had two operations: my appendix and my tonsils had to come out. I remained in contact with Brückner, as I had asked him to keep urging Hitler to consider my request and grant me leave to rejoin the navy.

It was Christmas. I received a telegraph requesting me to report at the Munich Central railway station that very evening. The Sonderzug would come through. I dressed in plain clothes and went to the station. Since everyone there knew me, I had no difficulties getting onto the platform, where Hitler's train would arrive. It stopped, I hurried to the Führer's carriage, was announced to the Führer by adjutant Schaub and was immediately shown through. I received my Christmas bonus. He extended to me his best wishes for my family, enquired after my well-being and took his leave, again with a handshake. I could not present my case with the request to join the troops. So I approached Brückner once again and asked him to please put in a good word on my behalf, seeing as I was physically fit again. Brückner's opinion was as follows: 'As you know yourself, the second the Boss even so much as hears your name, he absolutely refuses to contemplate anything which would even have the slightest thing to do with you' (among ourselves, Hitler was always referred to as 'the Boss').

I said goodbye and returned home. I still laugh today at the burning curiosity that befell me on my way home. I was extremely curious to see how much my annual Christmas present was, and yet it certainly wasn't greed that motivated me. I just assumed, after all that had happened, that the gift would be smaller than in the previous years. When I reached a street lamp, I decided to check and simply tore open the envelope right then and there. Well, would you believe it, it was nearly double the amount. It certainly helped me conclude that Hitler had calmed down and no longer thought that what had taken place was so very awful.

I had nothing to do, no occupation – nothing. It was March 1940, when, out of the blue, I was informed that the headquarters was set up once again in Berlin. I boarded the next train to Berlin, and was utterly determined to take matters into my own hands and put my affairs in order. I discussed this in depth with Brückner first. The other gentlemen wouldn't really look me in the eye. Well, yes, whispered some of the 'underlings', I had wanted to poison Hitler. I made quite sure to inform Brückner of these rumours and he assured me that he would set the record straight, which he did.

On one of the evenings, just before the usual time at which Hitler retired, I posted myself right in front of the library. I was well aware that only my successor[111] would accompany him up to that point and that this was my opportunity to speak to Hitler unhindered and without being fobbed off by somebody else first.

Hitler appeared and, upon seeing me, he asked: 'What are you doing here? How are you?' I responded: 'Mein Führer, if it may please you, do I have permission to return to the troops, as it is impossible for me to languish here in perpetuity and without any occupation whatsoever.' This time, I beseeched him to be good enough to set me free. He said: 'Well, fine, I will be in Berlin for another two days. During that time you can decide to which unit you want to return, to my Standarte or to the navy.' 'I have now had four months to think things through,' I answered right then and there, 'I started with the navy, and still belong to it to this day, and would politely request to be given leave to return to this particular unit.' Visibly furious at my answer, he said: 'If you really insist on having the last word, then go ahead, call the adjutant of the navy.' I was dismissed. I immediately contacted the adjutant of the Marines (Captain z.S. von Puttkamer)[112] and informed him to please come to the Führer now, concerning my transfer to the navy.

The door had remained ajar. I could still hear the conversation from the outside, with Hitler saying to the Captain: 'I have set Krause free to join the navy. Make sure that he gets a decent posting.'

A few days later I received my order to report in Kiel Wik. I was assigned to the destroyer (Bonte) and participated in the battles around Narvik.[113]

In total, I must have changed ships three times, and was also sunk three times. Later on, based on the fact that I had survived three naval disasters, Hitler ordered me back to join the Begleitkommando. Once the Battle of Narvik was over, I was given some leave. I reported to the Reich Chancellery. After that, Hitler once again allowed me to meet up with him in Munich. He wanted to know everything about how I had survived it all. He also enquired whether I had any special wishes. Just by the by I mentioned that my comrades and I would so much welcome it if I brought back with me a *Schifferklavier*[114] – at the time we were assigned to a *Vorpostenboot*.[115] This was immediately granted, and I received my accordion.

Once my leave came to an end, I immediately went back to Trondheim in Norway. While sailing from Denmark to Norway, my boat was torpedoed. Once again, I had to swim for three hours until I was spotted and saved. It was my third time, and this time round I had lost everything. Due to the long swim in cold water, I developed oedema in my leg and was transferred to the military hospital. I had nearly fully recovered when I was telegraphed and ordered to report to the Reich Chancellery just as soon as my health permitted it. On 26 October 1940 I arrived in Berlin.

It took a while before I was permitted to present myself and speak to the Führer. Brückner had been fired in the meantime, and all the rest of the adjutants just gave me the cold shoulder. A few days later Hitler was going to leave for Munich. I decided to put myself right next to his car, just at the spot where he would usually get in. All his adjutants filed passed and didn't even bother to throw me a glance. Then came the Führer. The chief guard of the Reich Chancellery protection squad made his report. I stood close by. Hitler passed by me without any acknowledgement. Just when he was about to take his seat in the car, that is, just when he was about to get in, he actually saw me, stopped, walked around the car to where I was standing and pulled off his gloves – something he rarely did – with the words: 'Well, wouldn't you know it, if this isn't Krause. You are already back here?' and shook my hand. But he was rushing off to catch the train, and no further discussion took place.

At that point, all these gentlemen then gathered round to greet me. A call came in from the railway station with the order that they should pack some food for me and my family, who were still living in the Reich Chancellery, along with a few bottles of wine.

This brief description of how things worked back then should offer just a bit of a glimpse into the typical environment adjutants worked and lived in. During my absence, which lasted some six months, and apart from Brückner, who had been fired, only the valet Hans Junge (Traudl Junge's – secretary to Hitler – future husband) backed me up, as did Gesche and Schädle, the two Kommandoführer of the SS-Begleitkommando.

What I Had Learnt

At the end of my reflections, I would like to put into perspective what the press has published about Hitler. Of course this is simply from the vantage point of what was my own experience and what information I had to hand. Above all, however, I would like to take issue with the so-called diaries by Eva Braun, which had been an especially controversial issue in the German press.

Every now and again rumours about Hitler's death will make the rounds. In my lifetime and after the war, there were a great many people who simply refused to believe that Hitler was dead. My own comment based on my well-founded conviction is that he is dead. Nobody could have truly known who Hitler really was as a person other than myself and my successor Heinz Linge, who then spent ten years in Russian captivity and was released in 1955.

Having lived together with Hitler for nearly ten years[116] and dealt with him on a daily basis, we got to know him much better and much more closely than anybody who just met him purely in an official capacity. Additionally I have spoken to several people who were with him in Berlin, to the end, and in close contact. They all agreed and confirmed that he is dead. His physical and emotional state alone would have not stood the test of time. A main reason was that Dr Morell had already run off several days earlier and could, therefore, no longer 'treat' him. This is because, during the end of his days, Hitler only survived on the injections which he had been given. And a body just collapses if it is all of a sudden deprived of the chemical substances (in part also poison) that had sustained it for such a long time. But he would have put his life to an end in any event, even had he been in a better physical state. The simple fact of the matter was that he had made up his mind and drawn his conclusions.

Why don't Germans ask themselves: 'What should he have done, had he continued to live?' Nobody can absolve him from the burden of his guilt, because it was he who had led us into this indescribable misery. Whether he did so knowingly or not – who can judge? This was unquestionably not what he originally wished for. He felt responsible for the entire German people. But he remained all on his own, alone, apart from one single man who would stand next to him with utter devotion to the end: Dr Goebbels.

All the rest knew how to manipulate Hitler in such a way that it would accommodate their own egocentric and dark machinations. I myself would compare Hitler to a banker to whom many honest people entrust their savings, seeing he obviously knows what he is doing. If then one of his employees – even a single one – commits a minor misappropriation, then this could probably be rectified. But if these misappropriations multiply and if ever more opportunists come along and join in, then one sunny day that bank will go bankrupt. The business will collapse. Whose fault is it then? According to me, blame can firmly be laid at the feet of the boss, of the owner, because he neither saw the maladministration nor did he uncover it. So all these good people who had entrusted their entire possessions to this man are now deceived. The question whether this banker is an honourable man or not, practically speaking, is no longer relevant. The masses out there will be judging him and him alone, and they will be entirely within their rights to do so, as it was he who was responsible for the business all along, but incapable of running it properly. He might then defend himself, claiming: 'I am blameless. I didn't want that. Blame those who have committed the misappropriations.' It doesn't change anything.

Hitler had drawn his conclusions. If he were still alive and returned to this place, what would there be left for him to do in the face of this crying shame of ours? He would have to gather the entire group of advisors and underlings he had, and who had decided on the fate of the German people, and he would have to hold them accountable. 'Why didn't you inform me and let me know how it really was?' he would probably be asking them. He would have to condemn them all, and then be his own judge. What I want to emphasise here again is that Hitler had no real sense of who people were, he had no insight into human nature. This is a hard and severe thing to say, but it's true. His advisors, Gauleiter, Reichsleiter, in fact all those who had occupied higher positions, were not men with whom the majority of the people agreed.

On the other hand, the Germans couldn't muster up sufficient energy to defend themselves. The fact was that people either trusted or feared him, and what they said to themselves was something like: 'He will surely know why he is doing it this way and not a different way.' They simply accepted their lot. Those in charge sadly took advantage of this situation, to the detriment of the people, but above all to the detriment of how the German people were viewed abroad.

The main culprits of most of the crimes committed against human beings, who lived and suffered in the German Reich and who were admittedly executed in Hitler's name, were Martin Bormann and Himmler, and blame must be firmly and squarely put on them. Both of them walked over dead bodies, no question about that. I was never able to tolerate Bormann. He was brilliant at knowing how to ingratiate himself; furthermore, and I have to be honest, he also was extremely hard-working. Once Dr Heim,[117] Bormann's adjutant, said this about him: 'He grew up among oxen, one just cannot expect him to be equally adept at dealing with human beings.'

What was more, Hitler wasn't actually informed about many things, regardless what the issue was. If indeed he was told, then it was likely only to a very small extent, or only to the extent that these two evil spirits would allow. Regarding the atrocities that happened in the concentration camps, nothing at all was public knowledge within the close inner circle surrounding Hitler. This was never spoken about. Only in the rarest of cases would someone mention that one or the other has ended up in the concentration camp. I, for example, only ever heard of the names Oranienburg and Dachau.

But they were presented in the light of merely being political education centres. People there were supposed to learn how to return to productive work. My colleague Toni, for example, was put into a KZ,[118] because once, when he was totally drunk, he had threatened to attack Hitler. He was, so we were advised, going to be taught how to break the drinking habit.

78

We were also told that only people who had committed a criminal offence, though not a severe one but which would have called for an immediate prison sentence, would be placed there. Until this day I just cannot see how this entire issue could have been kept secret at the highest level and that we didn't have even the tiniest inkling. This was obviously possible by virtue of the fact that only extremely few people knew about this, and they themselves didn't utter a word. Again I wish to stress here that these affairs – as well as the fight against the Church – originated with Bormann and Himmler. They only informed Hitler insofar as it was absolutely necessary, in their minds, to do so in order to properly stoke the fire.

They definitely also left Hitler in the dark when it came to what the real conditions were in the camps, and they would only inform him, if at all, of some of the more positive aspects. If somebody asks me what could justify what led to these thoughts of mine, here is how I respond that I draw this conclusion because I personally know of many small incidents in which instructions were relayed to us starting with the words: 'Der Führer has ordered . . . [or instructed],' where I know perfectly well that the Führer did not have the slightest inkling about any of this. Admittedly these were things that were of a personal nature and wouldn't have much interested the wider public. But they do shed light on how certain manipulating characters tended to phrase their sentences by invoking Hitler's name.

Let me mention an example: one day, Bormann arrived in Munich and gave a briefing on the Warsaw situation. Allegedly, a secret radio transmitter, which had been in contact with the outside world, had been discovered in the ghetto. Bormann requested guidelines as to what should be done. Hitler thought about it for a while and then said that if the report was true then punishment must be meted out. He did not, however, formulate a clear-cut order. It was left to Bormann, Himmler and the commander of Warsaw as to what shape this punishment should take.

Recalling such events, I should add that Hitler lived in a kind of fake world. He preferred to believe the good rather than the bad. If he was told, for example, that the SS had committed extremely horrific crimes at this or that location, he would comment that his boys wouldn't do such a thing, and if they actually had done it then inevitably they would have to be punished.

Another example: Berlin, February 1945. During an air raid Hitler turned to Heinz Linge, my successor, and asked him who the old woman was in the bomb shelter. He was told that she was the mother of Krause, his previous valet. Hitler said: 'They are from East Prussia, aren't they, and they have fled already?' Hitler committed a cardinal crime by waging this war and, in the end, an even worse crime by placing the Wehrmacht under, or rather behind, the Party. In the end, therefore, it was Bormann who directed the war. In any case it proved that it was entirely impossible for one single man to lead the people towards a good future, if, as was the case here, this one man is surrounded by men who are meant and are selected to support and advise him, but who fail him and if, furthermore, these very same men don't themselves have the good of the people at the forefront of their minds.

This is also a reason why we must no longer hand over the possibility to wield power over such a large number of people to a single person. People simply aren't in a position to guide this one person towards pursuing the common good. After killing off free speech, Hitler, in the final analysis, deprived himself of the possibility to ever get to the whole truth of matters. It is not right that just a handful of shady characters can do with the people as they please. In a healthy society, there have to be clear-cut parties where some are 'for' and some 'against'. Of course three or four parties would suffice, as if there are too many this could result in a fragmented situation which, in the end, would only benefit dictators who would capitalise on the situation. I would like to close this dark chapter with one last question: 'What on earth could Hitler really have done, had the army, the navy and the Air Force closed ranks and stood up against his inordinately excessive plans?'

Endnotes

1   Erich Raeder (24 April 1876 – 6 November 1960) reached the unusually high naval rank of Grand Admiral in 1939, and was in charge of the Kriegsmarine for the first half of the war; he resigned in 1943. He was sentenced to life imprisonment at the Nuremberg trials, but was released in 1955 as his health was failing.

Werner Eduard Fritz von Blomberg (2 September 1878 – 14 March 1946) was a German field marshal, Minister of War and Commander-in-Chief of the German Armed Forces until January 1938; he worked feverishly to expand the size and power of the army.

2   This building had been used as an SS prison and early concentration camp since 1933.

3   Julius Schaub was the chief aide and adjutant to Adolf Hitler until the latter's suicide on 30 April 1945.

4   The primary purpose of the Sturmabteilung (SA) was providing protection for Nazi rallies and assemblies, disrupting the meetings of opposing parties, fighting against the paramilitary units of the opposing parties and intimidating the political and racial enemies of the Nazis.

The Schutzstaffel (SS) originated as a branch of the SA before being separated. The SA became disempowered after Adolf Hitler ordered the 'blood purge' of 1934 – known as die Nacht der langen Messer (the Night of the Long Knives). The SA was effectively superseded by the SS, although it was not formally dissolved until after the Third Reich's final capitulation to the Allied powers in 1945.

5   Gut Neudeck was a rural estate which was von Hindenburg's last residence.

6   Nationalsozialistisches Kraftfahrkorps (NSKK; National Socialist Automobile Corps) was a paramilitary organisation of the Nazi Party that officially existed from May 1931 to 1945. Martin Bormann founded the NSKK, which Hitler made an official Nazi organisation on 1 April 1930. It was responsible for co-ordinating the use of donated motor vehicles belonging to Party members, and later expanded to training members in automotive skills.

7   SS-Obersturmbannführer Erich Kempka (16 September 1910 – 24 January 1975) was a chauffeur for Adolf Hitler between 1934 and 1945. He was present in the Reich Chancellery on 30 April 1945, when Hitler and Eva Braun committed suicide in the Führerbunker, and delivered the petrol to the garden behind the Reich Chancellery so the remains of Hitler and Eva Braun could be burnt.

8   Wilhelm Brückner (11 December 1884 – 18 August 1954) was until 1940 Adolf Hitler's chief adjutant, supervising all of the Führer's personal servants, valets, bodyguards and adjutants. He was well liked by applicants and everyday visitors at the Reich Chancellery for his straightforwardness and affability. He lost ever more importance with the war's outbreak, yielding more and more ground to Wehrmacht and SS adjutants. He was fired on 18 October 1940, which may have been due to a controversy with Hitler's housekeeper Kannenberg. He entered the Wehrmacht and had become a colonel by the end of the war. He was succeeded by Julius Schaub.

9   Hitler's comments refer to the fact that during the Weimar Republic members of the Reichswehr had no right to vote, or become politically involved but were subject to the jurisdiction of the Reichswehr, likened to having been a state within a state.

10   This refers to the oath to the leader, or Hitler oath, an oath of allegiance sworn by the

officers and soldiers of the German Armed Forces and civil servants of Nazi Germany between 1934 and 1945. The oath pledged personal loyalty to Adolf Hitler in place of loyalty to the constitution of the country.

11 In 1999 the Bahlsen/Leibniz company, a Hanover family business created in 1889, faced up to its moral responsibility and joined the Foundation Initiative for the Compensation of Former Enforced Labourers during the Second World War.

12 Steckenpferd-Lilienmilch: this soap advertised that it gave a tender pure face, white velvety skin and a youthful fresh look – obviously emphasising the 'fair complexion'.

13 The Deutsches Nachrichtenbüro (DNB) was the official, central press agency of the German Reich at the time of National Socialism. Disguised as an independent private enterprise, it was in fact owned by the Reich, the board members of the DNB were appointed by Propaganda Minister Joseph Goebbels. Most DNB news reports were not sent to the press, but, colour-coded, were received by only certain people in the Party and the state.

14 Jakob Werlin, who was an Austrian car salesman, became acquainted with Adolf Hitler in 1923, because the Benz dealership was located next to the office in Munich where the *Völkischer Beobachter* was printed. That same year he sold a Benz to Hitler and thereafter would regularly supply limousines for the Party. Along with Ferdinand Porsche, Werlin was involved with Hitler's attempt to build the Volkswagen (the People's Car).

15 A Gauleiter (leader of a district) was a political official governing a district under Nazi rule. In the early years of the Party's rise, Gauleiters were essentially Party functionaries without real power; but in the final years of the Weimar Republic, as the Nazi Party grew, so did their power as regional Party leaders. They would wield immense power, and be in large measure untouchable by legal authority.

16 Hans von Tschammer und Osten (25 October 1887 – 25 March 1943) was a German sport official, SA leader and member of the Reichstag. After 1933 von Tschammer und Osten led the Deutscher Reichsausschuss für Leibesübungen (DRA) (German Reich Commission for Physical Exercise). He introduced many innovations and improvements regarding the organisation of sports events, some of which, like the Olympic torch relay, are still in use today.

Joachim von Ribbentrop (30 April 1893 – 16 October 1946), German diplomat, Foreign Minister under the Nazi regime (1938–45), and chief negotiator of the Nazi–Soviet Pact. In 1936 Ribbentrop became ambassador to Great Britain; by 1938, when he left his post, he had become a thorough Anglophobe. His advice to Hitler, that Britain would not aid Poland effectively, proved correct.

Konstantin Hermann Karl Freiherr von Neurath (2 February 1873 – 14 August 1956) was a German diplomat and Foreign Minister of Germany between 1932 and 1938. At the Nuremberg trials in 1946, he was sentenced to fifteen years' imprisonment.

17 Vyacheslav Mikhailovich Molotov (25 February 1890 – 8 November 1986) was a Soviet statesman and diplomat. Molotov served as Stalin's Minister of Foreign Affairs from 1939 to 1949. He negotiated the Nazi–Soviet non-aggression pact of 1939 (also known as the Molotov–Ribbentrop Pact), which included a secret protocol stipulating an invasion of Poland and partition of its territory between Nazi Germany and the Soviet Union.

18 Otto Wilhelm Rudolf Caracciola (30 January 1901 – 28 September 1959) was a German

racing car driver. He was a member of the Nazi paramilitary National Socialist Motor Corps, but never a member of the Nazi Party. His record of six German Grand Prix wins remains unbeaten.

19   Alfred Ernst Rosenberg (12 January 1893 – 16 October 1946) was an influential Nazi intellectual. He is considered one of the main authors of key National Socialist ideological creeds, including its racial theory, persecution of the Jews, Lebensraum, abrogation of the Treaty of Versailles, and opposition to degenerate modern art. At Nuremberg he was sentenced to death and executed.

20   Ernst Friedrich Christoph 'Fritz' Sauckel (27 October 1894 – 16 October 1946) was a Nazi politician, Gauleiter of Thuringia from 1927 and (on the recommendation of Martin Bormann) the General Plenipotentiary for Labour Deployment from March 1942. At Nuremberg, Sauckel was sentenced to death and executed.

21   Julius Streicher (12 February 1885 – 16 October 1946) was one of the Nazi Party's earliest members. He was the founder and publisher of the anti-Semitic newspaper *Der Stürmer*, which was an important part of the Nazi propaganda machine.

22   Josef 'Sepp' Dietrich (28 May 1892 – 21 April 1966) joined the Nazi Party in 1923, worked at various jobs including being Hitler's chauffeur and bodyguard, and founded the SS unit that evolved into the SS-Leibstandarte Adolf Hitler. After the 1934 purge known as the Night of the Long Knives he received rapid promotion, reaching the rank of Oberstgruppenführer. After the war he was imprisoned for war crimes.

23   Hjalmar Schacht (22 January 1877 – 3 June 1970) was a German economist. A supporter of Hitler, he served as President of the Reichsbank from 1923 to 1930, and again following Hitler's appointment as chancellor, from 1933 to 1939. Appointed Minister of Economics in 1934, he resigned in November 1937, but Hitler retained him as Minister without Portfolio between 1937 and 1943. After falling out with the Nazi regime, Schacht was further jeopardised by the failure of the 20 July Bomb Plot. Arrested in the aftermath, he was sent to three concentration camps – Ravensbrück, Flossenbürg and Dachau. After the war he founded a private banking house in Düsseldorf.

24   Walther Funk (18 August 1890 – 31 May 1960) was an economist, prominent Nazi official and Reichsminister of Economics from 1938 to 1945. He was a major driving force behind the rearmament campaign, and behind the systematic expropriation and exploitation of Jewish property. At the Nuremberg trials Funk was sentenced to life imprisonment.

25   Julius Lippert (9 July 1895 – 30 June 1956) was a prominent Nazi Party member because of his fanatical anti-Semitism and connection with Joseph Goebbels. From 1937, as Berlin's mayor, he was responsible for much of the early persecution of the city's Jews.

26   Unter den Linden is one of the most famous streets of Berlin. Named centuries ago for its thousand lime trees, it was the most elegant street in the city.

27   *Der Zerbrochene Krug* (The Broken Jug) is a comedy written by the German playwright Heinrich von Kleist, which gently mocks the failings of human nature and the judicial system.

28   Constructed in 1875, the Kaiserhof, a luxury hotel, was located on Berlin's Wilhelmplatz, opposite the Reich Chancellery, and was often used by senior Nazis as a temporary residence. In November 1943, it was destroyed in a bombing raid.

29   Hans Heinrich Lammers (27 May 1879 – 4 January 1962) was a German lawyer and early

member of the Nazi party. From 1933 until 1945 he was head of the Reich Chancellery under Adolf Hitler. Tried after the war, he was sentenced to twenty years' imprisonment , later reduced to ten.

30 Otto Lebrecht Eduard Daniel Meissner (13 March 1880 – 27 May 1953) was a bureaucrat who became State Secretary in the Office of the President of Germany from 1923, during the entire period of the Weimar Republic and then under Adolf Hitler. In 1937, the Nazi regime appointed him 'Chief of the Presidential Chancellery of the Führer and the Chancellor'. Despite this, his political influence in the Hitler regime was distinctly minor.

31 Krause uses the diminutive for *Nachtkastl* (night table) by ending the word with 'l' or 'erl', a commonly used form by Austrians to describe people or items in an endearing form.

32 A D-train/D-Zug, a short form of Durchgangszug ('through train'), was an express train service known for its particularly comfortable seats and being extremely punctual. It comprised first and second class coaches, dining and sleeping cars (on night trains).

33 Hitler used his special train throughout the war when he travelled between Berlin, Berchtesgaden, Munich and other headquarters. It included a Befehlswagen (command car), including a conference room and a communications centre, a wagon containing washing facilities, one allowing room for guests, a wagon for the Begleitkommandos, dining car, etc.

34 The Kripo (Kriminalpolizei) were mostly plainclothes detectives and agents, who worked in conjunction with the Gestapo and the Ordnungspolizei (the uniformed police branch). The Kriminalpolizei was mainly concerned with serious crimes such as rape, murder and arson.

35 Horch was a car named after the German engineer and automobile pioneer August Horch, the founder of the manufacturing giant which would eventually become Audi. He was not a member of the Nazi Party.

36 Maybach is a German car marque that today exists as a sub-brand of Mercedes-Benz. Between 1921 and 1940 it produced a variety of opulent vehicles, now regarded as classics. The company also built heavy-duty diesel engines for marine and rail purposes.

37 Volkswagen (VW) is a German car manufacturer founded on 28 May 1937 by the German Labour Front to produce the eponymous 'People's Car' – a basic vehicle capable of transporting two adults and three children at 100 km/h (62 mph).

38 In German, this is a play on words as 'pulling up' also signifies making fun of somebody.

39 A tailcoat is a coat that has, since the 1850s, come to be worn only in the evening by men as part of the white tie dress code, also known as full evening dress, for formal evening occasions.

40 A dinner suit or dinner jacket is a semi-formal suit distinguished primarily by satin or grosgain facing on the jacket's lapels and buttons and a similar stripe along the outseam of the trousers.

41 The cutaway or morning coat derives its name from the cut corners of the crank. As a festive day suit, it is worn at weddings, high-class funerals or state receptions.

42 The Day of Potsdam, otherwise known as the Tag von Potsdam, was a ceremony for the opening of the new Reichstag after the German federal election, and took place on 21 March 1933.

43 Paul and Gerdy Troost were architects during the early 1930s. In the autumn of 1933 Paul Troost was commissioned to rebuild and refurnish Hitler's dwellings in the Reich

Chancellery in Berlin, and was then involved in planning and building state and municipal buildings throughout the country. After Paul Troost's death in 1934 Hitler remained close to his widow Gerdy, whose architectural taste frequently coincided with his own.

44 Whitsun, even though a religious holiday, was (and continues to be) celebrated in Germany as official holidays on a Sunday and Monday.

45 The Führerbau (Führer's building) was built from 1933 to 1937 according to the plans of architect Paul Troost, in Munich. During the Nazi period it served as a representative building for Adolf Hitler. The Führerbau has historical significance as being the place where Neville Chamberlain and Adolf Hitler signed the Munich Treaty in 1938. Today the building houses the Hochschule für Musik und Theater München (University of Music and Performing Arts Munich).

46 The Haus der Deutschen Kunst (House of German Art) was also constructed from 1933 to 1937, following plans by architect Paul Troost, as Nazi Germany's first monumental structure of Nazi architecture and as Nazi propaganda. The museum was opened on 18 July 1937 as a showcase for what the Nazi Party regarded as Germany's finest art and was intended as an edifying contrast to the condemned modern art on display in the concurrent Degenerate Art Exhibition.

47 Das Braune Haus (Brown House) was the name given to the Munich mansion located between the Karolinenplatz and Königsplatz, previously known as the Palais Barlow, which was purchased in 1930 and became the headquarters for the Nazi Party. Many leading Nazis, including Hitler, maintained offices there throughout the Party's existence. It was destroyed by Allied bombing raids during the Second World War.

48 *Semmelknödel* (bread dumplings) are a specialty of the southern German, Austrian and Bohemian cuisine. They are traditionally served as a side dish with sauerkraut or red cabbage, and mainly consist of a moistened white bread rolls-and-egg mixture, shaped into dumplings and cooked.

49 *Leberknödel* are usually composed of beef liver, though in the German Palatinate region pork is used instead. The meat is ground and mixed with bread, eggs, parsley and various spices.

50 400 Reichsmark would today equal some €2,500.

51 Fachinger is a medicinal and mineral water of the Heil- und Mineralbrunnen GmbH, based in Fachingen in Rhineland-Palatinate.

52 *Boonekamp* is a generic name for a digestif. In Germany it is sold as Underberg in small paper-wrapped dark bottles.

53 *Stollen* is a fruitbread often containing dried or candied fruit, nuts and spices, and usually covered with powdered sugar or icing sugar. It is traditionally eaten during the Christmas season, when it is called Weihnachtsstollen (after Weihnachten, the German word for Christmas) or Christstollen (after Christ).

54 Horcher was, between 1904 and 1944, one of the best-known restaurants in Berlin, and had good connections with the top of the Nazi hierarchy.

55 Gervais is a type of cream cheese.

56 The Four-Year Plan was a series of economic measures initiated by Adolf Hitler and put under the control of Hermann Göring. Though its ostensible aim was to economise and improve living standards, in truth it was to prepare for war.

57 The National Socialists called for an annual National Solidarity Day, in which prominent Party officials and artists with their collecting boxes asked for donations towards the Winter Relief programme.

58 Franz Seraph Lenbach, after 1882 Ritter von Lenbach (13 December 1836, Schrobenhausen – 6 May 1904, Munich) was a German Realist painter known primarily for his portraits of prominent people including Otto von Bismarck and Richard Wagner.

59 Around 1935, address books were published in 575 German cities and municipalities, as well as 350 specialist address books on registration, occupations and branches. Every few years, new editions were published. A particular value of the address books is in the indication of occupation of the householder and details of his assets.

60 Harold Sidney Harmsworth, 1st Viscount Rothermere (26 April 1868 – 26 November 1940) was an important British newspaper proprietor, owner of Associated Newspapers, and pioneer of popular journalism. In 1896 he launched the *Daily Mail* and in 1914 acquired the *Daily Mirror*. He was a known supporter of Nazi Germany and he cultivated contacts to promote British support for Germany.

61 Italo Balbo (Ferrara, 6 June 1896 – Tobruk, 28 June 1940) was an Italian Fascist leader who served as Italy's Marshal of the Air Force, Governor-General of Libya and Commander-in-Chief of Italian North Africa.

62 Gian Galeazzo Ciano, 2nd Count of Cortellazzo and Buccari (18 March 1903 – 11 January 1944) was Foreign Minister of Fascist Italy from 1936 until 1943 and Benito Mussolini's son-in-law. On 11 January 1944 Count Ciano was shot by firing squad.

63 According to art historian Birgit Schwarz, the painting represented for Hitler the natural struggle between the superior Germanic race and the inferior race; 450,000 Reichsmark equals some €2 million today, but differs from the amount which Döhring estimated. Gobelins are woven tapestries.

64 Johann Rattenhuber (30 April 1897 – 30 June 1957), also known as Hans Rattenhuber, was a German police and SS-general.

65 Peter Högl (19 August 1897 – 2 May 1945) reached the rank of SS-Obersturmbannführer (lieutenant colonel) and was a member of one of Adolf Hitler's bodyguard units. After escaping from the Führerbunker in Berlin at the end of the Second World War, Högl died from his wounds on 2 May 1945.

66 SS-Obersturmbannführer Bruno Gesche (5 November 1905 – 1980) was a lieutenant colonel of the SS in Nazi Germany. He was an early Nazi Party member and among the first of Adolf Hitler's personal bodyguards. He was put in charge of what was originally known as the SS-Begleitkommando des Führers, and later the Führerbegleitkommando, for the periods June 1934 – April 1942 and December 1942 – December 1944.

67 Franz Schädle (19 November 1906 – 2 May 1945) was the commander of Adolf Hitler's personal bodyguard (the Führerbegleitkommando; FBK) from 5 January 1945 until his death by suicide.

68 Sovereign of the whole world.

69 It is reported that Hitler shot himself in the Bunker with his own Walther pistol.

70 On 20 July 1944 Claus von Stauffenberg and other conspirators attempted to assassinate Adolf Hitler inside his Wolf's Lair field headquarters near Rastenburg, East Prussia. The name Operation Valkyrie, originally referring to part of the conspiracy, has become

associated with the entire event. The purpose of the assassination attempt was to seize political control of Germany and its armed forces from the Nazi Party (including the SS) and to make peace with the western Allies as soon as possible.

71 Between 1940 and 1945 *Die Deutsche Wochenschau* was the centralised and synchronised weekly newsreel programme shown in the cinemas of the German Reich, usually before the main feature.

72 The Camaraderie of German Artists was a National Socialist organisation founded in 1934, organising Kameradenschaftsabende (evenings of friendly get togethers).

73 The League of German Girls and the girls' wing of the Nazi Party youth movement, the Hitler Youth. It was the only legal female youth organisation in Nazi Germany.

74 Two popular actresses with Brigitte Horney marrying a Jewish art historian after the war and Olga Tschechova apparently working as a Soviet spy during wartime.

75 No historical documents seem to actually verify this.

76 In German, *Sie* is used in formal settings, while *Du* is used as a familiar form between friends.

77 The year is not specified by Krause, but was obviously after the war had ended in 1945.

78 The Spruchkammer was a court-like institution, which was used for denazification in Germany after the Second World War.

79 Opened in 1933, KZ Dachau was originally designed for holding German political prisoners and Jews, but in 1935 it began to be used also for ordinary criminals. It was used as the chief camp for Christian (mainly Catholic) clergy who were imprisoned for not conforming with the Nazi Party line. After and during the war, Germans always referred to concentration camps as KZ (pronounced: ka-tset), and rarely said the full two words 'concentration camp'.

80 The 'Night of the Amazons' was a bombastic event, staged with several hundred horses and scantily clad dancers in the summers of 1936–1939 at Nymphenburger Schlosspark.

81 On 12 February 1938 Austrian Chancellor Kurt Schuschnigg met Hitler in his Berghof residence in an attempt to smooth the worsening relations between their two countries. To Schuschnigg's surprise, Hitler presented him with a set of demands which, in manner and in terms, amounted to an ultimatum, effectively demanding the handing over of power to the Austrian Nazis.

82 Historical documents to this effect cannot be found.

83 *Der Stürmer* (The Stormtrooper) was a weekly German tabloid-format newspaper published by Julius Streicher, the Gauleiter of Franconia, from 1923 to the end of the Second World War. Vehemently anti-Semitic, it was increasingly a cause of embarrassment for the Nazi Party. Although Streicher and his paper were increasingly isolated in the Nazi Party, Hitler continued to support him and, contrary to what Krause says, was said to have been an avid reader of *Der Stürmer*. Also, contrary to Krause, it was Göring, not Hitler, who forbade the paper. Streicher was condemned to death by hanging at the Nuremberg trials.

84 Karl Friedrich May (25 February 1842 – 30 March 1912) was a popular German novelist who wrote adventure novels including on American Indians. He is one of the best-selling German writers of all time with about 200 million copies worldwide (compared to some 500 million Harry Potter books). The stories, indeed, were so popular that Nazi Germany

did not ban them despite the heroic treatment of coloured races; instead, the argument was made that the stories demonstrated the fall of the American aboriginal peoples was caused by a lack of racial consciousness.

85 Lutz Graf Schwerin von Krosigk (22 August 1887 – 4 March 1977) was Minister of Finance of Germany from 1932 to 1945 and became Leading Minister of the German Reich (Chancellor) in May 1945.

86 The Papal conclave of 1939 was convoked on the eve of the Second World War with the death of Pope Pius XI on 10 February that year in the Apostolic Palace. With all sixty-two living cardinals in attendance, the conclave to elect Pius's successor began on 1 March and ended a day later, on 2 March, after three ballots. The cardinals elected Eugenio Cardinal Pacelli, then Camerlengo and the deceased pontiff's Secretary of State, as the new pope. He accepted the election and took the pontifical name of Pius XII. The cardinal Krause might be referring to was George William Mundelein (2 July 1872 – 2 October 1939) who served as Archbishop of Chicago and was a liberal, a unionist and fought against anti-semitism.

87 Hanns Kerrl (11 December 1887 – 15 December 1941) was, from July 1935, Reichminister of Church Affairs, heading a newly created ministry. He was derisively called Kirchenfürst (Count of the Church). On the one hand, Kerrl was supposed to mediate between those Nazi leaders who hated Christianity (for example Heinrich Himmler) and the churches themselves and stress the religious aspect of the Nazi ideology. On the other hand, in tune with the policy of Gleichschaltung (the process of Nazification by which Nazi Germany successively established a system of totalitarian control and coordination over all aspects of society), it was Kerrl's job to subjugate the churches and subordinate them to the greater goals decided by the Führer, Adolf Hitler. He died in office.

88 Everyone should be happy in his *façon* goes back to a comment by the tolerant Prussian King Frederick II with respect to Roman-Catholic schools.

89 The term Alte Kämpfer (Old Fighters or Old Guard) refers to the earliest members of the Nazi Party, i.e. those who joined it before the Reichstag elections of September 1930, with many belonging to the Party as early as its first foundation in 1919–23. Those who joined the Party after the electoral breakthrough of September 1930 were known to the Alte Kämpfer as Septemberlings while those who joined the Party after the assumption of power on 30 January 1933 were known as the March Violets.

90 Heilige Abend, which is the night of 24/25 December, is called Holy Night, Christmas Night or Christmas Eve in German-speaking countries, such as Austria and Germany.

91 The tuxedo jacket was worn with the tailcoat's usual accompaniments: bow tie, waistcoat and a stiffly starched shirt with a high-standing, detachable wing collar.

92 In connection with the reconstruction of seven houses in the centre of Munich, a large inner courtyard was built between 1886 and 1888, which was used by architect Otto Lasne to erect a magnificent café, the Luitpold Café. The floor plan of the café was determined by that of the gathered courtyards and formed a longitudinal rectangle with transverse bars. The square large dome hall and the mirrored room were linked by a column-lined aisle. Fine materials such as bronze and black marble as well as rich jewellery along with wall paintings underscored the luxurious character of the establishment. At the Luitpold Café the artist group Der Blaue Reiter was founded in 1911 by Wassily Kandinsky and Paul Klee.

93 The Königsplatz was renamed Königlicher Platz under National Socialist rule, with Paul

Troost reversing Karl von Fischer's all-green concept. At the eastern end, the Führerbau was built north of the Brienner Strasse, and the administrative building of the NSDAP was positioned symmetrically to the south. Instead of Fischer's residential buildings, two Ehrentempel (honour temples) were erected as a common grave facility for the National Socialists who died during the Beer Hall Putsch in 1923. Their bodies were transferred there and reburied in bronze sarcophagi.

94   The New Reich Chancellery, designed by Albert Speer, opened in January 1939, after just twelve months of construction and at a cost of some 90 million Reichsmark.

95   Karl Brandt (1904–1948) and his wife were members of Hitler's inner circle at Berchtesgaden. He was tried at the 'Doctors' Trial' in 1946.

96   Ernst-Robert Grawitz (8 June 1899 – 24 April 1945) was a Nazi German physician who participated in a programme of human experiments, using concentration camp inmates in Dachau, Sachsenhausen, Ravensbrück and elsewhere. He killed himself and his family in April 1945.

97   Carl Otto von Eicken (31 December 1873 to 29 June 1960) was a highly experienced German ENT specialist.

98   Dr Hugo Johannes Blaschke (14 November 1881 – 6 December 1959) studied dentistry in Berlin, America and London and served as a military dentist in the First World War in Germany. After treating Hermann Göring in 1930, he joined the Nazi Party. As well as Hitler, he also treated Eva Braun, Joseph Goebbels and Heinrich Himmler.

99   Strychnine is a highly toxic, colourless, bitter, crystalline alkaloid used as a pesticide, particularly for killing small vertebrates such as birds and rodents. Strychnine, when inhaled, swallowed or absorbed through the eyes or mouth, causes poisoning which results in muscular convulsions and eventually death through asphyxia. While it has no known medicinal effects, in the past the convulsant effect was believed to be beneficial in small doses. Strychnine was popularly used as an athletic performance enhancer and recreational stimulant in the late nineteenth century and early twentieth century, due to its convulsant effects.

100 Ludwig Stumpfegger (11 July 1910 – c.2 May 1945) was a German doctor who served in the SS during the Second World War. He was Adolf Hitler's personal physician from 1944 to 1945, and was in the Führerbunker in Berlin in late April 1945.

101 Hitler is widely considered to have been at least psychologically dependent on Morell's injections by the latter stages of the war.

102 In December 1931 Himmler introduced the 'marriage order', which required SS men wishing to marry to produce family trees proving that both families were of Aryan descent to 1800. If any non-Aryan forebears were found in either family tree during the racial investigation, the person concerned was excluded from the SS. Each man was issued with a Sippenbuch, a genealogical record detailing his genetic history. Krause's comment on Hitler being so interested and generous vis-à-vis couples wishing to marry was not entirely without purpose.

103 On 18 August 1941, elements of the German 1st Panzergruppe seized the outskirts of Zaporizhia, a city in southeastern Ukraine, situated on the banks of the Dnieper River; the occupation lasted two years. Hitler flew several times to the city, meeting the army group commander Field Marshal Erich von Manstein (24 November 1887 – 9 June 1973),

German commander of the Wehrmacht, and his air force counterpart Field Marshal Wolfram Freiherr von Richthofen (10 October 1895 – 12 July 1945).

104 Wilhelm Keitel (22 September 1882 – 16 October 1946) was a German field marshal who from 1938 to 1945 was head of the Oberkommando der Wehrmacht (OKW) (Armed Forces High Command). At the Nuremberg trials, Keitel was charged with war crimes and crimes against humanity and was executed.

105 The Reich Chancellery hosted the various ministries of the Reich. Belonging to the Reich Chancellery were two newly built residential buildings running along the then Hermann Göring Strasse. These were allocated to Hitler's two personal escorts and their families. There are only these two references in Krause's book which refer to his own family.

106 The invasion of Poland, known in Poland as the September Campaign and in Germany as the Polenfeldzug (Poland Campaign) or Fall Weiss (Case White), was a joint invasion of Poland by Nazi Germany, the Soviet Union and a small Slovak contingent, which marked the beginning of the Second World War. The German invasion began on 1 September 1939, one week after the signing of the Nazi–Soviet Pact, while the Soviet invasion commenced on 17 September. The campaign ended on 6 October with Germany and the Soviet Union dividing and annexing the whole of Poland under the terms of the German–Soviet Frontier Treaty.

107 Führerhauptquartiere (Führer Headquarters) were the official headquarters used by Adolf Hitler and various German commanders and officials throughout Europe during the Second World War. At the beginning of the war there were no permanent headquarters constructed for the German supreme leader, the Führer. Hitler visited the frontlines by using either aeroplane or his special train, the Führersonderzug; thus, the Führersonderzug can be considered as the first of his field headquarters. Perhaps the most widely known headquarters was the Führerbunker in Berlin, where Hitler committed suicide on 30 April 1945. Other headquarters were the Wolfsschanze (Wolf's Lair) in East Prussia, where Claus von Stauffenberg in league with other conspirators attempted to assassinate Hitler on 20 July 1944, and Hitler's private home, the Berghof, on the Obersalzberg near Berchtesgaden, where he frequently met prominent foreign and domestic officials.

108 It is not clear what event this might refer to.

109 Karl-Heinrich Bodenschatz (10 December 1890 – 25 August 1979) served in the Luftwaffe from 1933 and was the liaison officer between Hermann Göring and Adolf Hitler during the Second World War. In 1944 he was seriously injured when the bomb exploded during the 20 July Plot at the Wolf's Lair headquarters in Rastenburg, East Prussia. After the Nuremberg trials he was imprisoned for two years.

110 The Fieseler Fi 156 Storch (Stork) was a small German liaison aircraft built by Fieseler before and during the Second World War.

111 Krause's successor was Heinz Linge (23 March 1913 – 9 March 1980) whom Krause had trained up for the position and who was one of many SS soldiers, servants, secretaries and officers who moved into the Reich Chancellery and Führerbunker in Berlin in 1945. There he continued as Hitler's chief valet and protocol officer and was one of those who closely witnessed the last days of Hitler's life.

112 Karl-Jesko Otto Robert von Puttkamer (24 March 1900 – 4 March 1981) was a naval adjutant to Hitler and was injured on 20 July 1944 when the bomb exploded during the

20 July plot. He joined Hitler in the Berlin bunker in 1945.

113 The Battle of Narvik took place during the Second World War, when Norway was occupied by naval, land and air forces. The occupation of Narvik was the task of Naval Group 1 consisting of ten destroyers under Commodore Friedrich Bonte. All ten deployed German destroyers were either destroyed or had to sink themselves.

114 An accordion in German can be called *Schifferklavier* (piano for marines) as it looks like a piano, but can be much more easily transported onto a ship than a piano.

115 The Kriegsmarine employed hundreds of auxiliary *Vorpostenboote* (outpost boats) during the war, mostly civilian ships that were drafted and fitted with military equipment, for use in coastal operations.

116 Krause was valet to Hitler for only five years (1934–9).

117 Heinrich Heim (1900–1988) studied law and worked with Hans Frank, who eventually became Hitler's personal lawyer. From 1939 to 1943 Heim was an aide to Bormann, and was responsible for recording Hitler's informal conversations. His reference to oxen relates to Bormann having attended an agricultural trade high school and having worked in a cattle-feed mill and as manager of a large farm.

118 Krause refers here to what might be considered the first phase of concentration camp building, lasting from the establishment of the Nazi dictatorship until the early summer of 1934. Larger or smaller detention centres all over Germany were built and existed next to state prisons – among them Dachau and Oranienburg.

Part 2

Herbert Döhring: Hitler's Housekeeper

Foreword

Contemporary witnesses from among Adolf Hitler's entourage are rare. Nearly all have died long since, and many have taken their stories to the grave without anybody ever having heard their voices or being bothered to listen to their accounts. Several of the dictator's followers have, however, either written about their experiences or captured them on film. This is what the erstwhile housekeeper of Hitler's mountain home in Berchtesgaden, a small town in the Bavarian Alps, has done.*

Unlike Albert Speer[1] or Martin Bormann,[2] Herbert Döhring did not belong to Adolf Hitler's innermost circle. Yet he spent several years living close to him, and his recollections manage to convey interesting events that were happening around the Führer during that time.

These recollections, therefore, serve as an additional piece in a puzzle that allows further insights into the personality of the last but one chancellor of the German Reich. The most fascinating bits in these accounts witnessed by the erstwhile manager are, of course, the coincidental events and the anecdotes he recounts, while the complex relationships, political decisions and other far-reaching historical turning points certainly play no part in them. Döhring was not privy to such issues, neither was he assigned a rank or position that would have justified his being involved in them.

---

* In August 1998, for nearly a week, the erstwhile manager of Hitler's Berghof made himself available for a comprehensive film interview. Standing next to historical places on the Obersalzberg and the region around Berchtesgaden, Herbert Döhring described his experiences and revealed secrets of those immediately surrounding the dictator. Old documents and pen portraits handwritten by Döhring himself were evaluated, while the manager then supplemented these with fascinating responses to the film's interviewer.

To him, as for so many of Hitler's secretaries, guards or other employees, Hitler was merely the Boss, who behaved towards his underlings in a friendly and polite manner but who could bear grudges and whose temper could flare up if something was not to his liking.

It is precisely this proximity to Hitler that placed Döhring in a special position – as a witness of these times. The BBC, among others, held Döhring's contributions in high regard, as the latter was still able to remember precisely what happened on certain days of the week and all sorts of particular details. A certain amount of innate 'curiosity', which was part of Döhring's personality, no doubt came in useful. This particular witness made it his duty to scout out certain spots in the green area surrounding the Berghof, from which he could listen in on discussions. The Hess 'flight' or the attack on the Soviet Union would, therefore, not have been surprising news to this eavesdropper.

The reader, however, needs to be aware that these recollections reflect only subjective impressions. It is a sign of years gone by, when certain viewpoints became idealised and events mixed up, but, given our recourse to other sources, these can easily be clarified. This notwithstanding, people who happened to have found themselves on the pulse of time were in a position to offer proof for assumptions made and, in particular, to shed light onto dark and hitherto unknown circumstances. Thus, a contemporary witness may offer something only rarely encountered: a first-hand account of that period in time.

It is a credit to this book that it publishes recollections by the Berghof's caretaker – who has died in the meantime – which portray Hitler also as a human being and offer some insight into his psyche. This dictator was, undeniably, a human being – even though many see him as the reincarnation of evil itself.

Alexander Losert
August 1998

Herbert Döhring: Hitler's Housekeeper

Alexander Losert's interviews with Herbert Döhring

How did you, a twenty-two-year-old man from East Prussia, make it to the Begleitkommando[3] and one year later end up in Hitler's personal employment?

On 1 August 1934 a circular letter arrived, written by some military authority, which said that they were looking for young, tall men. They wanted to set up a division to protect the Führer, called the SS-Leibstandarte Adolf Hitler,[4] based on the model of the Lange Kerls of Friedrich Wilhelm I.[5] And when I heard that, I thought to myself: 'Hold on a minute, what might that be? Off to Berlin, what fun. Normally not such an easy place to get to (for people like me) . . . why not sign up?' It said two years of service, but then two years turned into four years, and fate took its course.

I applied, was accepted and met all conditions. Training was extremely hard. Everything was kept secret. The Treaty of Versailles was still in place, and on 12 October 1934 the training was finished. Then Jüterbog, the 'Old camp', a training base for the troops . . . After that, I arrived in Berlin Lichterfelde and looked after some assignment there – guard duty. Was put through military training and I enjoyed a good relationship with my superiors. Fully carried out my duties, because, after all, I had signed up of my own free will. I was a very good shot, was a real 'poacher' and that was widely approved of by my superiors.

Another of those circular letters from the 1st Battalion of the SS-Leibstandarte Adolf Hitler arrived in the summer of 1935. A so-called Führerschutzkommando was being formed, which was some thirty men strong. Only those who demonstrated above-average performance and who had not stood out at any roll call were going to be considered. I just want to make a brief note here: we had three roll calls each week: one for weapons, one for clothing and one for a health check. Because my superiors respected me so highly, they had already put forward my name for this Kommando without my prior knowledge. This was only brought to my attention late one evening in the barrack room. We were ten men, distributed in two rooms, with one spare bedroom. The sergeant had come along, the leader of my platoon, and the company commander. The leader of my platoon just said to me: 'Döhring, you're on.'

My first thought was that they were dispatching me as a courier to army units in Döbritz and Zossen. They had always sent me there in the past, but then the following day I found out what was actually happening. My company lined up for the roll call and the sergeant announced that a Führerschutzkommando was being formed. By the end of August 1935 we would be marching towards Nuremberg, and during the Party Congress we would be in charge of the Führer's security at the Hotel Deutscher Hof. After that we would be marching towards the Obersalzberg and there the Führer would build himself a large house – the old house being expanded.

During the summer months, hundreds of visitors would gather there nearly every day and want to see Hitler on the Berghof. We constantly received complaints from the building management because of visitors being on the construction site. Already there was one accident – a woman had got hurt, and management would no longer accept responsibility. So, after being carted off onto the Obersalzberg, we were put in charge of the area's security. The whole construction site was secured and sealed off.

Shortly after arriving on the Obersalzberg, I was immediately posted to take on a different assignment – I became an operator at the Berghof. The telephone was in use around the clock. There were eight-hour shifts, each with three men on duty. And as an operator we came into contact with all sorts: with people from the construction management; from delivery firms; with architects; with the aide; and once, it was late in the evening and I was on duty, even with Herr Hitler himself. It's well known that Hitler was a night person. Shortly before midnight I answered the telephone: 'This is the operator', I said. 'Reich Chancellery' came the response and the lady then connected me with the Führer.

There he was, immediately on the line, asking whether he could speak to my future wife (Anna Krautenbach). No, she wasn't here. Neither was architect Schatz. Then Hitler said: 'I would have liked to find out what's happening with the roof structure, whether anything was done about that. Please inform the building management that they should call me tomorrow morning.' As I had always been a curious chap and one who was thirsty for knowledge, I had made it my business to look around the building site and had actually been observing the building process all along. That's why I could inform Hitler on the phone that the entire roof structure had been fully erected. Hitler was very surprised.

I had obviously supplied him with a concrete piece of information. 'You presumably also come from the building trade?' 'No, I've nothing to do with construction, my background is in agriculture.' 'You've done very well.' And that was the first time I had any contact with Hitler by telephone.

Later, my future wife Anna revealed the following to me: 'Do you know what the Führer said to me? I would have to find a clever man for myself, one who can present well, who is good with his hands, who is organised and who is fully capable of managing a large company.' My first response to her was quite blunt: 'Just do me a favour and stop this nonsense, I'm going back to my farm.' This was an ancestral farm and I was the only son. It had been in the family for 380 years, it was a business, measured seventy-two hectares, and ten of it was woodland. I wanted to go home again. But fate had other ideas for me.

Originally, our stay at Berchtesgaden was extended by three months, but the building management then submitted yet another extension request because, according to them, we harmonised so well with everyone in the company. They wanted to keep us on for longer. The request was granted and we remained there until 1 May 1936. One thing was certain: I was bound to get the position of housekeeper.

Preliminary talks had already progressed quite far, and on 12 May 1936 I was in Berlin, having hitchhiked there. On the following day I had to report to the building management of the Obersalzberg-Berghof. After my briefing, I had to sit through countless training courses: how to use the ventilation and the electric systems, the oil heating, the modern kitchen appliances and so on. And that is how I ended up there. What followed was eight years of personal service to Hitler.

Can you still remember your first personal encounter with Hitler?

My first face-to-face meeting took place on the last Sunday of March 1936. It happened just in front of the Haus Hoher Göll guest house. During the construction of the Berghof, Hitler lived in the Haus Hoher Göll. It was a Sunday morning and I was assigned to position two. Then, all of a sudden, Hitler comes out, followed by his entourage, in order to inspect the construction. At that moment, I should have announced my name, as per the rulebook. Then Hitler says to me: 'Are you the one who wants to marry my Anna? Stand at ease.' He continued chatting to me for quite a while, then patted me on my shoulders and descended with his retinue to the construction site. That was my first direct encounter.

In July 1937 Hitler had selected my wife to be the kitchen chef. Assisted by twelve to fourteen staff, sous-chefs and kitchen helpers, she became responsible for the daily well-being of at least fifty people. There were more guests, especially later on when there were constant meetings, conferences and state receptions. It was a real beehive of activity with constant comings and goings, day and night. And when Hitler invited particularly important guests, such as military people, foreign royalty and government leaders, he reserved the right to call in my wife the night before. Together they would then put together the menu.

She was responsible for the entire kitchen, and I for the housekeeping. But we were given totally free rein in our work. We managed it as if it were our own business – nobody interfered with us. Everyone had to follow our instructions, even the Hohe Herren.[6] I thought that this was quite normal at the time, but with hindsight, after sixty years, I have sufficient perspective on the whole thing.

How did it come about that your wife was offered the post at the Berghof?

My wife learnt to be a cook in Vienna and got a temporary job in a hotel in Berchtesgaden in March 1931. Already times were difficult and there were no jobs to be found. The job centre in Berchtesgaden, its department for hotels and restaurants, found her a position with an Angela Raubal at Haus Wachenfeld[7] on the Obersalzberg. Nobody knew who that was. My wife was told that she was to do ordinary housework, plus anything else that would come along, such as serving at tables etc. My wife accepted the position.

A while later Hitler arrived there. My wife, still a young girl at the time, didn't even know who he was, and actually didn't much care. Long story short, she arrived and quickly rose to the challenges that presented themselves on the Obersalzberg establishment. She grew into it very quickly and ended up running it like a regular government operation.

You got married in 1936 in Berchtesgaden. What was special about your wedding?

It was Hitler himself who organised the wedding for me and my wife. Since I belonged to the Waffen-SS[8] I was required to bring along several certificates, and that took a while. Hitler, however, insisted that I was allowed to get married without these certificates. I handed in the papers later on, but our wedding was nevertheless delayed several times. Hitler made a particular point of attending the wedding in person. The ceremony followed on 10 December in Berchtesgaden.

On that very day, the heating didn't work at the Berghof. I arrived in the cellar and all warning lamps were flashing up red and the entire technical system was registering a fault. Since I had already changed and was in a huge rush, I couldn't do a thing, unfortunately. After my first shock I told myself: 'Just go down and fix it straight after the meal.' Fortunately the dietician on the staff, Poldi, had already informed Karl Hebel (my stand-in) about the fault. While having lunch I already noticed that the heating is working again and that the chilly rooms are slowly turning warm. This took a great load off my mind.

We then returned from the Berchtesgaden civil registry to the Obersalzberg, the Boss had just arrived at Berchtesgaden and, as usual, he was in a great hurry. He called us to his study and presented my wife with a picture of himself with a handwritten dedication and presented each of us with an envelope with one thousand Reichsmark (about €5,500 today).

A few evenings before our wedding the phone rang at midnight. Hitler's aide Julius Schaub called asking: 'Döhring, how do you write your name?' 'What is it you are wanting?' I replied. 'The Führer wants to write a letter to your wife. We didn't know how to write your name.' So I spelt him my name. On our wedding day, Hitler hands the photograph to my wife and it says on it: 'Frau Anni Döhring, née Krautenbacher, wishing you warmest congratulations and blessings, Adolf Hitler, 10 December 1936.'

The number of visitors and state receptions at the Berghof increased steadily. The first conversion of the Wachenfeld Haus was carried out in 1936. What were the resulting changes for you?

The newly renovated Berghof was furnished from top to bottom during the summer of 1936. That is when the old Wachenfeld turned into the well-known Berghof. In my opinion every room felt comfortable – simple, traditional, not exaggerated, no chandeliers and so forth. Frills, such as I had read about after the war, did not exist. All of the hanging lamps were mostly made out of slightly browned brass.

After the second renovation of the Berghof, which took place in spring 1938, the housekeeping wing alone measured some ninety metres. The ground floor was taken up by a new switchboard, a dining room for the Begleitkommando, a further dining and common room for the staff, a scullery, toilets and an office.

There were seven lovely single rooms for the female staff on the floor above. As far as I can remember, each room had a radio, and we are talking early days.

Looking down from the large corridor, there was a toilet for women on the right-hand side, next to it a large cloakroom area, and behind that was the men's toilet. Further along there was a staircase, which led to the upper floor. Walking past the staircase, you ended up in the dining room with a large table that could sit up to sixteen people. The aides and secretaries mostly ate back where the bay window was and, depending on the arrangement, six to seven people could sit there at a round table. At the back of the dining room, they built a modern kitchen fitted with a Cromargan[9] oven, which worked either on electricity or on wood and coal.

Down in the basement, directly behind the dining room, Hitler had a modern bowling alley installed, which staff would sometimes use late at night. At the beginning, the Boss would also play, but the place just got busier with constant meetings, conventions and receptions. Eventually the bowling slowly stopped. But the bowling alley could double up for shooting exercises. Hitler himself wasn't interested in this, but Eva Braun happily sought out such opportunities. On the occasions when she challenged me to a game, I purposely missed the mark to let her win.

In the main building, as well as in the adjoining houses, there were rooms for management, machinery, guest rooms and lounges, bathrooms, broom cupboards and a dark room. In total some 131 rooms.

It is hard to believe but Hitler had all of a sudden run out of money in spite of him fighting to receive royalties from the sale of stamps with his portrait on them. When the roof went up on the Berghof, he had no money left. At first the plan was to cover the roof rafters with larch-wood shingles, as is customary in the Berchtesgaden area. However, this was also very expensive, and there also was a rush on completing the roof. So the decision was made to use the cheaper zinc sheeting. The fact that Hitler had run out of money at that point was something I learnt from his aide. All of us laughed into our sleeves.

In spite of all this, the Berghof very quickly turned out to be too small, as the number of visitors and guests kept increasing, and the operation got bigger and bigger. The presents alone proved an additional burden. It was unbelievable, what was arriving at our doors. It really became a problem after the annexation of Austria – we received thousands of parcels. People were completely crazy and sent really valuable gifts, but people also gave some kitsch and even some of their inventions. They just sent us anything and everything – and we simply didn't know where to put it all.

Did you also receive some unpleasant gifts?

At the time we would never have thought that people could send letter bombs. Thankfully nobody came up with such an idea. We unpacked everything ourselves: apples, cakes, the so-called Baumkuchen[10] from Dresden, and so on. The staff ate it all. Hitler never took a bite. Not even with these food gifts did it ever occur to us that something could have been poisoned.

Some packages were then sent on as presents to government offices, to children's homes and old people's homes, usually with an appended letter. These letters would be piled up, twenty to thirty high, and sent to Hitler's private Berlin Chancellery. There was room there, and donors would receive their thank you and response letters.

Please describe the routine of your work at the Berghof and that of the staff.

In the Berghof, the highest-ranking servant always had his twenty-four hour shift followed by one day off. Karl Wilhelm Krause, Heinz Linge, Hans Junge – all valets of Hitler – and myself, we all got along very well, both at work and privately.

In the end it was we who were responsible for the smooth operation at the Berghof. We were idealists, and had been used to assuming heavier duties during the war. Nobody would have come up with the idea of calculating overtime, and ask what he might be paid for that.

It was essential that all state visits and important meetings were planned and executed with military precision. But even the day-to-day schedule was meticulously organised from early to late, from one Sunday to the next.

The chief valet and us staff members were dependent on each other, and we had to make sure to coordinate between ourselves. An example would be organising the receptions. Also those who were not on duty were always informed in detail about everything that took place at the Berghof. Only these prior arrangements allowed us to ensure the successful and seamless running of the entire operation.

Hitler held Hans Junge in incredibly high esteem. In his opinion this man was the most capable among the staff. Unfortunately Junge was killed in August 1944 in France, as a result of a low-flying Allied aircraft attack. As it happens I too found myself very close to the place where the attack happened, and sadly had to live through all of this. Only once did I get to see his wife Traudl Junge (Hitler's last private secretary), and then only briefly. But I knew Hitler's other secretaries well: Johanna Wolf, Christa Schröder and Gerda Daranowski.

What was Hitler's behaviour towards his staff at the Berghof like?

Hitler felt socially responsible for his staff. Depending on how long an employee had been in his service, Hitler was happy to give each one of them a monetary gift. Some four to five weeks before Christmas he would distribute a wish list at the Berghof and people could put down their personal wishes, with anything from a wristwatch to a handbag.

In 1938 I put down my wish for a wristwatch and I actually received one. It had the engraving 'Christmas 1938 – Adolf Hitler'. I was to wear this watch throughout the war. Later on it became oxidised and stopped working. As my children weren't interested in it, I then sold it to an American collector.

At Christmas my wife and I would be presented with one thousand Reichsmark (€5,500) and a personal thank-you note from the Boss. Unfortunately all these documents went missing in the war. In one of these letters Hitler thanked us personally for all our efforts over the years.

As housekeeper I was a sort of factotum and I wouldn't even think about a holiday. At the end of 1939 the Boss asked me when I had last been to see my parents. When he heard that I had not seen them since 1935 he suggested that, immediately in February, I travel to East Prussia and visit them. After many years, that was my first holiday.

In 1940, in response to pressure applied by the East Prussian provincial authorities, I received a further ten-day leave in order to take over the farm from my parents on 12 September 1940. That was the last holiday I was granted.

The Berghof without electricity . . .

It was the middle of winter at the beginning of 1937 and the Berghof was full of guests. Suddenly we heard a deafening bang. Within a second the whole house was left without power. While some of the guests suspected sabotage, this did not even come to my mind. It took a while until the engineer in charge of the electricity board at Berchtesgaden, along with his team, could find a cause. Due to the extensive construction work on the Obersalzberg a mains cable had become damaged and had caused the power cut. Immediately, candles were lit throughout the Berghof, and both Hitler and his guests accepted the incident with good humour. On top of that, tiled fireplaces had been installed in seven rooms as a precaution, and in the Great Hall there was an open fireplace, with a further tiled fireplace in Hitler's study. This was a clever precautionary measure in the event that the central heating might stop working.

Hitler had given architect Josef Schatz power of attorney and sent him to all the places where the building works were somewhat delayed. That's what happened with the tiled fireplaces at the Berghof. All the important architects including Schatz had already arrived on the Obersalzberg. Schatz said: 'Mein Führer, what we need now is a trusty fireplace builder. A company that can at long last get started, so that we can finish the job here as well.' They were talking about a greenish tiled fireplace, surrounded by a bench. The tiles showed designs representing various Germanic regions: for example, the Münchner Kindl or the Berliner Bär.[11]

Hitler turned to Schatz asking: 'Well, do you know of such a good fireplace builder?' 'Yes, I know of a very good one', answered Schatz, 'but some four or five weeks ago you put him into the Dachau concentration camp.' Hitler asked: 'But why? What on earth did he do?' 'He was distributing some flyers', answered Schatz, 'for the KPD. They caught him and immediately locked him up.'

At that moment Hitler became quite agitated: 'The man should be released at once. Brückner, make sure that he is here within a few hours.' The Braune Haus[12] put a vehicle at our disposal and, indeed, barely four hours later this tiled fireplace builder was at Berchtesgaden on the Obersalzberg. He was a small man and seemed rather intimidated. Can you imagine, there he is with Hitler at the Berghof, someone who came directly from the concentration camp in Dachau.[13]

This was a big order and would take a few weeks. Hitler asked the fireplace builder: 'Can you take care of this job for me?' The man, his whole body trembling, answers: 'Herr Reichskanzler, if I may I will gladly do it.'

During that time I became more acquainted with the fireplace builder, and we would sometimes have a beer together. He was a totally innocent workman and the Nazis had simply incarcerated him.

'Do you have a particular request? First of all, I will make sure that you and your firm will be compensated for your stay at Dachau', Hitler said to him.

'Yes, Herr Reichskanzler, I actually do have a request, seeing that you had me locked up. May I have permission to manufacture one tile on which my image is immortalised. With bars in front of me, as I was imprisoned?' 'Yes, that will be done. That will get done immediately. Schatz, make sure this happens.'

The tile was manufactured using the same green shade as the tiled fireplace, and this man's picture behind bars was one of them. Standing in front of the fireplace, that tile could be found on the left-hand side.

Are you able to remember after so many years some details of Hitler's study at the Berghof?

Hitler's study at the Berghof was not connected to the central heating – the room was exclusively heated by a tiled fireplace. Everything was in the greenish colour favoured by the Boss. The Party had brown, but his favourite colour actually was green. The tiled fireplace was greenish, the sofa suite in front of the small fireplace was greenish, his desk was covered in green leather and the carpet was greenish as well. His favourite soap, Palmolive, was green, and his leather coats were also green.

Then there was a small table in his studio made out of walnut; one could extend it to seat two people and it was kept in his studio's wardrobe. Hitler only sat there when important people came to visit. The table was covered with a reed-green cloth and even the napkins were green. His signet 'AH' and the Swastika were embossed on it in a stronger green. That was his favourite colour. This seems to be entirely forgotten today.

At the Berghof there was a so-called Blomberg Room. What's the story?

Field Marshal Werner von Blomberg was Minister of Defence from 1933, and after 1935 he was commander-in-chief for the entire Wehrmacht.[14] At first, Hitler was on very good terms with von Blomberg. Because of the 1936 conversion of the Berghof, a whole number of rooms had been added on and each one was to be dedicated to a specific person. The most beautiful Hitler named himself and he dedicated it to von Blomberg. It was situated on the top floor and had a splendid view onto Salzburg, the Kneifelspitze and the Untersberg. This good man had met a most exciting woman whom he married in 1938. Shortly after the wedding it was revealed that this woman had modelled for pornographic photos. Nothing doing – von Blomberg had to take his leave. The room was then renamed Untersberg Room due to its lovely view onto the legendary[15] mountain of that name.

Having walked along the hallway and past a small vestibule, you would reach the large sitting room with the beautifully tiled fireplace. The room was panelled in larch wood, and that is also where the large desk stood, as well as some side tables and the lounge suite. A bedroom as well as a bathroom also belonged to the Untersberg Room.

The balcony offered an extraordinary view over the valley of Berchtesgaden, and to Salzburg and reaching as far away as the Salzkammergut. The Untersberg Room was exquisite and offered a good spot to take special photos. A great scene, for example, was Berchtesgaden covered in clouds, with only the rooftops of the two churches peeking out. I myself took countless pictures, but unfortunately nearly all my photos have gone missing, what with the upheaval of the war.

When he came for meetings on the Obersalzberg, this is where Rudolf Hess, Hitler's deputy, would stay. Rudolf Hess struck me as a strange person. He was a very withdrawn, calm and modest man, but there was also something impenetrable about him. One day Hess came to my wife requesting thick, black curtains. Because he likes to sleep late in the mornings and because in the summer it gets light early in the day, he was no longer able to sleep. The curtains we had were no longer sufficient, and so we procured additional heavy and black curtains and put them up for him.

Late one night, when all residents had already gone to bed, Hess came to me and asked me to hand him the keys to the house. He would then take a walk into the starry night, all on his own, for about an hour to an hour and a half, even if it was −20°C. For security reasons I would immediately contact the SS security forces so that the guard on duty would inform his sentries.

You have a rare picture among your documents showing a group of tourists standing on the green lawn in front of the Berghof and waiting for their Führer.

In the thirties, groups of visitors would gather nearly every day in front of the Wachenfeld House, waiting for Hitler to come out and greet them. Later on, at set times, the SS security forces would pick up groups at the Platterhof and take them at precisely 3 p.m. to the Berghof. If the Boss was in residence, he would stand at the entrance to greet the visitors. Sometimes he would even invite the BDM youth groups or the Jungvolk for coffee and cake.[16]

It was entirely possible for groups to take more than an hour to march past the building. The Boss was very irritated when he had to stand there in the sun for long periods of time. Bormann solved that particular problem. On 17 July 1937 it was Bormann's birthday, and very early that morning gardeners planted a fully grown lime tree. It would have taken too long to wait for a small lime to grow sufficiently tall in order for it to shed some shade. Head gardener Bühler along with his helpers – it was pouring with rain – dug a hole, then reinforced the newly planted lime with ropes so that no wind would harm the tree during its first season, and from then on there was plenty of shade.

Among the visitors would be many admirers and also hysterical women who liked to kiss and embrace Hitler; there was no special barrier. What would often happen is that a few aides and two or three men from the Begleitkommando accompanied the Boss up to where the entrance drive began.

In later years, when foreign and military dignitaries were guests at the Berghof, such receptions for regular visitors happened less frequently.

Please describe the security measures that were in place to protect Hitler at the Berghof

If you compare it with today, then the security measures taken at the time were pretty much useless. Hitler didn't attach much importance to them. He even expressly rejected them. He said to me these exact words: 'If someone wants to eliminate me, then he will eliminate me even if I have personal protection.'

The ultimate responsibility for Hitler's personal safety rested with Johann Rattenhuber, the head of the SS-Reichssicherheitsdienst.[17] When Hitler was on the Obersalzberg, there Rattenhuber was as well. During those times the office of the RSD was housed in what today is the Zum Türken Hotel and some eight to ten RSD officials would occupy it.

On top of that, Hitler's chief aide Wilhelm Brückner had his adjutancy within the Berghof area, and everything was under his responsibility. He was an easy-going, friendly and uncomplicated Party comrade. Unfortunately there was something slack about the work taking place in his office and that rubbed off on the Begleitkommando. I was used to the brutal drill at Berlin Lichterfeld, but in the adjutancy it was the exact opposite.

When Hitler stayed at the Berghof, it would just be one guard who patrolled around his Alpine home and nobody else. If the Boss stayed overnight, only one sentry from the escort squad would stand outside – there wasn't anything else. A single guard would accompany him on his walks to the teahouse at the Mooslahner Kopf[18] – that was the extent of his protection throughout the whole area.

In photos Hitler is often portrayed with his dog. What is this all about?

The question about Hitler's dogs is not new. The Boss had a white Alsatian named Sirius, and visitors and the so-called Obersalzberg pilgrims were just mad about the dog's fur. They would constantly cut this poor dog's fur and take it home as a memento. They would even hack off pieces of the fence belonging to the Führer's nature reserve and consider them as souvenirs. After Sirius died, the Boss had another Alsatian, called Wolf, who would fight and bite. He was quickly given away. Then there were also Muck and Blondi. Muck was still around during my service, but then died of old age. Everyone knows that Blondi was definitely Hitler's favourite dog.

In 1939, for his birthday, a breeder from Düsseldorf presented Hitler with an unusually beautiful animal called Beroll, a male dog. I was totally besotted with that dog and constantly had him by my side. Beroll closely guarded the entrance door to my office, he didn't allow anyone to enter, not even my wife. Every time a stranger would enter my office, Beroll would stand in front of me protectively and would turn his eyes to me and my guest, back and forth, back and forth. Unfortunately, in December 1941 and at Hitler's request, the Wehrmacht requisitioned this dog to be deployed in the fight against the partisans in Russia. Hitler only kept Blondi . . . until his end in the New Reich Chancellery in Berlin. She also had a litter and all of them were poisoned at the end as well.

As of 1937 the Boss rarely went on walks with his dogs because of constantly having to attend receptions for diplomats, heads of the armed forces and states. But all his dogs were kept in kennels located above the Berghof. Those were very nice kennels, and Betty, our employee and a real treasure, looked after them. Betty cared for the dogs, fed and, time permitting, even bathed them.

Was Hitler a strange man?

Hitler decided that for himself he would maintain a spartan lifestyle. He was unpredictable, impulsive, strict, inflexible and hard on himself. If you knew him well, you would be able to ascertain and sense what the right moment was to speak to him and whether he would even hear it, or whether he wasn't just lost in thought and hatching a plan.

Some occasions I specially remember: for example, some valuable, expensive paintings decorated the walls of the hall – all meant one day to be shipped off to Linz. In the mornings, when Hitler would come down from his study on the first floor, he walked past each picture humming a melody and allowing himself a lot of time. At that point he was his approachable self, and one could enjoy his company; you would even be able to inform him of something perhaps slightly unpleasant. But if he descended and was whistling then beware. get out of the way and keep your head down.

Once I had an inner conflict. Hitler had descended the stairs while whistling and I had to tell him something important. It was 1 January 1937 and, being −20°C, it was freezing cold in Berchtesgaden. Despite the temperature, the construction work was in full swing. Day and night. But during winter neither the electricity nor the water pipes could keep up with the demands that came with such a severe spell. Additionally, because of the extensive building works on the Obersalzberg, we suffered enormous fluctuations in the electricity supply. The winter garden belonged to the old Wachenfeld House and was not connected to the central heating. For this reason two radiators had been placed in the winter garden's room so it would be heated up. I once told my wife: 'Those are really old things, and what with the electric fluctuations it is possible that the coils will burn up' – and this is exactly what happened one day.

As was often the case, Hitler was sitting in the winter garden, poring over his construction drawings and plans. All of a sudden Hans Junge, the valet, comes to me and says: 'Herbert, the Boss is asking for you as it is very cold in the winter garden.' I immediately knew what had happened. I took one of the radiators along with me and measured the current. Although there was electricity, the appliances were cold. I immediately called the Berchtesgaden electricity board. It only took twenty minutes before two of their fitters, Hildebrand and Köberlein, arrived. With us everything happened as fast as lightning. And just as I had said, they confirmed what I had suspected. The old radiators had burnt out and were beyond repair.

All of a sudden I remembered that Johannes Hentschel, a master electrician, worked at the Berlin Reich Chancellery. He had previously been employed by the firm that had produced these radiators. All it took was a call to him, and on the morning of the following day a courier plane landed at the Ainring airport delivering two new radiators.[19] The plane was able to land despite the bad weather, snowfall and the fog. Without delay, I picked up the radiators, brought them to the winter garden and connected them up. After a good half an hour, we had managed to reach a pleasantly warm temperature. And just as I left the winter garden to make my way to my office, Hitler comes along and whistles a tune. I stopped and looked at the Boss. 'Döhring, you've got something for me?' 'Yes, mein Führer. I can report that you can now use the winter garden again.' I then briefly told him what had happened.

With this type of service you were able to gain quite a few brownie points. But it was far easier to lose these. If something went wrong and it was an important issue you would be thrown out on your ear immediately.

One of Hitler's special habits were his fast-paced marches

Always depending to the weather, these fast marches would take place in three different areas. If it was hot in the summer, Hitler would run at a fast pace back and forth in front of the adjutancy, lost in thought. This is where he forged his plans, and under no circumstances was he to be addressed at that time.

In bad weather he would use the area under the arcades at the main entrance of the Berghof. Should a sharpshooter have wanted to murder him this would have been an ideal and open shooting space, offering someone a safe distance of one hundred metres. Under the code name Operation Foxley, the English Secret Service had already planned such an operation.[20]

During the winter Hitler's fast marches took place within the Berghof site itself. He would run from the main entrance, which was on the ground floor, to the dining room and from there to the winter garden in the old Wachenfeld House.

Was Hitler a lonely person?

He was a very lonely person. I would so often think, where does this man take his energy from? When other people would visit friends on a Saturday or Sunday or engage in some leisure activity, the Boss sits there, upstairs, and works. Through countless long nights he would prepare construction drawings, whole city districts, bridges and new buildings; and then there were these endless plans for city reconstructions. Initially he wanted to rebuild forty-seven of the large German cities in their entirety.

In March 1939 his list increased to include the city of Memel, because the Memel Territory had become absorbed into the German Reich. Additionally there was Bozen and Meran, so that a total of fifty of the main German cities were to be completely turned upside down: they were to enjoy good air, sun and public parks. And this is what he worked on night after night, producing his ideas and making countless handwritten notes.

Downhill from the Berghof, at a distance of around 200 metres as the crow flies towards Berchtesgaden, is situated Villa Bechstein,[21] and this is where our large studio was located. There, some six to eight architects worked on Hitler's plans nearly non-stop. They would suggest drafts, changes and new designs. That's how it came about that I would drive down to Villa Bechstein several times a week, picked up construction plans and models, and then return them to the villa. That's how it went, back and forth.

Here is a small anecdote which was based on a misunderstanding. Hitler had gone to his teahouse at the Mooslahnerkopf and, as usual, the idea was that his chauffeur Erich Kempka would then pick him up along with the other guests, down where the so-called Führersperrgebiet ended.[22] What happened sometimes is that Hitler would return on foot from the teahouse at the Mosslahnerkopf to Villa Bechstein. This was the case on that day. Kempka was already sitting with his passengers in the waiting room at headquarters. All of a sudden the phone rang and the operator was on the line. Döhring was to immediately come to Villa Bechstein. I thought the architects had called and that, once again, I was to pick up some construction drawings or plans and bring them back to Hitler's study. I drive down and what do I see? At the circular driveway there stood the Boss, along with Major Schmundt, chief of the personnel department of the Wehrmacht, Heinz Linge, his valet, Obergruppenführer Wilhelm Brückner and Karl-Jesko von Puttkamer, Hitler's naval adjutant. I stopped the car, got out and, following the tradition at the time, said: 'Mein Führer, present at your command.'

'Why, who has sent you?' asked Hitler, quite puzzled. 'What do you want?'

'I was told to come to Villa Bechstein. I concluded that I was once again to pick up some construction plans and models.'

'Let's all go in Döhring's car,' said the Boss.

At the time I was driving a cabriolet Opel Admiral, which Hitler had received as a present from the Opel manufacturers. And that was my company car, seeing as I was the housekeeper. A brilliant car in those times. Hitler got in next to the driver's seat and his entourage sat in the back. A lot of people would fit in that car. So I drove off and, arriving at the top, just after the hairpin bend, there stands the chauffeur Kempka with his other drivers and sees that I am the one driving.

'You drove well, Döhring,' said Hitler, and slapped me approvingly on the back. And thanks to this mistake, I too was allowed to drive Hitler this one time.

Much has been written about Hitler's vegetarian food habits – what was your impression of this?

He sometimes dictated his speeches until the early hours of the morning, sometimes even till 4 a.m. When he went to bed so late, he would also sleep in, until eleven or twelve o'clock. On the other days he was woken up towards half past nine. The newspapers were brought to him and he would read them still in his bedroom. For breakfast he was served tea, rusk biscuits and milk. Until the outbreak of the war, he drank full-fat milk; after that, the Boss would have only skimmed milk, tea and curd cheese for breakfast.

Hitler, as we know, was completely vegetarian. All the stuff that was written about him after the war, much of that isn't true. He ate a lot of vegetables, curd cheese, rice and soups. My wife would also have this so-called sour soup – it was made with fried batter pearls and roasted breadcrumbs. Because of his being vegetarian, Hitler never ate meat. The things that Hitler's chief aide Julius Schaub said are not correct. What is conclusive and true is that when the operation was still very small, he would often come all by himself to the kitchen and ask my wife: 'So, Anna, what might you be cooking today? Just make sure that it's not meat, you know, ever since suffering from gas poisoning during the First World War I cannot even smell meat. That is abhorrent to me, my mucous membranes are all in a mess, I don't taste anything and have to throw up.' It was the gas poisoning that caused Hitler to give up meat. My wife and also his half-sister, Angela Raubal, confirmed this.

But then, over the course of time, Professor Theodor Morell[23] totally exaggerated the vegetarian diet. That's what we also said to the staff: 'How can a man who carries such a heavy burden survive on a diet of raw cabbage, red carrot juice, cucumber juice and this special brew?' The brew even had a special name, and came from a health-food shop in Berchtesgaden. Every lunchtime, a vehicle was dispatched especially to fetch the brew. The shop was close to the Grand Hotel, later called the Berchtesgaden Hof.

And that was in addition to us having our own diet-specific cooks at the Berghof. I just cannot explain why Hitler went along with this. I assume that this Professor Morell would have made sure to work his magic on the Boss. All this came about via Heinrich Hoffmann,[24] Hitler's official photographer, who somehow smuggled Morell into Hitler's life. Hardly any of the doctors accepted Morell as a colleague.

We know that Hitler and Goebbels were film fans. Is it true that at the Berghof films were shown on a regular basis?

Before the war, dinner was at half past six and after the meal the film screenings took place. Most of the time two films were watched. Additionally, the *Deutsche Wochenschau* (German newsreels) were shown. I can still remember exactly that one of his favourite films was *Carl Peters* with Hans Albers[25] in the starring role.

Hitler took his seat along with the other guests and often additional chairs were put up so that the entire staff could also watch the films. He often waited for the last latecomers to get there. With the outbreak of the war in 1939 there was a sudden change. No longer would entertainment films be shown but, instead, just the current weekly newsreel.

It was quite cold in the Great Hall, but every room was permitted to be warmed up to only 18°C. Those who were cold should move around was Hitler's motto. Hitler, for himself, lived like a Spartan. This was his explanation: 'Seeing that my soldiers don't have anything out there, I am not allowed to have anything either.' This was his bottom line, while he additionally imposed some further restrictions on himself.

Shortly before the annexation of Austria, a meeting took place at the Berghof between Schuschnigg and Hitler. You were an eyewitness. Can you remember any details?

On Saturday 12 February 1938 Dr Kurt Schuschnigg, the Austrian chancellor, arrived at the Berghof for an important meeting. Initially the discussions should have lasted until three o'clock in the afternoon but, as the topic was so complex, talks went on much later. The regular mealtimes were not kept to on that day, and all preparations were thrown out of the window. Then finally, at half past seven in the evening, Schuschnigg left. Hitler then withdrew with his generals to the small sitting room.

The chambermaid and the valet went to the Great Hall to tidy up. What a scene. Coffee cups everywhere, chairs had been shoved around, and the map of Austria was still spread out on the card table. I was just about to roll up the map when I suddenly heard: 'Hold on. Stop. Nothing is to be removed.' Surrounded by his generals, Hitler approached the card table.

'Well, gentlemen, for today you are released. Your presence was of enormous importance. We would like to ask the Almighty to help us and that all may turn out for the good, both for Austria and for ourselves.' With this Hitler meant the forthcoming annexation of Austria into the German Reich.

'Gentlemen, it is never possible for two stags to rule in the same deer park.' At moments like this Hitler was very strict – very forceful. His remarks referred to Mussolini. The deer park was Europe and the two stags were Mussolini and himself. Since his meeting with Mussolini in Venice, in May 1934, he had developed a quiet hatred towards the man.

There is another anecdote in connection with Schuschnigg's visit: the Austrian chancellor was accompanied by someone charged with security – a pleasant, friendly Viennese – who was being looked after in our common room by our Begleitkommando's security officers. They enjoyed a good old time, drinking Schnapps together, and soon that jovial man was totally tipsy. All of a sudden the Viennese says: 'If I were Schuschnigg, I would say to Hitler, "Oh, Herr Hitler, just take Austria and do with it whatever you want."'

After the annexation, Hitler's car stops right at the entrance to the Berghof drive, and I open the door for him. 'See, Döhring, there is this old tale of Barbarossa who lies all curled up in the Untersberg on German land; now, after the annexation of my homeland, he can finally stretch out, down there.'

Hitler had all the shutters of the Berghof lacquered in the colours of Austria's national flag – red, white, red. The job centre in Berchtesgaden hired unemployed Austrian decorators to do that job and they got to work immediately.

What do you know about Hitler's private art collection?

The plan was to deposit his private art collection in a large studio in Linz. At one point the idea was to build a huge gallery. Spitzweg[26] was his absolute favourite painter, but he also liked Bürgel and Rubens. He collected pretty much any of their works that he could lay his hands on. The *Kampf der Zentauren* by Ludwig Bürgel[27] was his absolute favourite.

The Boss had even charged somebody in Breslau – I forget the name – to buy up, along with Heinrich Hoffmann, interesting art objects. In the Berghof alone hung some fifty to sixty valuable paintings, which should have been taken to the gallery in Linz. Linz was the actual place Hitler had chosen for his retirement, not the Obersalzberg.

What was the story about the notorious 'Table Talks'?

One day Hitler returned from his teahouse at the Mooslahnerkopf and it was just when Heinz Linge was on duty. Linge comes to me and says: 'Herbert, the Boss sends his best regards. While he is having his meal, you are to go upstairs and get the study ready. Above all the desk, as he intends to sign some documents.' So I went upstairs and opened the three French doors to the balcony; it was a magnificent summer evening. On the slope down the mountain there was a group of deer jumping about, quite close to the edge of the forest.

All of a sudden, Heinz Linge shows up and asks: 'What do you think he is doing now? He is holding one of his Table Talks. Once again he will be taking them all for a ride. There he is, telling some tales, drawing people's attention to something else, telling them some fibs and what do they do? They believe him.' Those were the famous Table Talks.[28]

Then, abruptly, Hitler enters the room and slaps his thighs. My immediate thought was that he would dance a *Schuhplattler*.[29] 'My goodness, gentlemen,' he says, 'did I ever make something up for them.' I myself pretended not to know anything.

During that time preparations behind closed doors for the campaign to invade Russia were already taking place. That's when Hitler always knew to adeptly distract the others and change the subject.

Was architecture really Hitler's passion?

When Professor Ludwig Troost died, Hitler suffered a great loss. At the time Troost was Hitler's preferred architect, and he believed him to be a genius. He wanted to build, build and build again. Berlin, Munich, Linz, Weimar and Nuremberg were in the middle of being remodelled. In those five cities some major construction projects were already under way. The next city on the list would have been Vienna. Berlin was the capital of the German Reich, Munich the capital of the Movement. Nuremberg was the city of the Party rallies and congresses, and Vienna was intended as the city of music. The plan was to extensively develop Vienna with some gigantic opera houses and concert halls. Models, sketches and drawings had already been prepared, but no decision had yet been taken. After the war I only got to see one of the drawings. Julius Schaub probably threw the rest into the fire he made on the terrace of the Berghof.

And there was even the thought of turning Berchtesgaden into a veritable gem. The plan was to build a Thingstätte (open-air theatre) at the foot of the Faselsberg, near the Jenner, intended to seat thousands.

I still have stuck in my memory countless models showcasing sport facilities and theatre venues. His goal was to have these other cities outdo Salzburg.

With his books Hitler in his mountains *and* Hitler Away From It All, *Heinrich Hoffmann knew to present Hitler in the desired propaganda as someone close to his people, as a man who loves walking in the woods and climbing the mountains of the Berchtesgaden Region.*

It's a fact that the Boss very often and very much loved using the Professor Linde footpath for his walks. Be it alone with his dogs, with guests or with Party comrades, this was always his preferred route. Depending on how fast he or his guests would walk, it did not take them more than one hour to reach the Hochlenzer. This restaurant is where he enjoyed taking his lunch, where he praised their cocoa and their outstanding cheesecake. I too enjoyed walking along this trail and, given the odd break, I would take the dogs along with me.

The path can take you further up, to the Graflhöhe and from there, in a straight line across, you then reach a mountain pasture called the Scharitzkehlalm.

Throughout the whole time that I worked as the Berghof's housekeeper, Hitler never once carried a pistol with him. In some rare private photos you might detect Hitler on his walks carrying a bull whip.

There are photos showing Hitler surrounded by children, were these pure propaganda pictures?

It wasn't propaganda. It was actually his normal behaviour towards children. Of course this sounds paradoxical. On the one hand he loved children, wanted many of his own, and on the other hand he provoked a war that took the lives of millions. But that was typically Hitler. For Germany, he wanted many children, and he wanted them to grow up in comfortable circumstances.

A story comes to my mind which relates to this. It was towards the end of 1938, Austria and the Sudetenland had been amicably annexed into the Reich and the German film corporation broadcast the current and important events of the past year. Then comes the weekly newsreel with its images of troops and many young soldiers marching into the Sudetenland. All of a sudden, up jumps Hitler, right in front of his staff and guests and says: 'Oh children, I am just lost for words of how to thank the dear Lord. Just take a look at all these young boys. Had it come to a shoot-out, how many of them would have been killed?'

In October 1929 Hitler made the acquaintance of the seventeen-year-old Eva Braun in the Munich studio of his photographer Heinrich Hoffmann. Were you aware that Frau Braun was Hitler's girlfriend?

The first time I saw Eva Braun was on the last Saturday of March 1936. At that time the Berghof was just in its first stage of renovations, and Hitler had moved into his quarters in the guest house of the Party, the Hoher Göll. Anna, later my wife, said to me at the time: 'Just listen to me, there'll be a a young blonde lady turning up, that's Adolf's girlfriend.'

I was totally lost for words. The public had absolutely no knowledge of the fact that the German Reichskanzler had a girlfriend.

Late at night, from what was then my bedroom, located in the attic of the Berghof, I glanced down to the terrace of the guest house Hoher Göll, and that's when I saw Eva Braun for the first time, walking up and down the terrace with Hitler. She looked sporty, had an elegant manner about her and was smartly dressed. In my mind there was something moody about her, but then that might have been understandable. After I was married to my wife, Anna shared more details with me about this strictly secret relationship. Within the 'company,' the rule was that Eva Braun was never to be spoken about, not to anybody.

During Hitler's presence on the Obersalzberg, Eva Braun was first put up in the Platterhof Hotel.[30] *After the Berghof renovation in 1936 she received her own room there.*

Late one night, Hitler sat in his study on the top floor of the Berghof and, totally lost in thought, he worked on some construction plans. The Boss ordered me to come up in order to help him sort out and register his documents. He sat there, poring over his plans, as if transported into a trance, and did not hear the knocking. He kept on measuring and drawing on his plans. After a while someone knocked and knocked again. All of a sudden the door separating his study from his bedroom opened and in came Eva Braun. She was surprised to see me so late in Hitler's study. So Fräulein Braun approached him from the side and addressed him. Hitler totally lost it and belted out: 'You always come when I don't want to be disturbed. You surely must see that I am knee-deep in my work. I have absolutely no use for you now.' Eva Braun turned red, furiously lifted her head, looked at me angrily and then she was gone.

Fräulein Braun and Hitler would never have been close to each other under normal circumstances. At Hoffmann's photographic studio in Munich-Schwabing she was hired as a secretary, and Hitler often went there. Hoffmann cleverly took advantage of this opportunity and literally fixed up Eva Braun. As we say in the army: 'This broad was served up on a silver platter.' That was my personal take on it.

There had already been one death at the Führer's flat, at Prinzregentenplatz 16 in Munich.[31] There, on 18 September 1931, his niece Geli Raubel had committed suicide. And Eva Braun as well had tried to commit suicide several times. In my opinion this was the reason why Hitler was simply not in a position to prevent this relationship.

Heinrich Hoffmann was actually the real cause of all of this. It was he who had cleverly snuck Fräulein Braun into the Führer's life. Only later on, through Hitler's aides, would the relationship become more public knowledge.

Hitler did not like to keep having new employees join him in his private surroundings. Ideally they should all have remained in their jobs forever. This did not work in Hitler's favour, not with respect to his private or his political life. Keeping this affair secret made an open recruitment for appropriate staff impossible. The consequence was that no new and capable manpower was hired at the Berghof.

I had a fine relationship with Eva Braun, although something or other would always bother me. She was simply not capable of adhering to the constraints imposed on us because we were living in times of war. She certainly was one to indulge in a sophisticated lifestyle, and luxury items were part of that. At the start of the war, surprisingly, we had quite high stocks of food and luxury goods, but even the most generous supply tends to run out eventually. While other people had nothing, she desired turtle soup for dinner, freshly pressed orange juice and confectionery. Things like this really upset me.

When these sweets were actually close to running out, I had a word with Gretel Mittlstrasser, head-housekeeper at the Berghof, and my wife Anna. I got carried away and decided to write to a praline and chocolate factory in south Germany, which at the time was very well known for its product. Having lived in East Prussia in the past, I was familiar with the area's large sugar factories, and with the sweet and chocolate shops they were supplying. I therefore sent a note, which had the letterhead 'Berghof – Obersalzberg in Berchtesgaden' written at the top, asking for some samples to be sent.

After about eighteen days the postman brought a package weighing some ten kilograms – all fine pralines and chocolates. I thought to myself: 'Well, I'll be damned, but if the Boss gets wind of this he will chuck me out immediately.'

Eva Braun was often bored. For her, life was hugely monotonous, and this is why she was also so moody towards Hitler. She preferred an elegant wardrobe, she was keen on modern music and liked to dance. My wife and I would have really liked to take her along with us to dances in Salzburg just to make her happy. But we were not sure if this would one day become an issue. We didn't want to take the risk. And the minute handsome people such as Hermann Fegelein,[32] a liaison office on Hitler's staff, entered the room, she was besotted.

What was the relationship like between Eva Braun and Reichsleiter Bormann (head of the Nazi Party Reich Chancellery)?

If Bormann had had his way, he would have thrown her out immediately, as this relationship was entirely unsuitable in his eyes. According to him, all Eva Braun ever did was cause unnecessary expenses due to her high demands and exclusive desires. For him, Eva Braun represented a kind of parasite.

On the other hand, Eva Braun didn't like him much either, because he was such a rough guy, a real brute.

Until today the true background of the relationship between Hitler and his niece Geli Raubal remains unclear. What is it that you know about this?

It was Easter 1940 and Hitler was, once again, on the Obersalzberg. Based on the meetings with high military officials it was clear to us that fighting would commence in the West any day. And that's how it happened that the Boss once again very abruptly terminated his stay at the Berghof. Within two hours the whole group had disappeared again.

Just before their departure, his valet Heinz Linge came to me in a rush and said that Hitler wished to see us. My wife, in the meantime, had brought a grey envelope from our flat in which, much to my surprise, there was an unusually beautiful picture of his niece Geli. Here was a tall, young woman sporting a fashionable hairstyle, and her eyes had a sensual look. There was a strange expression on Hitler's face and he asked my wife: 'Anna, can you be so kind and let me have the photo? When the war is over, I will give it back to you immediately.'

It never came to that. Nobody knew what happened to this picture. At that very moment there was his partner Eva Braun, sitting back in the Berghof, only a few rooms away from him. From that I gathered that he had loved his niece, and still loved her.

In 1931 my wife made an interesting comment: during the summer of that year Geli Raubal and Hitler took more walks than usual. One day Anna thought that both of them had gone out, so she went to make up their rooms. When she entered the living room she saw Hitler and Geli sitting in full embrace on the couch. She immediately left the room and quietly closed the door.

Hitler's niece occupied her own room in the old Wachenfeld House. This was a simply furnished room on the top floor, combining living and bedroom, just when you come up the stairs, on your right. An old wooden bed, a wooden cupboard with a mirrored door and a chair – that was it.

After Geli Raubal shot herself in the apartment on Prinzregentenplatz 16 on 18 September 1931, a Friday, her funeral followed quickly afterwards on 23 September 1931 in Vienna. Straight after a Party convention that took place on 24 September in Hamburg, Hitler secretly called for somebody to drive him to her grave in Vienna. After that he just locked himself into Geli Raubal's room in the old Wachenfeld House for an entire week. He mentioned to my wife that he wanted to shoot himself. He was also refusing food. Eventually my wife was able to convince him to eat something. She then brought him up rice soups, salads and puddings. After that, the room was called the Geschenkzimmer (gift room). As we were constantly receiving presents on the Obersalzberg, and there were some very valuable things among them, we had very little space. All presents were sorted, catalogued and stored away in what once was Geli Raubal's room. The story about this room was an extremely closely kept secret, and I only got to know about what happened there through my wife. Nobody else knew, though perhaps Julius Schaub, Hitler's chief aide, might have had some inkling.

When it was time to renovate the Wachenfeld House, Hitler ordered that this room remain forever untouched.

Reichsleiter Bormann is often referred to in the literature as an obscure, devious 'Brown Eminence'.[33] *What was your impression of him?*

The first time I set eyes on Reichsleiter Bormann was in the summer of 1936. It was just when I was making my rounds, passing by Hitler's kennels. I was coming down the steps and saw below me a man standing on the terrace dressed in a grey suit and wearing a floppy hat and black boots. I approached to see who it was. All of a sudden he looks at me, turns on his heels and approaches me. 'Oh, it's you Döhring, I have already received my information, I am aware of the situation and I know who you are.' That was my first encounter with the so-called Lord of the Obersalzberg. Later on, when Hitler spent time at the Berghof, Bormann would come nearly every day for lunch, together with his wife.

Then Bormann started buying up land on the Obersalzberg. When I hear what the prices were that people were prepared to pay, I thought that everyone had gone mad. Back home in East Prussia, you would have been able to purchase large feudal estates or properties of some hundred to a hundred and fifty thousand hectares for those amounts. In those days on the Obersalzberg for a few hundred square metres you would pay approximately 100,000 Reichsmark (€550,000).

Some time later I had a chat with Bormann and asked him about this particular issue. He responded: 'Döhring, I understand your complaints, but the Führer had expressly ordered this. If the inhabitants of the Obersalzberg have to move away from here because of us, then you have to pay them not only for their property but also for the loss of their homeland.' That was the justification for the steep prices that were being paid. At the beginning of this property purchasing, the prices paid were especially high, and the reason for this was to sway the minds of those inhabitants who still wanted to stay put.[34]

'Go to Bormann, we here have nothing further to say' is what the aides at the Berghof would respond when they were questioned regarding these transactions. And that was, unfortunately, indeed the case. When Hitler would make only the slightest comment, Bormann would immediately pounce on it and make it become true and real. Examples of this happening are the Eagle's Nest, atop the summit of the Kehlstein mountain, and then there was the Manor House, a prototype of a farm or, yet another example, the greenhouses. Then came the shocking demolition of the house of farmer Rasp, Hitler's neighbour.

And that's how it came about that Hitler would always criticise the aides who surrounded him as complete slouches, but would at the same time applaud Reichsleiter Bormann for his work. 'Although Bormann is a philistine and a rogue, he is still the man I can wholly and fully rely on. He carries out my orders to perfection, dotting all the "i"s and crossing all the "t"s' is what Hitler would say.

Why did Martin Bormann get the nickname 'Napoleon' on the Obersalzberg?

The employees on the Obersalzberg feared the Reichsleiter for several reasons: his constant surveillance, his firings without notice and then there were these harassments, circulars entitled 'Anschiss durch Rundschreiben'.[35] At the time, the cinemas screened a new film called *It's All Napoleon's Fault* and, because Bormann had a similar build to the old Frenchman, somebody from the staff came up with this nickname.

The Eagle's Nest is an absolute magnet for visitors to the Berchtesgaden Region. How did this impressive building come about?

The construction of the Eagle's Nest can be traced back to a casual comment Hitler had made. During one of his frequent walks along the Professor Linde path, up to the Hochlenzer mountain and then further to the Scharitzkehlalm, the Boss noticed another mountain which was much favoured by hikers – the Kehlstein.[36]

This mountain was also well known in the region for the storms and lightning that erupted in that particular area. Hitler commented to the people accompanying him that it might be a good idea to have some solid tables and chairs put up atop the summit so that mountaineers and hikers could stop off there for a snack and enjoy the magnificent view over the Berchtesgaden valley. Again this quite random remark by Hitler was grist to Bormann's mill. He immediately embraced it and straight away set to work turning this idea into a course of action. It wasn't long before he thought of erecting right on the rocky ridge of the Kehlstein mountain not just seats for a snack but also a solid building. Instantly he drummed up his colleagues from among the Party elite and requested they draw up architectural and operational plans. Eminent architects, engineers and even Dr Fritz Todt – the inspector-general for German Roadways and later Reich Minister for Armaments and Ammunition, where he managed the entire war military economy – were enlisted.[37] Bormann's idea was along the lines of 'let's give Hitler in 1939 the Eagle's Nest as his fiftieth birthday present.'

After some initial discussions, an inspection of the Kehlstein and its surroundings took place. From the very beginning, this Kehlstein project was enormously complicated, the first reason being its extremely steep face, another was the so-called hornplates – rock-hard stones that most tools couldn't cut through. In spite of all these adverse conditions, construction of the Eagle's Nest began at the end of March 1937, at full speed and without pause. Workers laboured in three shifts at several construction sites simultaneously, and even during the winter, when weather conditions were impossible, they pushed forward with the project.

During the day, holes for the explosive devices were drilled, day after day, month after month. At around 6.30 p.m. the explosives were detonated. This caused an echo in the surrounding mountains, and the reverberations sounded like unbelievable thunder that reached as far as the Berchtesgaden valley. This went on throughout the whole summer of 1937 – through the day the drilling and the positioning of explosive devices. The detonations were followed by the gathering of the accumulated rock pieces and gravel, all of which were then transported away.

Hitler would then tend to make some rather cynical comments to Bormann, making a play on words with his name.[38] 'The "Bormann, the Drill-Man" is drilling and blasting away and driving the entire valley crazy.'

The construction of the approach road leading to the Eagle's Nest[39] required special security measures. The explosions necessary to create the tunnels and the steep rocky mountain surfaces were even more difficult. In spite of all the security measures put in place, a few labourers still lost their lives during this extraordinary construction project.

Following torrential rain there were huge mudslides, and I personally knew one truck driver who got killed after his vehicle fell over on a sharp bend. The avalanche disaster in 1938 proved once again that the Kehlstein was a dangerous and treacherous mountain.

Even your brother-in-law belonged to the Obersalzberg Trägerkolonne.[40] What made this dangerous work so attractive?

Labourers on the Obersalzberg made good wages, considering the times. Then a whole range of supplementary payments existed too: those depended on the labourer's distance to the workplace, there were then height bonuses, bonuses for danger, and so forth. For years, my brother-in-law transported the heaviest loads imaginable, and that was before there were paved roads. Sacks with gravel and shingle, cement and also large and heavy wooden beams.

When payday fell on a Friday, there were frequent fights among the labourers after their drinking binges, and the so-called Trägerkolonnen would be called in to bring order. These were all sturdy, robust types. Later on, Hitler issued an order that drastically reduced the consumption of alcohol. Instead, free drinks were offered all day long, and alcohol was on tap only after hours. There was just too big a risk of having an accident at this height. From then on, the canteens served free non-alcoholic drinks, pork sausages and additional food.

During Christmas 1936 all labourers were offered a thick, woollen jacket as a present. These were all three-quarter jackets with a herringbone pattern, so the builders were easily recognisable in the village. All in all there were eight thousand men who were employed at the Kehlstein, working both on the supply roads and on the Obersalzberg.

All the Berchtesgaden inhabitants would immediately recognise the jackets and say: 'That's the real "Obersalzberger", he works on the Obersalzberg.' For Christmas in 1937 each labourer received a pair of good, solid boots made by a manufacturer in Pirmasens.[41] What with this incredibly large workforce, such an order caused a huge amount of expense and placed high demands on the supplier, just to get all the sizes right and the boots delivered on time. The following year the Christmas presents were replaced by cash.

Is it true that there was a brothel in Berchtesgaden?

One day the head gardener Bühler came to me at the Berghof, informing me that he would have to go to the Laroswacht guest house in order to mow the lawn 'of the brothel'. Until then I had no idea that there was a brothel there. I then drove with him to this place, and we actually went in, just to have a look, mind you. It all looked very tidy, everything was very clean.

In the Berchtesgaden quarter called Unterau near the Ache river, the so-called floozies had set up their home in the Laroswacht guest house – diagonally opposite the Freimann-Lehen. Initially some seven girls worked there; later, in 1940, there were already some twenty-five ladies. These girls were attracted by ads and job centres located in France and Belgium, and were then hired. Initially it was the military doctor of Obersalzberg who was entrusted with their medical care, and later it was a doctor from Salzburg.

Just shortly after the Eagle's Nest was completed you went on some trial runs, accompanied by Erich Kempka, the chauffeur. What kind of a feeling did you get from that?

The whole project is a true masterpiece of architecture, engineering and workmanship. It starts with the ambitious road, which leads up to a car park situated 1,700 metres high. Behind large brass gates lies the tunnel, measuring 125 metres long, which continues deep inside the mountain before you reach what seems a near-sacred copper hall. Visitors were all deeply impressed when they were taken from there by a lift with the interior decked out in fine polished brass, leading up to the actual building. The Eagle's Nest is located at 1,834 metres, and the lift manages to cover the elevation between the car park and the house, some 134 metres. By mid-September 1938 this imposing construction was completed. Alongside Hitler's chauffeur Erich Kempka, it was I who made the first test drive to the Eagle's Nest. The ascent was incredibly exciting and we barely had time to admire the magnificent view as, in parts, the road is extremely steep and there are very sharp bends to negotiate.

What was Hitler's attitude towards the Eagle's Nest?

As far as I knew, and from what I gathered from his comments, Hitler's attitude was always negative about the Eagle's Nest. He himself never really wanted to drive up there. He said: 'I don't feel well up there, and the air at that height is too thin.' These were the excuses he wanted the world to accept, but in truth he just didn't want to go up there.

What Hitler really feared was being struck by lightning. During construction work several unbelievable storms raged up there. Once, during a severe lightning storm, several hundred metres of electrical cable was totally scorched. Hitler knew of this incident, and he was frightened that lightning could one day strike the lift at the Eagle's Nest.

At the beginning of August 1939 a large Hungarian delegation arrived at the Berghof for a meeting. It was planned that coffee, tea and cake would be served at the Eagle's Nest. Hitler called for me and ordered that I drive up there. I set off, along with two maids, two servants, the lift engineer and the chauffeurs. Josepha from the Hoher Göll guest house had brought along two cakes, and everything was set for twenty-five guests. Much to our surprise, no phone call came letting us know that Hitler was on his way with his guests. So I contacted the operator of the Berghof and was told that Hitler had cancelled everything and was having tea with his Hungarian guests in the Great Hall.

We then decided to make ourselves comfortable at the Eagle's Nest. We had coffee and packed up all leftovers and took them back to the Berghof. And that was one of those instances when Hitler declined a visit to the Eagle's Nest at the very last minute.

Also, much that has been said about the costs of the Eagle's Nest is not correct. No tax money was used, and everything was funded by donations to the Party and the 'Adolf Hitler donation'. The Eagle's Nest was to be the Party's present for Hitler's fiftieth birthday.

How did the construction of the greenhouses and of the Manor Farm come about?

Hitler liked taking frequent walks on the Obersalzberg. There, even in the early months of the year, say February or March, we would have splendid weather with bright sunshine. As soon as the sun had melted away the snow on the southern slopes of the mountains, the Boss would go for walks with his guests. Once he made a random comment: 'The sun seems to shine down over those slopes so beautifully, some wonderful greenhouses could be built over there.'

That was not an order, not an instruction, yet Bormann immediately picked up on these words and instantly translated what just minutes ago was an idea into a reality. Two greenhouses were built straight away. They grew vegetables there and different sorts of flowers. This allowed my wife to put in her orders for fresh flowers on practically a daily basis, on demand, for the Berghof. This was extremely important to Hitler.

On the afternoon of 7 July 1942 an unimaginable hailstorm hit the Berchtesgaden region. Nearly all the glass panes of the greenhouses were destroyed and, because of all the many thousands of shards everywhere, the soil was rendered completely useless. At the Berghof as well there was damage, and many window panes on the attic floor were destroyed. Bormann had been informed by his deputy and had put everything in motion. Already by the following morning a glazier was to come to renovate the windows at the Berghof. One should not forget that this was in the middle of the war, and it wasn't so easy to procure window panes. But Reichsleiter Bormann looked after the matter and ensured that, after the unusable soil had been replaced, the greenhouses themselves were completely renovated, including their window panes.

The real pet project of Bormann's was the Manor Farm. Here he bred pigs, Haflinger horses[42] and many other animals. Bormann constantly tried to convince the Boss to inspect the Manor Farm, in an attempt to persuade him of this estate's benefit. On one of those days this was once again the case, and the Boss accepted the invitation. They took a good look at everything and marvelled at the vast valleys and the magnificent views. Hitler then commented with a smile: 'So, Bormann, your pigs really are getting a wonderful view.' Those were the types of teasing remarks Hitler made to Bormann, who of course did not respond to them.

The forceful removals and expropriations of farmers with homes in the Führersperrgebiet are used nowadays as examples of the ruthlessness of the Nazis. What have you personally experienced in connection with this?

Underneath the Berghof lay an estate called Freidinglehen, and it belonged to old farmer Josef Rasp, also known as 'Fleck'. During this time, Bormann had already bought up nearly all the houses, farms and estates situated in the Führersperrgebiet. He then ordered the whole area to be razed to the ground and had a new lawn put down. Looking down from the Berghof terrace, this allowed for an unbelievably gorgeous view. As for the Freidinglehen, Hitler had given express orders that this estate should not be touched until further notice.

When, as usual, the Boss was standing with his guests on the terrace enjoying the beautiful view, he casually mentioned that, in fact, this particular estate did indeed bother him. Once again Martin Bormann overheard this comment. A little while later, when Hitler went on a trip to Munich, Bormann already had everything in motion: diggers, trucks, as well as organising a whole team of labourers equipped with axes, saws, shovels and picks, who immediately set to work and tore down the Freidinglehen. They removed the dwelling house, sawed down old trees, dug out the foundations, and in no time everything was transported away.

An unimaginable number of people and machines worked under enormous time pressure. Like clockwork, in came the trucks transporting topsoil and turf, which was instantly laid. No gaps were allowed to show.

After some forty-eight hours, Hitler returned from Munich to the Obersalzberg, and Martin Bormann was ready with his report. Listening, the Boss just shook his head, but generally accepted the facts, and his reaction was friendly. That was typical of Bormann. He acted with lightning speed and tended

Above: In 1936 the erstwhile Wachenfeld House was converted to the Berghof; the picture shows the topping-out ceremony, in March, traditionally celebrated by placing a tree on the roof.

Below: In this view of the Berghof, the two windows above the balcony on the left belong to the flat of the housekeeper – Herbert Döhring at the time; the shutters are lacquered in red and white, which indicates that the photo was taken after the annexation of Austria in 1938.

Above: Adolf Hitler greets Italian head of state Benito Mussolini on 25 September 1937 at the Munich Central railway station. In the background is Hitler's valet Karl Wilhelm Krause.

Below: Hitler in his Mercedes-Benz, Type 770, seen driving through the site of the Reich Exhibition called Schaffendes Volk *(The People Who Create) in Düsseldorf, 2 October 1937. Krause sits behind Hitler.*

Above: Hitler greets SA Obergruppenführer Heinrich Knickmann while Krause waits in the background.

Below: Hitler and Krause in front of the Jägerhof Castle, offices for the Düsseldorf Gau leadership.

Hitler's housekeeper Herbert Döhring and Anna Krautenbacher were married on 10 December 1936 in the Berchtesgaden's Evangelical Church.

Above: After the wedding ceremony, Hitler joined the guests of Herbert and Anna Döhring in the Berghof's Great Hall.

Below: Employees at the Berghof celebrate new year 1938 with a 'liquid' party; in the middle, Herbert Döhring, in civilian clothing, reaches for a glass; on his right is Hitler's valet Krause; next to him is Anna Döhring.

Above: The Berghof staff in 1938 among whom is Döhring (on the far left). The second woman on the right (looking sideways) is Gretel Mittlstrasser, the maid of Eva Braun and wife of Döhring's successor Willi Mittlstrasser.

Below: Döhring outside the Berghof.

Above: Herbert Döhring with his wife and two friends, standing by the landing stage for the Königssee boat.

Below: Döhring and his family.

*Hitler received an Opel Admiral from the Opel Works, which Döhring used as an official car (**above** and **below**). On one occasion, he happened to stand in as Hitler's driver. Erich Kempka, Hitler's full-time chauffeur, observed the scene from afar and afterwards praised Döhring for his driving skills.*

Above: Many people visited Berchtesgaden in order to see Hitler with their own eyes. Here, Döhring stands behind Hitler, watching him.

Right: Döhring on the Berghof terrace in 1937, with Eva Braun (with camera). His wife Anna is kneeling next to the fawn.

Above: *Hitler very much enjoyed taking a walk along the Professor Linde Path, behind the Berghof, in the foothills of Hochlenzer mountain. Here, he is followed by his adjutant Wilhelm Brückner, an SS man with a camera and Herbert Döhring in uniform (far left).*

*Above: For the Berghof's employees the period spent on the Obersalzberg remained a lifelong and unforgettable experience. Arthur Kannenberg (**insert**) here reminds Herbert Döhring, in 1958, of the 'big times they had between 1932 and 1945'. Kannenberg was the housekeeper at the Reich Chancellery, in charge of the catering services and official receptions.*

Below: In August 1988 Döhring gave an extensive film interview for which he opened up his treasure trove of memories. Even after so many decades had passed, he still vented his anger about Anna Plaim's dismissal from the Berghof, by Martin Bormann.

Above: Chambermaid Anna Plaim (née Mittlstrasser) with her family. Plaim's father Franz (far right) was a committed 'black' Austrian. His political and religious affiliations were to impact on Plaim's life while in Hitler's employment.

Left: Plaim in 1941 at the Berghof, shortly after she started her new position, which she received based on the recommendations of her cousin Willi Mittlstrasser and his wife Gretel.

Below left: Plaim, on her arrival at the Berghof.

Below right: The car in which Plaim was picked up at the Salzburg railway station was the same one in which Döhring (far right) caused an accident that had serious repercussions. Also in the picture are Gretel Mittlstrasse (2nd from the right), the film projectionist Ellerbeck (far left) and chambermaid Plaim (2nd from left).

Above: Plaim on one of her leave days with her parents in her hometown of Loosdorf, which is in Lower Austria – at the time called Lower Danube. Coincidentally, both of Plaim's brothers were also there.

Below: Hitler's blotting paper which Plaim removed from his desk at the Berghof. As she later commented: 'Somehow it also is a document. And clearing away a piece of used blotting paper was part of my duties.'

Above: *The chambermaids at the Berghof: Elfriede König (left), Resi Stangassinger (right) and Plaim (centre).*

Opposite above left and below left: *Hitler's long absences from the Berghof proved to be more of an advantage to the staff than a disadvantage. Even though they had to combat isolation and loneliness, there was, as compensation, sufficient time to play, dance and sing.*

Opposite above right: *After the official Christmas 1941 celebration with the ladies of the house, a private celebration with staff followed. The photo shows Elfriede König and Plaim sitting in the staff room.*

Above: Along with Eva Braun and her dogs, Plaim often travelled to Munich, where Braun owned a house on the Wasserburgstrasse. On one such trip, the party made a stop at the guest house on the Chiemsee. With Braun in this picture are Gretel Mittlstrasser and Plaim.

Braun's Scotch terrier Negus (below left). In 1941 she bought a bitch, Stasi, to keep Negus company. After Plaim had been dismissed from the Berghof, she received a dog from Braun, which was sent by train from the Berghof to Loosdorf (below right). It was one of Stasi and Negus's puppies. Plaim called her Stasi, like her mother. This was the last contact Plaim had with Braun.

Anna Döhring with Hitler's dogs Muck and Blondi.

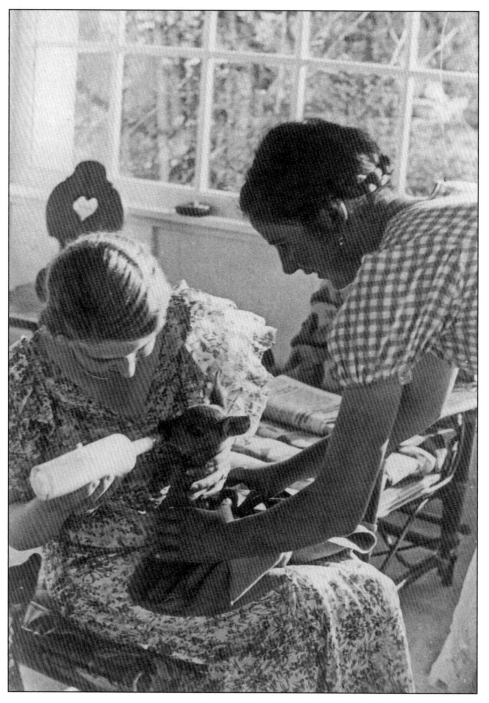

Magda Goebbels and Anna Döhring feeding a fawn in the Berghof's conservatory.

Above: The Berghof's conservatory and terrace. In the first room on the right, Eva Braun ate her dinners nearly every evening. Part of the Untersberg is recognisable in the background.

Below: The Berghof: a world still intact. In 1943 Plaim received this photo from the Berghof. In it, Anna Döhring is having coffee on the Berghof terrace, with the chambermaids Resi Stangassinger and Elfriede König.

Above: This photo of Braun was taken at the Berghof. She presented it to Gretel Mittlstrasser on her birthday, adding a personal dedication. Hitler was also presented with this photo.

Right: Braun, once an employee at Hitler's personal photographer Heinrich Hoffmann, was keen on photography. This is one of the pictures thrown away by Braun, which was retrieved by Plaim. It shows Braun in Hoffmann's studio. Still visible on the studio window is the name of Hoffmann's business. It remains unresolved why Braun kept tearing up photos and throwing them away.

Right: Plaim's cousin Willi Mittlstrasser and his wife Gretel. Willi enjoyed a special relationship with Hitler and at times worked as his driver. His wife was also employed at the Berghof. She was Plaim's immediate superior.

Below: Gretel Mittlstrasser hands Hitler flowers for his birthday. Those in the background include her husband Willi.

Bottom: Willi Mittlstrasser (left in the front), his wife Gretel and their three-year-old son belonged to the last group of people who stayed until the end at the Berghof. Nothing came of Hitler's alleged plan to flee to the Berghof.

Above: Gretel Mittlstrasser sits on the bench that surrounds the tiled fireplace in the living room.

Left: Braun's living and dining room. After dinner she was handed a daily list of cinema films from which she could pick those she wished to see afterwards, in the Great Hall.

Above: Cook Lilli surrounded by her Berghof kitchen assistants. Although in the entire Reich food could be purchased only with food stamps, there was an abundance of groceries available for the Berghof. Turtle soup at two o'clock in the morning was not a rare occurrence.

Right: Hitler knew all of his staff members by name. Here he greets cook Lilli, who baked his favourite pastry, which was regularly sent to him when in Berlin, by special courier.

Above: The Great Hall, which was 146 × 12 metres, had a lounge suite arranged in front of the red marble fireplace. The 1941 Christmas celebrations took place here. As was customary for the Berghof, festivities lasted until the early hours of the next morning.

Below: The Great Hall with its large conference table and view towards the Untersberg. The window, measuring 9 × 3.6 metres, consisted of ninety individual glass panes. The globe, on the left, became world famous in Charlie Chaplin's classic film The Great Dictator.

Behind this Gobelin tapestry was the film screen. Prior to screenings, all chairs were turned into the right direction for guests to have a perfect view. For the ladies of the house these films were the highlight of the day.

Above: A grand piano stood in another part of the Great Hall. Plaim was allowed to play it when there were no guests in the house.

Below: This cupboard in the Great Hall stored all Hitler's certificates for honorary citizenship.

Above: A different aspect of the Great Hall. The door on the left of the piano led into the dining room.

Below: The entire Berghof dining room was clad in pine. Hitler usually sat in the middle on the side facing the windows, rather than at the head of the table.

Above: Hitler in his study at the Berghof.

Below: Hitler liked fresh flowers in the house. These were grown in the Berghof greenhouse.

Above: From his study, Hitler had direct access to his bedroom, via the door in the far right of the picture.

Below: Three French windows led from Hitler's study to the balcony at the Berghof. Between the doors hung paintings of Hitler's mother (left) and his father (right).

Left: Hitler at the entrance to the Berghof. The Führer loved grand appearances. His goal was to impress and intimidate state visitors coming to the Berghof, and he succeeded in achieving that. Meanwhile Eva Braun had to recede into the background, especially during such state receptions. No one ever got to see her face to face.

Below: The Untersberg Room in which Rudolf Hess stayed while at the Berghof shortly before his ill-fated trip to Scotland in 1941. Plaim had to clean this room and in it she found a stash of medication.

Above: Plaim's cousin Willi Mittlstrasser had his office in Haus zum Türken, the local headquarters of the SS and the criminal police. This is where the reports against Plaim came in.

Below: The Eagle's Nest, Hitler's teahouse on the Kehlstein, was situated at a height of 1,834 metres. He had it built to impress state visitors, and its construction cost 30 million Reichsmark, yet he visited this sumptuous building perhaps less than a dozen times.

The Berghof had a panoramic view over the Latten Mountains and the Untersberg.

to put into operation what had been a mere thought just seconds beforehand. He earned himself a lot of brownie points with Hitler. But it was different with the rest of the staff. Woe to him who might have got something wrong – then he would be much more than just strict. The culprit would face immediate dismissal. An additional three-month salary would still be paid, but this time you would have to try and find an appropriate job elsewhere.

You had a fight with Martin Bormann during your work as housekeeper at the Berghof. What was the cause?

Bormann accumulated more and more power for himself. He was a very difficult man and generally didn't get on well with people. One day I also got into an enormous fight with this 'Almighty man on the Obersalzberg'. It happened the day after Hitler's fiftieth birthday, on 21 April 1939. For his party, the well-known Chilean pop singer Rosita Serrano, who was an admirer of Hitler, presented him with an album containing ten of her most recent records. We already had five records by the Chilean lady in our record archive, among which was the world renowned song 'Red Moon'.

Hans Junge, the valet and husband of Traudl Junge, had been given the order to immediately hand me the new album the moment it arrived. That evening, just to indicate how the timing was relevant with respect to what happened the next day, late towards midnight, Hans Junge returned from Salzburg where he had attended a dance at an elegant, exclusive restaurant – a place, by the way, that both my wife and I also liked to visit.

Well, the following day, lunch was served at 1 p.m. and finished at 1.30 p.m. The valets and staff cleared up the dining room. The entire kitchen staff was busy and both my wife and I were extremely concerned that the whole operation was moving along swiftly and smoothly. All of a sudden Bormann enters and starts screaming at me: 'Döhring, you are to immediately come with me to the Great Hall and see the Führer, we want you to put on the new Serrano records.'

I let him know that we actually have no new records, just the five old vinyls, yet Bormann continues bellowing at me: 'You must surely know where the new records can be found.' All of a sudden I just get furious and shout: 'For crying out loud. I don't have any other records, where on earth should they be?' I screamed in such a loud voice that staff immediately lowered their heads.

As it happens Bormann was significantly smaller than me and, while we were having this argument, he constantly moved backwards, and when I screamed at him the way I did he eventually just said nothing. Frankly I was just about to slap him across the face . . . when in comes Junge, the valet. Obviously he had heard from all the way up in his room all the commotion happening downstairs and immediately realised that he had actually not yet had a chance to hand me the new album. So he gives it to me right then and there, and it of course contains the ten new Rosita Serrano records. Bormann sees this exchange, doesn't utter a word, turns on his heels and departs from the Berghof within minutes.

I then took the ten new records to the Great Hall, and Hitler listened to three or four of them. In the meantime the weather had cleared up; as it had stopped raining Hitler then made his way down to the Mooslahner tearoom.

Well, you wouldn't imagine the high regard Bormann showed me after this incident. It actually wasn't my intention, but by God he sure had respect for me, like you wouldn't believe. From then on, and for many years later, we enjoyed a relatively harmonious working relationship.

Bormann was a workhorse of the first order; he was extremely strict and very frugal, even though the Nazis had huge amounts of money. During the construction phases he was working on site day and night. He always needed to inspect what was going on, even if it would be in the middle of the night. In this regard, the man was a sort of a model for me, but there was this other side to him which was unpredictable and hard.

It was 1 January 1939, New Year's Day. It was still early in the morning, and Bormann was full of ideas. Hitler had taken leave from his New Year's Eve guests only at 1.30 that night. And all of a sudden, Bormann arrives late at night on the Obersalzberg, accompanied by his party revellers. It was −15°C, it was freezing and there was one-and-a-half metres of powder snow on the ground. The streets were, as was always the case, clear of snow, and the whole gang was driving their heavy vehicles up to the Eagle's Nest in order to continue celebrating up there. That's in the middle of the night and in the middle of a deep winter. The Eagle's Nest wasn't heated of course. A number of valets and maids also had to come along. What complete madness.

At the Berghof, staff had celebrated until the early hours in the morning together with Hitler's Begleitkommando. When it was about 5 a.m. I told them: 'Well, it's about time to put an end to this.' It was just then that Bormann and his gang returned from the Eagle's Nest. Then, all of a sudden, it dawned on me that this man is still going to be checking this very morning on all the heads of department, regardless of where they were, whether in the barracks, in the garages where the official cars were parked or in the Party guest house. This man is going to be making his tour this morning and will check up on anybody who might have overslept.

Up there, at the Berghof, we normally started work at 6.30 a.m. With respect to that particular day I had requested the maids and all the kitchen staff to commence work at 9 a.m. I myself got up at 8.30 a.m. and I was downstairs, on the ground floor of the Berghof, by about 8.45. All the maids and the entire kitchen staff were all assembled and ready. All of a sudden, the door opens and in comes Reichsleiter Bormann asking: 'Döhring, how are things? Has anybody overslept?' 'No, Herr Reichsleiter, as you can see for yourself, everyone is present.' 'Goodbye', he said and he was gone.

But had anybody overslept, that person would certainly have lived to regret it. Bormann was hard as iron, indestructible, and constantly went on inspection drives, travelling to every single spot around the Obersalzberg.

Based on an intrigue that could be traced back to Bormann, adjutant Wilhelm Brückner was fired in October 1940 in Berlin. It came as a huge surprise to everyone. It was all about some controversy between Arthur Kannenberg,[43] Hitler's steward, and two other aides – Max Wünsche[44] and Wilhelm Brückner.[45] Kannenberg had taken it upon himself to issue orders to the two aides and, because they didn't care for this too much, they would not toe the line and refused to act on the order.

At some point Hitler had said: 'All I have in Berlin are slouches whom I have to get rid of one by one, but from where should I take good people? Let's take the Berghof as an example and let's take a look at how things are run there. What I have there are the Döhrings, so I know that everything will be in *Ordnung*.'[46]

That's exactly what he said to the secretaries and aides in Berlin. Of course staff made sure to convey to us Hitler's praise. This made my wife and me feel slightly awkward, of course.

There were some people within Hitler's private circle about whom we would like to learn a bit more. What impression did, for example, Heinrich Hoffmann make on you?

Hoffmann was an old Party comrade and private friend of Hitler's. Naturally he was favoured when it came to art commissions. When expensive paintings were being bought, Hoffmann was brought on board as an advising art expert to the Boss.

As far as I was concerned, being the simple man that I am, Hoffmann's drinking binges rubbed me up the wrong way. Night after night he got together with any old pals of his. I was truly distraught by this and wondered how it was possible that one could come across people like that – and allow such people to become so close to Hitler. It really had a very negative influence on the entire entourage and community on the Obersalzberg. At some point later on, Hitler would mention Hoffmann's red nose saying: 'If you set Hoffmann's nose on fire, it would burn for a very long time what with all the alcohol.'

Dr Theodor Morell, Hitler's personal physician, was recommended to him by Reichsleiter Bormann.[47] Apparently he was an eminent doctor from Berlin, but then the doctor introduced this completely idiotic diet to the Berghof, which consisted purely of these stupid juices. According to the opinions of our dieticians and my wife, this way of eating practically ruined Hitler.

For a time, Reichsminister Joachim von Ribbentrop[48] visited the Berghof nearly every day and, when Hitler stayed there, von Ribbentrop would even come twice a day. Von Ribbentrop had purchased Fuschl Castle located in the Salzkammergut as this property was close to where Hitler stayed, should Hitler require him.[49] Towards us staff von Ribbentrop appeared to be very upstanding and pleasant, always praising the meals and the desserts my wife would serve.

As a sign of gratitude for having been our guest so often, around Christmas time he handed me – in the presence of an adjutant – an envelope with 500 Reichsmark (€2,750). He wished that this amount should be distributed among the entire staff, including my wife. I then drafted a thank-you note to Reich Foreign Minister von Ribbentrop on special stationery with the Berghof Obersalzberg letter heading, and asked all employees to sign it. Later on, I handed the letter to him in person.

What was Hitler's relationship to Great Britain?

In the years between 1936 and 1938 a number of the guests we received were English. Lord Harold Sidney Rothermere,[50] the so-called press baron at the time, even occupied the beautiful Untersberg Room. In September 1936 David Lloyd George, British prime minister during the First World War, visited the Obersalzberg.

Hitler truly wanted, for his own reasons, to cultivate a very intensive and friendly relationship with Great Britain. He intended to befriend the people, not the 'stuffy' English lords – for them he cared little. He regarded England as a model for quite a few things. Often Hitler would say: 'Such a small country with only forty million inhabitants ruled over an entire world empire.' He would always take the British Colonial Empire as a leading example. On the other hand he would also malign the English and drag them through the mud, as the saying goes, simply because of the 'English disease'.[51] He made a lot of fun of the children's bowed legs.

The 10th December 1936 was a special day. I remember it exactly as it was my wife's and my wedding anniversary. An important phone call from the German Embassy in London came at lunchtime. The newly appointed ambassador to the Court of St James's, Joachim von Ribbentrop, phoned and informed Hitler that Edward VIII, later known as the Duke of Windsor, was going to abdicate. During lunch, which lasted for two hours, Hitler must have been called to the phone at least ten times, and after each call he returned to the lunch table looking more downcast. Hitler had had high hopes for Edward VIII. He was, as we know, particularly fond of Germany and, had he remained as king, much might have turned out totally different.

Hitler had to accept a similar blow when Józef Piłsudski[52] (the Polish Head of State at the time) suddenly died in 1935. Later on, he would always say: 'If Józef Piłsudski had stayed alive, England would not have been able to influence the developments in Europe.' Piłsudski was an outspoken hater of communism. Germany and Poland would have waged a united war against communism in Russia. From the start Hitler was convinced of that. Poland would have risen to glory like never before in its history. Hitler often and repeatedly emphasised this point. But the English made everything null and void through their clever politics.

The German-Polish Non-Aggression Pact 1934 essentially provided Poland with the power to behave aggressively towards the German Reich. Thus, repeated attacks on ethnic Germans living in Poland were allowed to take place, and the dispute over Danzig definitely aggravated the situation between the two countries. Added to this, we had the 1939 test flights of the Royal Air Force with its long-range bombing squadrons to the south of France. Newspaper articles reported on these test flights, which reached as far as the Pyrenees, Andorra and Biarritz.

Walter Hewel – Joachim von Ribbentrop's chief of staff, diplomat in the Foreign Ministry and a close friend of Hitler and myself – was, like us, a very skilled Skat[53] player and often, when we used to play in the evenings, Erich

Kempka and Gretl Braun would also join our game. One time Hewel all of a sudden exclaimed: 'The English are mobilising this very minute. There is no turning back, it's not possible. We are head-on approaching a war.' That was spring 1939. A total shift from peace to war.

How was Hitler's Halt Order[54] – halting the advance on Dunkirk as part of the Battle of France – viewed?

The generals were totally taken by surprise that the German tank squadrons – based on the expressed order of Hitler – were stopped prior to reaching Dunkirk. From our perspective this was only motivated by some sentimental sympathy towards the English.[55] Hitler was still hoping that the English would change their politics if he allowed the British Expeditionary Force to withdraw. Hitler's opinion was that his image in England would improve immensely based on this decision. But this was not the case.

He could have taken the soldiers belonging to the British Expeditionary Force prisoners, maybe England would then have even surrendered? But Hitler always speculated that England would reverse its politics. This was his mistake, and his mistake alone. Unfortunately he often didn't accept the advice given to him by his political and military advisers.

Until today Rudolf Hess's solo flight to Scotland on 10 May 1941 remains shrouded in mystery and controversy. Can you tell us any details about it?

After the so-called solo flight, Reichsminister Hess was portrayed by the Nazis as a crazy man and as an idiot. The public doesn't even know that the whole affair was, in my eyes, one big con. Based on what I observed, and the discussions I accidentally overheard, I am firmly convinced that Hitler himself gave the suggestion or even an order to embark on this voyage. Hess was Hitler's most trusted deputy and was requested to fly to England in order to prevent a war on two fronts, as had occurred in the First World War.

I believe that the rumours that circulated after the flight were just that. No crazy, total idiot of a man can fly a Messerschmitt Bf 110 to England, or rather Scotland to be precise, and, on top of that, accomplish this by flying blind. Additionally Göring's air defence did not even register the flight.

During the first days of May 1941, the Boss was extremely nervous and unsettled. It was exactly at that time that he would often have phone conversations with Rudolf Hess. Valet Hans Junge would say to me that Hitler was having phone conversations till late at night. Of course we wanted to know with whom he was speaking. Hitler, however, knew precisely at what time the other person would call and made sure to answer the call himself. But there was a third party involved as well, though not a single person knew who it was.

By coincidence I was once privy to an important call. While I was not an actual aide of Hitler's, I always kept my eyes and ears open; they were always set to 'receiving mode', so to speak. There were three spots at the Berghof from where I was able to secretly listen in and remain undetected. I stood in the cellar, right next to the ventilation shaft, which led to the big window of the Great Hall, and listened in on the secret discussion between the Boss and Nicolaus von Below, Hitler's personal adjutant in the Luftwaffe. This conversation lasted some twenty minutes and touched on the specialist area of night flights and blind flights. I listened to the entire conversation because it was so interesting. Von Below explained to the Boss the various ways to fly an aircraft such as this in order for it not to be spotted by the air defence. It emerged that what is important is that the pilot flies at an extremely low altitude so that he may make optimal use of the terrain.

At the time I was unable to recognise any connections and did not give this any further thought. Days later, when I found out that Hess had flown to England and that Göring's air defence had absolutely no information on that, it dawned on me. Reichsminister Hess flew at extremely low altitude from Germany to Scotland.

That was Hitler's last attempt to avoid a two-front war. In Hitler's book *Mein Kampf* he described the dangers of a two-front war, which were based on his experiences in the First World War. All efforts to make a peace agreement with Great Britain had failed, and the Hess flight was Hitler's last attempt. Everyone can say or write what they want, but personally I am firmly convinced of that fact.

Hitler summoned all Reichs- and Gauleiters[56] to the Berghof in order to swear in all these high-ranking Party members. They were to be faithful to him, even during difficult times. After Hess had flown to England, all the 'faithful' members were gone. Hermann Göring had long ago lost favour in the Reichskanzler's eyes.

Often Hitler would not hesitate and say the following to his servants and workers in his employment: 'Once again, General "Meier" spoke total nonsense.' By General Meier he was of course referring to Göring, as Göring once famously said that his name would be 'Meier' if even a single hostile plane managed to fly over the Reich. I also know that engineers from the Research Department and

Industry had approached the German Luftwaffe in order to submit their tenders for the further development and deployment of radar technology. And Göring's predictable response was: 'By the time you have developed the radar, we will have long since won the war.'

Josef Stalin was an adversary who needed to be taken seriously. What did Hitler think of him?

Hitler accepted Josef Stalin even though he was a communist. Stalin knew exactly what he was after. I look back to the year 1939. The Memel Territory, the most northern part of the German province of East Prussia, had been ceded to Lithuania after the First World War. At the end of March 1939 Hitler gave a speech in the Berlin Sports Palace to young officers in training, in which he stated that the Memel Territory had finally returned to Germany and would henceforth remain German for thousands of years to come. Stalin was informed of that speech via his secret service and responded: 'It will be me who will decide one day to whom the Memel Territory belongs.' Hitler knew precisely that Stalin was his biggest adversary.

Stalin enforced so-called purges in the Red Army, during which he had many thousands of army officers executed or deported to the Gulag. The German secret service and Hitler believed that these purges by Stalin could one day be helpful to them. Unfortunately the exact opposite was true. Since many military leaders previously serving under the tsar had now been replaced by new officers trained in the communist system, they were fighting much more fanatically for their communist ideals.

Stalin was known to have commented: 'If Germany should one day attack us, it will be the end of Hitler.' And that is exactly what happened.

The 23rd August 1939 was a very muggy day, and it remained hot until late in the night. Hitler had given a speech that morning to his commanders in the Great Hall of the Berghof and informed them that von Ribbentrop, the Reich's Foreign Minister, was already en route to Moscow, where the German–Russian Non-Aggression Pact would be signed. This news hit the generals like a bomb and they were left speechless, shocked; nobody really knew what was going on.

Wilhelm Keitel (Chief of the High Command of the German Wehrmacht) and Karl-Heinrich Bodenschatz (Göring's adjutant and liaison officer between Göring and Hitler) were assembled on the terrace of the Berghof and expecting an important phone call. Tension was so thick one could almost cut it with a knife. Will the signing come to pass or not? Suddenly the call came from Moscow. Count Friedrich-Werner von der Schulenburg,[57] the German ambassador, was asking to speak to Hitler urgently. Stalin requested to receive, at once, free rein over the Baltic states of Estonia, Latvia and Lithuania, as otherwise he could not sign the pact. There was quite a bit of agitation and an urgent meeting was called. Finally Hitler had no option other than to leave the Baltic States to Stalin.

At the very moment of signing the pact in Moscow, all of us were standing on the terrace of the Berghof and came to behold an exceptional appearance in the sky, which spread over the Latten Mountains and the Untersberg. Everyone was transfixed by this horribly beautiful, but equally terrifying shape appearing in the sky. First, the clouds shaded in various colour tones ranging from sulphur yellow to a fiery red to dark blue and then bulging into a deep black, then they literally came rolling towards the Obersalzberg. Those clouds did not move along normally, but would rotate and roll and tumble into one another – most unsettling. Our adjutant immediately called Salzburg to enquire whether any reports about a large fire or something similar had perhaps come in.

I was never able to forget that particular day, since I was never again to experience something quite so scary. It took about a quarter of an hour for this horrible and gruesome sight to disappear. Nicolaus von Below also mentions this awful occurrence in his book *At Hitler's Side: The Memoirs of Hitler's Luftwaffe Adjutant*.

There was a mysterious, elegant, blonde lady who was part of Hitler's private entourage. Her name was Marion Schönemann and she was a fortune teller from Vienna. All of a sudden she collapsed and when she came to she predicted, with all guests present: 'Mein Führer, this augurs nothing good. I saw blood, misery, distress, chaos and a cruel demise.'

Hitler was totally shocked and responded to her: 'Yes, well, if it must happen, then let it happen as fast as possible. Goodbye, ladies and gentlemen.' He turned on his heels and disappeared into the Berghof.

It's up to everyone to interpret this event as they wish. Summer lightning, phenomena in the sky, caused by supernatural powers or perhaps just nonsense. My wife was convinced that Hitler was guided and led by an invisible power.

Is it correct that Hitler called the Berghof on the day war broke out in order to warn you of the danger of an imminent air attack?

On Friday, 1 September 1939, war broke out with the invasion of Poland. On Sunday, 3 September, at around ten o'clock, the French and English ambassadors handed to the German government the declaration of war. Towards 1 p.m., just in the middle of our lunch, the phone rang at the Berghof and Heinz Linge informed me that the Boss wanted to speak to me immediately and that I was to go to his study as there was a direct line there and the operators would not need to be involved.

Hitler says: 'Döhring, you have heard what has happened. You need not take any special precautionary measures, but from now on you must be aware that you will be the first one to get a hit on the head. I would like to ask you, however, and as a matter of precaution, to have the paintings that have been earmarked for Linz moved into the cellar.' So we brought those valuable paintings, which had all been counted and registered, downstairs. Then I called the Reich Chancellery and reported that all the orders had been executed.

The code name 'Operation Barbarossa' referred to the invasion of Russia in the summer of 1941. What can you tell us about what happened prior to this?

The 31st July 1940 was a highly charged day. Hitler had informed the Wehrmacht Oberkommando of the plans to invade Russia. Based on what we knew from the military adjutants, both the servants and I were well aware that a war on communism was certainly going to happen one day.

A secret meeting at the Berghof took place at which the following were present: General Field Marshal Wilhelm Keitel, Major Rudolf Schmundt[58] and a spy who submitted his reports. At night, these men closely studied the documents provided by the spy, and concluded that an attack by the Red Army on the German Reich was imminent. Already during the 1940 campaign in France the Wehrmacht Oberkommando and Hitler were deeply worried that Stalin's army would actually go on the attack then and there. That's also the reason why the leadership of the Wehrmacht immediately attempted to agree on a ceasefire with France.

According to some rumour, a secret convention of the commanding officers was to take place at the end of August on the Obersalzberg. On the evening before, 30 August, the Boss ordered my wife to come to him so he could inform her that the commanding officers of all military services were going to attend a big conference. He discussed the menu with Anna and requested *Griessnockerl Suppe*[59] and further instructed his guests to take a trip to Salzburg or go bathing. Late that evening, before the start of the conference, he requested that I take all ordnance survey maps covering all of east Europe to him – from the North Pole down to the Caspian Sea. After I had brought these to him, I was allowed to go to bed.

The day of the conference was muggy, and for some reason the air conditioning[60] wasn't working. Karl Wilhelm Krause, Hitler's valet, informed me that I should only air the room by opening the large window of the Great Hall while the generals were at table. Otherwise everything was locked and the keys had been handed in. When I approached the card table close to the large window, I saw, spread out, all the ordnance maps I had taken to Hitler the evening before. Looking at them closely, I saw the two main strategic areas that were marked up. It all of a sudden hit me that these were the preparations for war with Russia. I was dumbfounded.

I didn't speak to anybody about what I had noticed. Then, in the evening, when we all sat together with the staff, the conversation was revolving around England and Russia. Everyone just said anything that came to their minds without really thinking. Hitler had given a secret order that only those who were directly involved with the matter may be informed.

Krause and I were probably the only ones who knew some further details. During our chat, Krause all of a sudden looks at me and then we both just leave the room so as not to give anything away inadvertently. It can quickly happen that something just slips out and then all hell breaks loose.

That was my experience with respect to Operation Babarossa. Hitler then issued an order of the day, which basically stated that Germany would have to wage a two-front war for a five-month period. The German troops would return by Christmas. But he had got that totally wrong.

The goal to push forward until they reached the Volga was not achievable. An alternative deadline was in place, summer 1942, but any later dates were just too precarious. Once Christmas 1941 was over and nothing decisive seemed to be forecast for 1942, the first doubts started creeping up inside me. This time, Hitler's prediction did not turn out to be true, and I asked myself whether this was the beginning of the end of the Third Reich.

One day after the attack on Russia, Hitler spent time in the Führer Headquarters called Wolfsschanze near Rastenburg.[61] The moist climate had turned spring into autumn, and the headquarters into one big, mosquito-infested area. At night, the Boss wasn't able to sleep because the mosquitoes practically ate him up. In 1941 he suffered a syncopal event and had a complete breakdown. That was never revealed to the public.

The whole excitement caused by the wars with Poland and France, in addition to England's refusal of a peace agreement, all deeply depressed Hitler. It was the cause of the stomach upsets. He indicated to my wife that these stomach problems had been caused by gas poisoning during the First World War. All of a sudden Heinrich Hoffmann had the idea to speak to Dr Theo Morell, and at the end of 1940 he started with this stupid diet of his – of juices and raw vegetables, pills and injections. When the Boss then suffered this circulatory collapse, Morell only further increased the dosage of the medication and the number of injections.

In 1941, just before the Russia campaign, it was like the Grand Central Station at the Berghof. Diplomats, military officials and ministers were coming and going in quick succession. First came Dr Jozef Tiso, president of the Republic of Slovakia. Then followed King Boris III from Bulgaria and Ante Pavelić from Croatia and, on 10 June, Marshal Ion Antonescu from Romania arrived. When such important guests visited, the house guests had to leave the Berghof. My wife was in Salzburg at the time. Except for one cook, the entire kitchen staff had left. Erich Kempka, Heinz Linge and I were on duty and it was an unbelievably hot day in Berchtesgaden. Back in the management wing we kept all the windows open, sat ourselves down in the staff lounge and played a game of Skat. Gradually a heavy storm started brewing in the north. Suddenly, at around 4 p.m., there was complete silence. We just felt that at any moment something like the sound of an explosion would pierce the stillness. All of a sudden it started getting dark everywhere, as if it were a real solar eclipse. I myself had this strange feeling that, once again, a creepy situation would befall us. It was eerily quiet and one felt that at any minute something would erupt. Suddenly a blaze of fire, an incredible crack, a deafening explosion. It was pitch black, and we had difficulties breathing because of the smell of sulphur. At this same moment the cook comes running to me and says: 'Herr Döhring, please look at the flag in front of the Berghof.'

Lightning had hit the ten-metre-high flagpole. There was no sign of the huge flag, nor of the flagpole that had always stood there. Thousands of wood splinters were spread out within a perimeter of ten or fifteen metres – they couldn't have been bigger than matchsticks.

Kempka, Linge and me – we couldn't utter a word. That does not bode well. Since this event coincided with the visit of Marshal Antonescu, I suspected some relationship to Romania. What might happen if Romania, the largest oil supplier to Germany, is lost to us? Those few oil-refining plants in Gelsenkirchen, Halle, Bitterfeld and in the Sudetenland will be unable to meet Germany's demands – I knew that.

During my deployment, I was the oldest Unterführer of the 1st SS Panzer Division Leibstandarte SS Adolf Hitler (LSSAH) and served as the transport leader for a convoy of tanks from Linz on the Danube to Normandy. As the train tracks had been destroyed, we were ordered to take detour routes leading out of Belgium. At lunchtime we arrived in Wetzlar and were cared for by the Red Cross. On that day it was the German Red Cross manager's birthday, and we celebrated in spite of this damned war. All of a sudden we heard, on the Volksempfänger[62] broadcasting, the news that Romania capitulated on 23 September 1944. The Red Army arrested Antonescu and occupied Romania. That's when I recalled the mysterious event of 1941 at the Berghof. My heart nearly stopped and from that moment on I was firmly convinced that Germany had for sure lost the war.

Hitler had never been appraised of this curious event because, of course, Bormann had been ever present as usual and took charge. Directly after this unusual incident, the phone rang at the Berghof. Reichsleiter Bormann was on the phone: 'Döhring, I saw what has happened and I ordered Bühler, the gardener, to immediately replace the flagpole. We have the exact same flagpole standing near the car park – it should be cleaned up and put in place. Not another word about this incident.'

You repeatedly mention curious natural phenomena in relation to important political decisions. What are your suspicions?

Hitler often spoke about providence. Whether he believed in a sort of predestination, I cannot say. My wife was a young girl when she started her service at the Berghof, and she got to know him rather well throughout many years of working there. She was also near him and in his proximity during many private events. Sometimes she thought that some invisible spirit steered him. Sometimes he was lost in thought, as if in a trance, and during those periods we knew that he was forging one of his plans and nobody was to approach or speak to him.

Anna said to me that Hitler was a man who was hard to define – a strange man. It is difficult to describe that because he was so full of contradictions. On the one hand he could be benevolent; on the other hand he was utterly brutal.

In my opinion the Boss was driven by a higher power, that's the impression I had gained in those many years. How all this hangs together still remains to be discovered, and I unfortunately cannot shed more light on it. In the first years of my service Hitler would often say: 'May the Almighty help us.' Many years later, when the Boss said goodbye to me and my wife, he said it again: 'May the Almighty assist and help us.'

After his mother's death, Hitler never had a Christmas tree again, as she had died during the Christmas period (on 21 December 1907). Eva Braun was finally able to change his mind so that a Christmas tree was put up in the Grand Hall. Hitler himself would appear at the Berghof only in the afternoon of Christmas Day (he was never there on Christmas Eve).[63] On 24 December he would always meet up with his Alte Kämpfer[64] in the Bürgerbräukeller – a large beer hall in Munich.

Hitler had an inner faith and didn't reject the Church either, unlike so many of his Party members. The only people he was at loggerheads with were the Church dignitaries who criticised him.

You knew the Berghof like the back of your hand. You have already spoken about the receptions and the conferences which you eavesdropped. What actually were the opportunities to do that?

There was this shaft-type room in the cellar with a large open window, where both the ventilation system and the technical equipment were located. From that passage it was possible to listen in on conversations. Access to that room was usually impossible due to two panels closing the area off. I would often unscrew the panels, just so some air could circulate and dry out the shaft. This was just a few metres down below and directly under the large conference table at which the military and the state visitors held their secret meetings. That's where I listened in on really secret and confidential stuff.

In the salon, which was located a few steps higher than the Great Hall, there was a long and thick curtain that hung down to the floor. If I stood behind the curtain, I could also listen in on nearly all the discussions. But there was a third spot, and I will keep this one to myself. My successor Willi Mittlstrasser certainly also knew of one or two such strategic spots.

In September 1941 I was on my way to the Führer's headquarters, the Wolfsschanze in Rastenburg. I was sent there as a messenger. My parents lived quite close by and I dropped in on them. All of a sudden the phone rings and the local innkeeper wants to know if I wanted to stop in for a beer, seeing as there were many of my acquaintances having a drink there just then.

I was quite relaxed as I sat in the pub chatting to them, and I told them a few things about life on the Obersalzberg. Rather thoughtlessly I also let it slip that there were some spots in the building from which you could listen in on secret conversations while remaining unnoticed.

Some two or three weeks after my return to the Berghof, two SS officers, whom I had never seen before on the Obersalzberg, suddenly appeared. They introduced themselves and informed me that I had revealed confidential secrets when I was performing my messenger duty at the headquarters in East Prussia. They wanted me to tell them precisely the spots from where one could secretly listen in on conversations while remaining undetected. I then showed them the spot behind the curtain. My interrogation ended then and there. I suspect that somebody who happened to be in that pub of my hometown had reported me. Well, that's how it was back then, but it's still like that today.

When did your work as Housekeeper on the Obersalzberg come to an end?

When war broke out on 1 September 1939, Hitler ordered by decree that none of his closest staff was to be drafted. This exempted his valets Karl Wilhelm Krause and Heinz Linge and his chauffeur Erich Kempka from active service. Nearly all the rest were unaffected by that order and could be drafted.

If I hadn't been drafted into the SS-Begleitkommando and become attached to Hitler's household, I would have been involved in the war from the very beginning. In the early summer of 1935, I had completed various training courses and was part of the process of the first Waffen-SS panzer units being set up. I quietly regretted that I could not be at the war front with the others. Otto Günsche, one of Hitler's personal adjutants, did in fact receive permission to join the front. So I also put in a request in 1942 to Hitler, asking to be transferred to the front. After several such requests, Hitler set me free and gave me leave to join the war.

So it came to pass that my last and longest conversation with Hitler took place in November 1942. Even at that time he still was intensely occupied with all his construction and city plans. Then, much to our surprise, he left the

Berghof because of the critical situation of the 6th Army, which was cut off and surrounded in Stalingrad.[65]

When news of the total encirclement of Stalingrad reached staff at the Berghof, something of an ominous atmosphere began to spread over the Obersalzberg. The Boss had, in fact, intended to stay at Berchtesgaden until the end of November, but then, on 22 November 1942, he decided to travel by chartered train to Leipzig and fly from there onwards to the Führer headquarters Wehrwolf, which was located in Ukraine.

I can still remember Hitler's parting words to me: 'If fate permits it, Döhring, we will see each other again one day.'

He wished me all the best, and also asked my wife to come to him. 'When you have become the famous farmer's wife in East Prussia, I will come and visit you and you will host me on your farm. Because you have served me with such faithfulness, you will receive a personal pension, as long as we both live.'

After suffering serious war injuries I was captured by the British and ended up as a prisoner of war. My home, all my property, everything was gone. Of course it made me think long and hard about so many things. But what should I say? He was, after all, my Boss. I even regarded Eva Braun as my Boss, as far as was humanly possible. I have done my duty, and I would have also done my duty if fate had put me in the service of Mr Stalin or Mr Churchill.

By nature, I was a helpful human being. During the war in Russia, too, I helped people wherever I could – that was simply my character. From day one, I condemned the acts of violence that are part of war.

Endnotes

1   Albert Speer (19 March 1905 – 1 September 1981) was Hitler's chief architect from 1933 to 1945. He was also appointed Minister of Armaments and War Production in 1943and in 1944 he headed the Jägerstab, a task force given extraordinary powers over labour, production and transportation resources, and over expanding the use of slave labour in the aviation industry.

2   Martin Bormann (17 June 1900 – 2 May 1945) was appointed overseer of renovations at the Berghof, Hitler's property on the Obersalzberg, in 1935. Hitler put him in charge of its construction, as well as that of the SS guard barracks, roads and footpaths, garages, a guest house, staff accommodation and other amenities. Retaining title in his own name, Bormann bought up adjacent farms until the entire complex covered ten square kilometres. Within it, members of Hitler's inner circle built their homes. Bormann was also responsible for the construction of the Eagle's Nest. He became head of the Nazi Party Chancellery in 1941, and in so doing gained even greater power within the Third Reich. He used his position as Hitler's private secretary to control the flow of information and access to Hitler.

3   The Führerschutzkommando (FSK) or Führerbegleitkommando (FBK) was an SS security force of Nazi Germany and became the Reichssicherheitsdienst (RSD, literally, 'Reich security service') under Himmler. Originally a bodyguard for Hitler, it later provided men for the protection of other high-ranking leaders of the Nazi regime. The RSD (Bav) and FBK worked together for security and personal protection during Hitler's trips and public events, but they operated as two groups and used separate vehicles. Döhring uses the terms interchangeably which is not incorrect.

4   The 1st SS Panzer Division SS-Leibstandarte Adolf Hitler (often abbreviated as LSSAH) began as Hitler's personal bodyguard, responsible for guarding the Führer's person, offices and residences. Initially the size of a regiment, the LSSAH eventually grew into a division-sized unit.

5   The Potsdam Giants was the Prussian infantry regiment No 6, composed of taller-than-average soldiers. The regiment was founded in 1675 and dissolved in 1806 after the Prussian defeat to Napoleon. Throughout the reign of Friedrich Wilhelm I of Prussia (1688–1740) the unit was known as the Potsdamer Riesengarde (giant guard of Potsdam), but the Prussian population quickly nicknamed it the Lange Kerls (tall guys).

6   Hohe Herren or Hohe Damen refers to the higher echelons of society.

7   This house was initially rented by Hitler's half-sister Angela Raubal on behalf of Hitler, who then bought it outright with funds he received from the sale of his political manifesto *Mein Kampf* and renamed it The Berghof.

8   The Waffen-SS was the armed wing of the Nazi Party's SS organisation.

9   Its stainless-steel material was made by WMF in 1927 under the name Cromargan, which is now world-famous. It cannot tarnish, is rustproof, acid-resistant, unbreakable, easy to clean and therefore extremely durable.

10   Baumkuchen (tree cake) is a tree-trunk-shaped cake, with a pale golden interior marked by dozens of concentric circles and often covered in chocolate. Baumkuchen is traditionally made on a spit by evenly brushing on thin layers of batter, then rotating the spit over a heat.

11   These were coats of arms respectively from Munich and Berlin, the former representing a

small child and the latter a bear.

12 The Brown House was the name given to the Munich mansion which was purchased in 1930 for the Nazis. It was converted into the headquarters of the National Socialist German Workers' Party, it's nickname coming from the early Nazi Party uniforms, which were brown. Many leading Nazis, including Hitler, maintained offices there throughout the Party's existence. The building was destroyed by Allied bombing raids during the Second World War.

13 see endnote 116, p.91, in the Krause memoirs.

14 The Wehrmacht (defence force) was the unified armed forces of Nazi Germany from 1935 to 1946. It consisted of the Heer (army), the Kriegsmarine (navy) and the Luftwaffe (air force).

15 Legendary, because of the many myths and stories surrounding the mountain that straddles the border between Berchtesgaden, Germany and Salzburg, Austria.

16 The BDM (Bund Deutscher Mädel) was the girls' wing of the Hitler Youth, while the Deutsches Jungvolk ('German Youngsters') was its separate section for boys aged 10–14.

17 See endnote 3, p.145.

18 The Mooslahner teahouse was constructed in 1936 on the side of the Mooslahner Kopf, less than a kilometer away from the Berghof. The main part of the teahouse was cylindrical in design, measuring some nine metres, and the Hitler monogrammed tea service and cutlery were silver. The building was destroyed by the US Army.

19 Reichenhall-Berchtesgaden airport was the government airport for Obersalzberg during the period of National Socialism. It lay in the area of the municipality of Ainring, now part of Mitterfelden. After the war the US Army housed concentration camp survivors in the barracks.

20 Operation Foxley was a 1944 plan to assassinate Adolf Hitler, conceived by the British Special Operations Executive. Although detailed preparations were made, no attempt was made to carry out the plan.

21 The Bechstein family, manufacturers of pianos, owned this villa in Berchtesgaden and were huge admirers of Hitler. The Nazis used the villa as a guest house for visiting dignitaries, most usually Joseph Goebbels.

22 After the former inhabitants had been driven out, the erstwhile resort around the Berghof up to the Kehlstein and including the Eagle's Nest was cordoned off and the area named specifically Führersperrgebiet (off limits).

23 Theodor Gilbert Morell (22 July 1886 – 26 May 1948) was Hitler's personal physician, who had a reputation in Germany for unconventional treatments. Morell gave Hitler daily drug injections and doses of vitamins, and Hitler became ever more reliant on him. Although Hitler recommended Morell to others in the Nazi leadership, it was to little avail.

24 Heinrich Hoffmann (12 September 1885 – 15 December 1957) was a close friend of Hitler's and, from 1921, his official photographer. Hitler used Hoffmann's photographs in his propaganda campaign to present himself and the Nazi Party as a mass phenomenon. Hoffmann became a millionaire because he received royalties from all uses of Hitler's image, even on postage stamps.

25 Hans Philipp August Albers (22 September 1891 – 24 July 1960) was one of the most popular German actors and musicians of the twentieth century, especially between 1930

and 1945. His relationship with the half-Jewish actress Hansi Burg started in 1925 and managed to survive the war years, during which Burg went first to Switzerland and then the UK. They were reunited in 1946.

26   Carl Spitzweg (5 February 1808 – 23 September 1885) was a German romanticist painter, especially of genre subjects.

27   Döhring seems to have made a mistake here. This painting was by Arnold Böcklin and Böcklin was indeed one of Hitler's favourite painters; Bürgel never painted an image with this title. The painting referred to had an estimated value of 200,000 Reichsmark (€1 million) and was deemed to be the most expensive painting at that time.

28   Bormann and others took notes of Hitler's thoughts expressed over dinner and in monologues late into the night and preserved them. The material was published after the war as Hitler's Table Talks.

29   The *Schuhplattler* is a traditional folk dance popular in the Alpine regions of Bavaria and Austria.

30   After the Nazis took over the Obersalzberg, the Platterhof was supposed to be a national people's hotel, where the common people of the Third Reich could stay when visiting their Führer. However, it ended up being an expensive luxurious building serving high-ranking Nazi dignitaries and other important visitors.

31   In 1929 Hitler moved into a luxury nine-room apartment at Prinzregentenplatz 16 in Munich. The apartment was on the second floor and important diplomatic meetings took place there after the whole building became the property of the Nazi Party.

32   Hermann Fegelein became Eva Braun's brother-in-law by marrying Eva Braun's sister Gretl.

33   'Eminence Grise' is the term for a loyal confidant of any powerful individual, and is based on Père Joseph, a monk dressed in grey robes and secretary to Richelieu, in the early sixteenth century.

34   What Döhring omits here is that if landowners refused to sell or leave their property, they would face incarceration in the concentration camp at Dachau.

35   The German 'Anschiss durch Rundschreiben' (lit. 'bawling out by circulars') conveys a double meaning: *Anschiss* can mean 'reprimanding' or 'shitting' on someone.

36   The Kehlstein is, at an elevation of 1,881 metres, a sub-peak of the Göll massif, a 2,522-metre mountain in the Berchtesgaden Alps.

37   The Todt Organisation (OT) was a civil and military engineering group in the Third Reich from 1933 to 1945, named after its founder, Fritz Todt, an engineer and senior Nazi figure. The organisation was responsible for a huge range of engineering projects in Germany, both before and during the war, as well as in occupied territories from France to the Soviet Union. It became notorious for using forced labour.

38   The German verb *bohren* (pronounced the same as the first segment of Bormann's name) means to drill.

39   In German-speaking countries this place is called the Kehlstein Haus. In this translation it is referred to as the Eagle's Nest as this is how it was known in the English-speaking world. It is situated on a ridge at the top of the Kehlstein. Paid for by the Nazi Party, it was completed in thirteen months but not used until a formal presentation on 20 April 1939. Its four-metre-wide approach road climbs 800 metres over 6.5 kilometres. Costing some 30 million Reichsmark (about €150 million) to build, it includes five tunnels but only one

hairpin bend. Today the Eagle's Nest is open seasonally as a restaurant, beer garden and tourist site.

40   *Trägerkolonnen* (columns of porters carrying heavy loads up the mountain).

41   Lying close to the French border in the Rhineland-Palatinate, Pirmasens is a city with approximately 45,000 inhabitants and has been known for its shoe manufacturing for more than 200 years. Still today the largest proportion of footwear production in Germany is based here.

42   The Haflinger, also known as the Avelignese, is a breed of horse developed in Austria and northern Italy during the late nineteenth century.

43   Arthur Kannenberg was Hitler's chief steward who, aided by his wife, headed Hitler's household, above all in the Chancellery. He was charged with hiring of staff, ordering of food and organising the catering service during state visits.

44   Having been one of Hitler's personal bodyguards, Max Wünsche then became part of his Begleitkommando.

45   Wilhelm Brückner was a long-time chief aide of Hitler charged with supervising all the Führer's personal servants, valets, bodyguards and adjutants.

46   This expression is kept in German because *Ordnung* (order) was paramount in the German mindset.

47   Most sources state that Heinrich Hoffman introduced Morell to Hitler. Hoffman certainly believed this to be the case.

48   Joachim von Ribbentrop was appointed Foreign Minister of Germany in February 1938. Convicted for his role in starting the Second World War and enabling the Holocaust, he was sentenced to death at the Nuremberg trials.

49   Ribbentrop had bought Fuschl Castle after the castle's owner, Gustav Edler von Remiz, had been incarcerated in Dachau concentration camp where he died.

50   Harold Sidney Harmsworth, 1st Viscount Rothermere (26 April 1868 – 26 November 1940) was an important British newspaper proprietor, owner of Associated Newspapers, and pioneer of popular journalism. In 1896 he launched the *Daily Mail* and in 1914 acquired the *Daily Mirror*. He was a known supporter of Nazi Germany and he cultivated contacts to promote British support for Germany.

51   The 'English disease' was rickets, which affected mostly children and was caused mainly by vitamin D deficiency. Because of muscle weakness, children might develop bowed legs.

52   Field Marshal Józef Piłsudski was leader of Poland from 1926 to his death in 1935.

53   Skat is a trick-taking card game devised in early nineteenth-century Germany.

54   The order to halt actually did not originate with Hitler, but with Field Marshals Gerd von Rundstedt and Günther von Kluge and then it was sanctioned by Hitler. They suggested that the German forces around the Dunkirk pocket should cease their advance on the port and consolidate, to avoid an Allied breakout.

55   It gave the Allies time to evacuate and build a defensive line and was known as the Miracle of Dunkirk or Operation Dynamo.

56   Reichsleiter was the second highest political rank of the Nazi Party and Gauleiter were political officials governing a district under Nazi rule.

57   Count Friedrich-Werner von der Schulenburg (20 November 1875 – 10 November 1944) was German ambassador to the Soviet Union from 1934 to 1941. Accused of being

involved in the 20 July Plot, in 1944, against Hitler, he was executed.

58 Rudolf Schmundt (13 August 1896 – 1 October 1944) worked closely with Hitler during the Second World War, as chief adjutant of the Wehrmacht. He was injured during the 20 July Plot against Hitler and died a few months later from his wounds.

59 *Griessnockerl Suppe* (a soup with semolina dumplings) is an Austrian speciality, and is not to be confused with the *Salzburger Nockerl*, which is a sweet soufflé dish.

60 The Berghof had what was deemed rather sophisticated technology built in, such as air conditioning.

61 The Wolfsschanze (Wolf's Lair) was the first of several military headquarters Hitler built, and the name 'Wolf' alludes to Hitler's chosen nickname. The top-secret, high-security site was in the Masurian woods about eight kilometres east of the small East Prussian town of Rastenburg (now Kętrzyn, Poland).

62 Volksempfänger refers to the German radio (People's Radio) introduced in 1933. Heavily subsidised, it was intended to help expand radio ownership and thereby facilitate the penetration of Nazi propaganda.

63 In Germany and Austria Christmas Eve is celebrated on 24 December and is called Heilige Abend.

64 This term Alte Kämpfer (Old Fighters or Old Guard) refers to the earliest members of the Nazi Party, i.e. those who joined it before the Reichstag elections of September 1930, with many belonging to the Party as early as its first foundation in 1919–1923. Those who joined the Party after the electoral breakthrough of September 1930 were known to the Alte Kämpfer as Septemberlings while those who joined the Party after the assumption of power on 30 January 1933 were known as the 'March Violets'.

65 The 6th Army was a field army unit of the German Wehrmacht during the Second World War. It is still widely remembered for its destruction by the Red Army at the Battle of Stalingrad in the winter of 1942/43.

Part 3

At Home with Hitler: Memories of Chambermaid Anna

In Memory of My Deceased Husband Karl, and for My Daughter Anna and Granddaughter Charlotte, As a Reminder

Anna Plaim

Foreword

At the time of writing her book, Anna Plaim was eighty-two years old (today, she is ninety-eight). Her life was essentially uneventful; ever since her husband Karl, a secondary school teacher, passed away some seven years prior to the book's publication, in 2003, she had been a widow. Before that, and since her wedding in 1948, she had been a housewife.

But Anna Plaim, whose maiden name was Mittlstrasser, had a story to tell. In May 1941, the then twenty-year-old daughter of a busy wheelwright foreman from Loosdorf in Lower Austria was recommended to take on the position of chambermaid at Hitler's Berghof – her cousin in Munich had told her about the job opening. She went into service 'overnight', so to speak, and thus became privy to the private lives of Adolf Hitler and Eva Braun, which were otherwise hidden from the public eye. Her account of Hitler's centre of power is honest and authentic.

Shortly after commencing her service at the Berghof, Anna Mittlstrasser decided to write letters to her parents, which resembled diary entries. During her time on the Obersalzberg, she managed to send home a total of thirty-seven letters, all of which have been preserved in their entirety to date. They actually should have been subject to censure and perhaps confiscation. Fortunately for us they were not and so they offer a unique insight into life at the Berghof – Hitler's private refuge – of a life that seemed to have been something of a banal, yet idyllic bourgeois existence in a golden cage, especially for Eva Braun.

Germany was in the midst of a war of aggression, while mass murder of Europe's Jews was pursued with the utmost brutality and the SS extermination and murder in the East revealed racial insanity and profound contempt for human rights. Millions of people died of hunger, were slain or shot dead and perished, and all this horror reigned all around the Berghof, which was an oasis of a seemingly sane world, an artificially created blissful space.

In this 'sane world' on the Obersalzberg, excess and boredom abounded, coupled with a system of double standards, intrigue, superficiality, all wrapped inside a consciously displayed opulence. Hitler, praised as 'the greatest military commander of all times' in the 1941 German press, used his home as a venue to welcome countless state visitors, whom he intended to both impress and intimidate. To this end Hitler had constructed the teahouse on the Kehlstein,[1] an imposing building erected at the top of a steep mountain, 1,834 metres high, and on which he spent an enormous amount of money (some 30 million Reichsmark) and which he may have visited less than a dozen times. At the same time, the state propaganda's intention was to continuously feed the public an image of Hitler's Berghof as a simple, clean and well-maintained mountain lodge of rustic decor. It went so far that even postcards depicting 'the little house of the people's chancellor' were distributed, thus further emphasising the misrepresentation of the man as someone who was merely a modest and simple leader of the people.

Part of this lie was Eva Braun. When Anna Mittlstrasser started her service, Eva Braun was a constant presence at the Berghof. However, the public was never informed of her role as Hitler's partner in life. During state visits at the Berghof, Eva Braun had to remove herself and step out of the limelight. In fact she was practically hidden away. Even vis-à-vis staff, she was known only as the mistress of the house or the *gnädige Fräulein*.[2]

After war with Russia started in June 1941, Hitler left Eva Braun for long periods of time, and she remained at the Berghof on her own. He was neither capable nor willing to show the love and care that Eva Braun – throughout her life – demanded. Even before that, she had resorted to the most extreme measures to secure Hitler's attention: namely, a number of suicide attempts. In 1932 she tried to take her life by shooting herself in the neck. Her goodbye letter rattled Hitler. He could neither afford a scandal nor did he want to raise any alarm bells. Only then did he grant her the warmth she was after. But this lasted only a short while. Her second suicide attempt followed in 1935 – this time with the help of thirty-five sleeping pills. Hitler once again wanted to avoid any scandal, and so intensified their relationship. Heinrich Hoffmann, his personal photographer and erstwhile employer of Eva Braun, was instructed by Hitler to purchase a house located in the Wasserburgstrasse in Munich. And Eva Braun started moving onto the Obersalzberg. Clearly, however, Hitler had no intention whatsoever of publicly acknowledging Eva Braun.

While he tried to portray himself as the 'greatest military commander of all times', Eva Braun lived a life of utter boredom up there, on the Obersalzberg, in her 'golden cage'. At that time Anna had already started her employment as a chambermaid, becoming one of Eva Braun's closest contacts, not only responsible for her residential requirements but also accompanying her on excursions.

Eva Braun did everything to make life at the Berghof as pleasant as possible for herself. And this is what Anna experienced first-hand, like the excursions to the Königsee[3] and to Munich, which offered welcome distractions. Every pretext to venture out and escape the narrow confines of the Berghof was seized on with relief. Hard to believe, but Negus and Stasi, Eva Braun's dogs, had to visit the grooming parlour. Eva Braun pursued her hobby in photography, and those pictures that didn't find favour in her eyes were simply thrown away.

Anna, the chambermaid, found these pictures and stored them away for safekeeping. She did the same with the blotting paper thrown away by Hitler, and likewise with a heretofore undeveloped photographic film of the Berghof – a unique finding, and all coloured by hand. These items, images and documents have been included in this book.

But of equal importance to these records are the memories harboured by Anna, the only living Austrian witness of those times, her memories of the time at the Berghof and its Obersalzberg protagonists. In order to replicate these in the most authentic way possible, and to convey to the reader this chambermaid's perspective in the most immediate, vivid and direct manner, this book is conceived as an interview. I decided on this format for no other reason than to allow the reader to experience the events at the Berghof as directly as possible.

Eva Braun was certainly Hitler's 'life-partner', but it was only at the very end that she had him all to herself – the day he married her on 29 April 1945 in the bunker of the Reich Chancellery in order to then commit suicide together. Up until that point, her only real duty was to recede into the background. That was to be the case everywhere, including the Obersalzberg, where the all-powerful Martin Bormann was the actual ruler. This radical anti-cleric was a former chief of staff of Hitler's deputy, Rudolf Hess, and after Hess's 1941 solo flight to England Bormann became Head of the Party Chancellery. Even before that, Bormann, in his role as private secretary to the Führer, was responsible for Hitler's private finances, including the running of the Berghof, where he along with his family occupied his own 'Bormann House'.[4]

Bormann belonged to Hitler's inner circle and, during Hitler's absences, would govern the Obersalzberg as its absolute ruler. It is not for nothing that he was considered the 'Lord of the Obersalzberg'. Each and everyone had to obey his orders. Eva Braun was no exception. The chambermaid Anna, above all, was subject to his rule and, in the end, was to be removed from the Berghof based on Bormann's decision. The reason was that 'she originated from a family who were church-goers'.

Kurt Kuch[5]
Vienna, February 2003

My Life on Adolf Hitler's Berghof

Kurt Kuch's interviews* with Anna Plaim

'. . . and you will talk to no one about this, is that clear?'

How did you, then merely a twenty-year-old girl from Loosdorf, a village in Niederösterreich, become the chambermaid to Adolf Hitler and Eva Braun, practically overnight?

Very simple. It was through my cousin in Munich. But, first, I need to tell you a little bit about my family's history. My grandfather was Johann Mathias Mittlstrasser, a skilled wheelwright from Bavaria who had travelled to Austria after becoming qualified.[7] After completing several placements in different cities, among them Vienna, he finally settled in Loosdorf. He got married and established himself as an independent wheelwright.

When his wife died, he all of a sudden found himself alone and with six children. Shortly afterwards, he married an older woman by the name of Anna Gruber, who brought her own child into this already rather big family. Later on, they had a child together – my father. At some point, my father's stepbrother Willi decided to return to Munich. He had a son who was also called Willi and who would become one of the first members of the NSDAP. That's how, early on, my cousin came into personal contact with Hitler, at a time when the NSDAP was still quite a small and unknown party. Willi was then with the SS, and was assigned a position on the Obersalzberg. He was the one who made sure that I actually got the job at the Berghof.

---

* This conversation with Anna Plaim, née Mittlstrasser, is based on the twenty-three meetings that took place between June 2002 and January 2003 in Loosdorf.[6]

You were born in Loosdorf?

Yes, in 1920. Father owned a workshop, a wheel-making business – something that, of course, doesn't exist any more today. Before that, Germans called it Stellmacher.[8] Besides that we also owned a small farm.

Was your father politically active?

Absolutely. He was master of his guild, which was the Lower Austrian Guild for Wheelwrights and Trade and Industry. As well as that, he founded the cooperative of wheelwrights of Lower Austria, and also acted as their chairman. Frankly, he was a true Conservative. He belonged to the Christian Social Party and was active in the local council. He was a devout Catholic. Furthermore, my father was acquainted with Julius Raab, who would later become Chancellor of Austria. When my father passed away in 1958, Raab, who was then already chancellor, sent a handwritten letter of condolence to my mother.

While journeying, my father, still a young man, also visited my grandfather's home in Bavaria. It is important to note this fact, as it made him a German citizen, and as such he was drafted into the German army during the First World War.

This is the reason why in Loosdorf he was considered to be somewhat of a German national. He was also active in the German Association for Athletics,[9] which was a classic meeting place for German nationals. Little wonder then that the National Socialists in Loosdorf later on tried to win over my father to their cause. They certainly failed.

But back to my father's stepbrother. I actually never knew him until it came to Austria's annexation to Germany. Up until 1938 we, in Loosdorf, had no contact with our Bavarian relatives. But soon after the borders between Austria and Germany were dismantled and Austria had become part of the German Reich, all the Munich relatives came to our front door. The reason was, of course, that at that time Munich already had a massive shortage of a whole range of consumer goods, while we in Lower Austria still had plenty of just about everything.

Tell us a bit about your cousin. How would you describe your very first meeting with him in 1938, and getting to know him?

Well, he was quite a bit older than me. Most of what I know about him stems from what he himself told me. I still remember that he tended to portray himself as a go-getter and an adventurer. He left home when he was still young. At the time, his parents owned a pub in Munich. His father was a bit of a showman, perhaps one would describe him today as 'one-of-a-kind'. This so impressed some of the Loosdorf inhabitants that they even travelled to Munich to visit him in his pub, just to see him 'live', so to speak.

My cousin left Munich for Hamburg as a young man. He sort of loafed about there and ended up travelling to America, turning himself into a stowaway. He must have done that journey about a dozen times: Hamburg to America and then back again. He was a butcher by trade, and then at some point he managed to get himself a regular job on an ocean liner. In any event Willi joined the NSDAP when he was still young and for that reason his Party number was very low. I would still hesitate to call him a political person. He simply found himself in the middle of the 1920s in Hitler's close proximity, and knew him at the very beginning of his rise to power.

At the time of Austria's annexation, you were barely eighteen years old. What was your experience of living in Austria during the Nazi period?

I don't have the best of memories when it comes to recalling the invasion by the Nazis. As we were declared 'black', we weren't really in the Nazis' good books.[10] Immediately after the annexation we were, therefore, very worried as to what might be in store for us. Everything really started turning ugly when we found out that the Nazis had picked up a good friend of ours and beaten him up. It then didn't take long until they also came to fetch my father. They brought him, together with two other men, into the large room of the pub and locked them up. I still remember this quite clearly as I was the one who brought my father some food. They kept him there for a few days. He wasn't mistreated in any way, however, and I myself rather looked upon this as a show of strength, as it was well known that he wasn't a Nazi.

This wasn't the ideal background for becoming a chambermaid at Adolf Hitler's house.

That's correct. Mind you, I only got the position thanks to my cousin Willi, who happened to visit us in Loosdorf with his wife Gretel in 1940. His wife originally came from Munich and was incredibly well trained in her field, which was hotel management. She was extremely clever. Willi had met her at the Berghof, where she was working for Eva Braun. He himself was also stationed there and had a position as Hitler's driver. Long story short, their honeymoon allowed them to visit us in Loosdorf. My mother went to great lengths to make them feel welcome and be a generous host, and she really did succeed. Willi and Gretel felt very much at home with us. They talked a lot about the Obersalzberg and the Berghof; how beautiful it was there, and how well they got on there.

'Goodness me', I exclaimed to Willi's wife Gretel, 'this certainly would be a place where I would also want to work.' Well, in view of my father's background, this actually was entirely unthinkable. In fact, it was out of the question, if I was honest to myself. However, one needs to bear in mind that it was the beginning of 1941, when people generally were no longer seriously concerned about which party anybody was active for. In 1941 there just was widespread euphoria. It is hard to imagine this today, but at that time practically everybody supported Hitler, and unconditionally so. The war simply gave you no other option.

Having said that, even before the war Hitler had – just in general – a lot of followers in Loosdorf. I can, therefore, unequivocally say that my hometown was no exception when it came to National Socialism. There was one academic in Loosdorf who even went so far as to financially support those Nazi Loosdorfers who needed to move to Germany, because, officially, belonging to the Nazi Party in Loosdorf was illegal at the time. A young girl had been caught by a policeman while she was standing on the street distributing flyers with a swastika on them, and subsequently she was even punished for this act. What I want to say by mentioning all of this is that many people among the population had for many years been enthralled by Hitler's ideas, as well as by the possibility of Austria becoming annexed to Germany. Then there were others who expected that Hitler would bring them employment and prosperity.

As you well know, the economic situation during the 1930s was anything but rosy. There was unemployment and poverty and, yes, even hunger. I suppose my father, as well, inwardly edged closer to the Nazis.

What did your father say about what was happening at the time? He would, in any event, have listened to what his nephew was saying when he was speaking about the Berghof, would that be fair to say?

He was interested in the Berghof, just as much as I was. We also, of course, always listened to the radio together, to all the propaganda and so forth. There was one broadcaster whom my father was really enthusiastic about. His name was Fritzsche[11] and he, according to my father, gave some really fantastic political commentaries on the radio. He certainly wanted to listen to this Fritzsche person.

Somehow this man managed to inspire my father. My father was someone who, in actual fact, wasn't particularly prone to being influenced by the normal Nazi propaganda slogans. Fritzsche's broadcasts just seemed to be more factual than those of other commentators.

And then the call came in from your cousin.

My father already owned a telephone at that time. All of a sudden a call came in. An operator simply said: 'from the Berghof'. This caused quite a stir, I can assure you. Who would receive a call from the Berghof? 'Anni, you may come to the Berghof' was the brief message. Shortly thereafter I received a letter. I was to go by train to Salzburg. There I would be fetched by someone who would then take me to the Obersalzberg. My father was also very excited. It is just so difficult to imagine today what this news meant for my family – our Anni will be at the Berghof.

What was your reaction?

What on earth should someone like me do in a place like the Berghof? I was at a total loss. While before I had wished for this to happen, I still just couldn't imagine what I would be doing up there. Gretel, my cousin's wife, called again and during our conversation she addressed my concerns regarding how I could possibly be of any use up there. Her response was short and dry: 'Well, you'll just be the chambermaid in that case. Just come.'

Did your parents comment in any way?

They were pleased that this turned out to be a real possibility. It had nothing at all to do with politics. They were simply proud that 'their Anni' would be working at the Berghof. A little bit later, at the end of May or beginning of June 1941, I took the train to Salzburg. I still remember it vividly: the train was totally packed – soldiers everywhere. When I wanted to board the train in St Pölten, there was not a single empty seat to be had. So I went up to the train manager on duty and said, in a rather brisk tone, that my services were required on the Obersalzberg, and that I needed to get onto the train, no matter what. That certainly did the trick, and he immediately put me into first class, even though I didn't even have the right ticket for that.

On the platform in Salzburg, ready and expecting me, was Gretel. She was accompanied by a tall man dressed in civilian clothes, who turned out to be the chauffeur. Introducing himself, he said his name was Döhring.[12] He was the housekeeper at the Berghof.

Surely it must have been enormously impressive to be picked up by your own car with your own chauffeur.

Absolutely. And especially when I set eyes on the car: it was a Steyr[13] in which we then drove from Salzburg to Berchtesgaden. This was, it turned out, a memorable journey, which subsequently made the headlines and ended up in court.

What happened?

It was really a big deal. At a very busy crossing in Berchtesgaden, a woman cyclist drove into us. There was huge upheaval. You can imagine, a woman cyclist hits the car of the Führer's housekeeper – that's quite something.

There is actually nothing more to say about this. We performed first aid right then and there, after which the heavily injured woman was driven to hospital. The term 'fractured skull' still clearly sits in my memory.

A few days later the whole story was spread all over the newspapers. What came after that was a court case. As such, the story was simple and there was nothing ambiguous about it. Döhring, after all, held quite a high position as the housekeeper on the Obersalzberg, and he had hit the cyclist. There was no question at all about who the guilty party was. The excitement intensified, however, by the fact that Hitler himself had been at the Berghof that very day. His personal doctor even drove to the hospital to check on the woman who, it transpired, had suffered a head injury, and he presented her with a large bouquet of flowers from Hitler. This was my first impression of what it meant when Hitler was in residence at the Berhof: every single thing had to be perfect, the SS were posted everywhere, everything was geared towards the Führer. Hitler held court. And this did not just impress state visitors from abroad.

Several weeks later the court case opened in Hallein, and Gretel and I were called in as witnesses. We were dressed smartly and wore make-up, which actually was unusual for those times. So there we were, standing in the small courtroom with a young judge presiding, sitting in front of a table on which stood a crucifix and two candles. He questioned us about the accident, what details we remember of how it had happened. After the hearing, Gretel and I were laughing at how we obviously had totally confused the young judge, what with our stylish appearance. By the way, the woman cyclist was found guilty and fined.

What impressed you most after your arrival on the Obersalzberg?

It might really sound ludicrous, but it was the kitchen; it was by far the largest and best-equipped kitchen I had ever come across. For those who are familiar with the hotel business, this kitchen might not have been anything out of the ordinary. But for me, until then I had never really been outside the most immediate confines of my home town. Also the kitchen was the first room I was brought to after my arrival.

Just in front of the kitchen, the atmosphere in the corridor was extremely hectic. SS service personnel were everywhere – about ten tall, young men, I would say. They all wore a white uniform. At those times when the Führer was in residence, it was only the SS men who were permitted to serve at the tables. Additionally I had never before encountered one of those servants' bell boxes. A bell would ring and a red light would appear to indicate from which room the guest had rung.

It might be best, however, if I read a bit from one of my first letters that I wrote to my parents:

Dear Parents.

I know I had promised to write to you on the same day of my arrival, but considering what is going on here this hasn't actually been as easy as you might expect. My journey to this place was quite awful, meaning that I nearly wasn't allowed to board the train in St Pölten. Forty people were left behind on the platform. But I told them that I was expected for work at the Berghof, and in the end it worked out. Upon arriving in Salzburg, I didn't see anybody right away, and so I just waited for a while in front of the station. But then Gretel literally whooshed by in a car, along with Döhring. They said that they had been looking for me for quite some time. The car in which they came to fetch me was rather fabulous. On our way, just after having left Salzburg behind us, there unfortunately was an accident: a woman cyclist drove straight into the side of our car. She suffered a fractured skull. It was really quite an upheaval.

At the Berghof itself (note that it consists of several buildings) it's very nice. I immediately received an official pass which I have to carry on me at all times.[14] Gretel, even after being there so long, has to keep showing it to the posts. Gretel immediately gave me some hand-me-down clothing as she now only wears dark blue dresses. We wear a red-and-white-checkered *dirndl*[15] with a white apron and a blouse with rounded collars. Now we are also due to receive dark blue silk dresses with aprons (we really do look quite attractive). In total there are three chambermaids, and I am one of them. We have to get up at seven o'clock in the morning, then we are off to the rooms.

One of my duties is to prepare everything in the dining room to the last and most exact detail (I have attached a photo). The male servants are in charge of clearing the dishes. They are rather elegant (the SS men). There are about ten of them. After about an hour I am finished with my work in the dining room and then I am off to the other rooms along with the other girls – you can also see them in the photo. You don't have the faintest idea as to how many courses are being served and how plentiful they are. Not even I myself have fully figured it out. Right now, we have quite a few guests visiting.

I won't have to spell out who it is. They all only get up at around eleven o'clock. The most awful thing about this for me is that we all have to keep very quiet during the daytime. We are to move swiftly through the house like shadows, speaking only in very low voices. When the ladies and gentlemen rise, we scurry from one room to the next. We do this in pairs. You can well imagine, Mother, how such a guest room has to be tidied up. My job is to do the toilet and bathroom (each room has a bathroom.), I scour the tub with Imi,[16] I clean all the tiles, wipe the mirrors, and I will give you one word as to how I do all of this – thoroughly. Happily all is cleared away by three o'clock in the afternoon. Then we have to prepare a fruit bowl for each room, which needs to be placed in the rooms by the evening, along with a bottle of mineral water and a glass (this takes us about one hour). Then there will always be an errand to run for one of the ladies. Once everyone goes to dinner, we return to the rooms and prepare the beds for the night. We might have to clean the bathroom again. All rooms have to be darkened.

I would say that it is generally ten o'clock at night, every day, before our work is done. If the Führer is residing in the building, I would also prepare his bed and bathroom. I get his fruit bowl ready and lay out his nightshirt, making sure that it lies in the right spot, perfectly pressed and folded (what else would you expect from such a man). But, otherwise, his accommodation is no better than any other guest's. He only uses a normal quilt (not even a duvet).

Whatever you get to read in the papers or see on the weekly newsreel, I will most certainly have seen it all in close-up.[17]

I hardly ever get to go outside during the day. Tomorrow I have off as of three o'clock in the afternoon until the following morning. I think Willi will come with me to Berchtesgaden. I will post the letter. The food is quite wonderful. The way it is served is very classy. Breakfast: coffee and milk. You can pour yourself however much you want. Butter, sausages, goose fat, bread, rolls – all in abundance. We receive the same lunch as the guests. You can easily picture how delicious it all is. There is always a dessert of fruit or ice cream, and cake as well. In the afternoon there is coffee and pastry. This evening we had roasted dumplings with large amounts of meat, cherries and apples – plenty of them – for dessert, cucumbers and green salad. At lunch and dinner we are offered beer or sweet apple cider to drink. As much as you want. There is always enough fruit, and I often have some oranges left over. Well this is how it stands with my *Arbeitsbuch*.[18] If I had the choice I would like to stay here for half a year to a year or so. I don't want to stay on longer, as by that time I will have seen and learnt it all. There are no Austrians working here. Most of them are Prussian. I don't understand any of them well at all.[19] Although Gretel assures me that it takes a few weeks until one finds one's feet and gets to know everything, I myself am just quite apprehensive. Otherwise I am really doing very well and it seems that I am virtually on a fattening-up diet.

I literally got stage-fright at the beginning when I was faced with having to speak to these high-up people, but it is good for me to learn how to deal with them and learn everything along the way. There is a lot of *gnädige Frau* here and *gnädige Frau* there going on.

Warm regards. Annerl

That was it for my first letter. I feel that what I wrote very aptly describes what my initial impressions were at the Hitler household. I still have to add something with respect to the pass: you always had to carry it with you, in order to identify yourself to the guards. I still clearly remember the one time that Frau Speer, wife of Hitler's favourite architect Albert Speer, had left her permit behind. She had travelled from Munich to the Berghof along with Eva Braun and myself. We simply weren't able to get past the guard on account of her missing permit. Nothing helped, even after Eva Braun personally vouched for Frau Speer. It was only after consultation with the Kripo[20] that we were given permission to pass through.

But let's go back in time, back to my arrival. First they handed me my uniform and then I was introduced to the other two chambermaids. One girl originated from Berchtesgaden, her name was Resi Stangassinger; the other girl was called Elfriede König. I was, so to speak, the third of the bunch, and actually replaced a girl called 'Betty' who had just left the Berghof in order to get married. At first I didn't really get the feeling that the girls welcomed me with open arms. Betty, my predecessor, had been very well liked. She had worked at the Berghof for many years, and, unlike me, she was not Austrian.

Were Austrians less well liked?

I wouldn't put it quite that way, but Austrians certainly were the exception in the house. I just have to recall how my dialect was cause for general amusement among the rest of the staff, including my colleagues. Those who spoke 'High German' were very amused by my way of speaking.

Herbert Döhring, the housekeeper, immediately picked on my dialect. He especially liked to make fun of the way I spoke German. He told me about the discussion Hitler had had with the last Austrian chancellor, Kurt Schuschnigg, at the Berghof. It had been Schuschnigg's last effort to save Austria. I remember vividly how Schuschnigg, after returning from the Berghof, had uttered the words: 'May God protect Austria'. In any event, Döhring made a point of ridiculing the presentations the Austrian delegation had made at the Berghof – above all he was referring to its Begleitkommando. Alluding to their heavy Austrian dialect, Döhring commented that 'they must have put marbles in their mouths'.

Well that's how it was. For an Austrian, incidentally, it wasn't exactly so easy to understand Döhring either, as he hails from East Prussia. It was quite a challenge for someone like him to hide his origins. There were further incidents having to do with my dialect, and it always contributed to people's amusement. Once we played the game – and it may sound stupid – 'Alles was Federn hat fliegt'.[21] As a forfeit, Döhring had to stand on a stool and follow my commands 'Turn left' and 'Turn right'. When I called out to him to 'Pay attention' to what I was going to ask him to do with respect to turning right or left for his forfeit, everyone burst into laughter, as in the German army my call 'Habt Acht' was actually the command to 'Stand still'.

In a letter to my parents, I told them how I had immediately taken revenge on Döhring: 'When it came to the next forfeit, I commanded this silly man Döhring to mess up his own hair – he was so terribly proud of his hairstyle – and while doing so he was to say the words: "If only I could be the Chief of the Negroes".'[22]

Apart from the rather sweet pleasure of promoting a convinced Nazi – albeit briefly – to the position of a 'Chief of the Negroes' at, of all places, the Berghof, it surely cannot have been easy for you at the beginning.

Due to my continued isolation, with only rarely being allowed to leave the house, I, who already was quite homesick, got increasingly more so. Also the fact that I was able to get this job only thanks to the intervention of my cousin Willi and his wife caused some bad feelings at the beginning. It was definitely not customary to immediately rise up to the position of a chambermaid. It was most certainly rare for the 'new one' to straight away be allowed access to the rooms.

How did all this continue?

First they showed me to my room. It was really a very nice space, situated on the second floor, with a view onto the mountain slopes. I was, of course, quite overwhelmed at the very beginning. The mountains, the impressive view, the SS parades – just everything. To be honest, I was completely intimidated. If the Führer held court, everything that had to be available was available. I was also elated by my room. It was a single room, nicely fitted out with green-varnished furniture. There was even a telephone on the bedside table, and I was allowed to make outside calls whenever I wanted.

I mentioned this in my letter to my parents as well:

> . . . So, Sunday we'll phone again. At ten o'clock in the morning, but do think of what to say. I don't want it to happen again that we just don't know what to say to each other. I can make as many phone calls as I want. The soldier at the switchboard who connects me does this as a favour to me. One girl's fiancé has been called up, and she phones him every day in Prague . . .

This way I was able to speak to my parents relatively often. Of course, bear in mind that it wasn't like using the phone today. At the time I always had to first contact the switchboard of the Berghof and, on top of that, the quality of the connection left a lot to be desired. It sometimes happened that you practically couldn't understand a word that the person on the other end of the line was saying. In any case, none of this was easy, as the man in charge of the Berghof switchboard was known for being very impatient. And when I called my parents, he would put the call through to Loosdorf saying just 'Switchboard Berghof' and brashly requesting that the other operator free up a line at once. So I wouldn't have thought that he was well liked by the people at the Loosdorf post office. At that time, staff at the post office were all enthusiastic Nazis who probably listened in on our conversations with great curiosity, and very likely passed everything on. This certainly fuelled resentment and jealousy – the consequences were going to come back to haunt me during the Russian occupation.

What was your first day of work like?

It started immediately after my arrival with a briefing by Gretel. It was really just to let me know what the running order for the day was: getting up at 6.45 in the morning, then off to the dining room, which I was to set up nicely. That was the dining room to be used by Hitler. As soon as I had finished with that, the guest rooms needed to be done, and these were to be cleaned by myself and the other girls.

Can you imagine my surprise when Gretel, who was a woman of some resolve, confided in me, with her deep voice and heavily accented Bavarian German: 'So, Anni, let me tell you straight off: Hitler and Eva Braun – they are together.'

I will never forget these first words of her so-called briefing session. And she then continued in the same tone of voice: 'This is the room of the Führer. And this thing here is the room for suitcases.' Just to explain, this was a small chamber-type room full of the most precious suitcases, most of them made of crocodile leather. They were stacked nearly up to the ceiling. This so-called 'suitcase room' had two doors. One opened into Hitler's room. And as soon as we went through the second door, Gretel came straight to the point: 'And this here is Eva Braun's room. Coming to grips with all this? I don't need to tell you more, do I?'

And, quite honestly, she didn't have to. I was speechless. Barely a soul knew that the Führer had a girlfriend – at the time one probably would have more appropriately referred to her as 'companion', and the fact that his and her room were separated from each other by nothing more than a sort of broom cupboard, this 'suitcase room', was known by a very select number of people – certainly not a twenty-year-old girl from Loosdorf.

So it was a secret?

That is how it was. Gretel immediately added: 'Everything which you now know, everything you have seen, everything you hear, must remain between ourselves. You are not allowed to speak about anything that happens here. To nobody.

Never. And you are not to talk to anybody about this. Let this be clear. And above all, not about the Führer and Eva Braun.'

Was it easy for you to keep to yourself such a delicate state secret?

With whom should I even have spoken about this? The only people I was in telephone contact with or wrote to were my parents and a small number of friends. The operator would have been able to listen in on telephone conversations and, as for letters, these correspondences would all have been subjected to a censorship in any case. I am, however, not quite sure whether my letters were even being opened prior to leaving the Berghof.

The letters you sent from the Berghof have been preserved in their entirety, and they offer a very thorough insight into the everyday life at the Berghof. How do you explain their continued existence?

Before the Russian invasion, my mother had buried them. She dug out a big hole in the barn and in a crate, which she lowered into the hole, she hid the letters. She excavated the crate only after the Russians had left. During those times the likelihood of being plundered was relatively high. In fact, up until the 1960s, I didn't even know that the letters had survived in their entirety, as I had moved away from my home in 1948, the year I got married. I never even gave them another thought. Then one day, out of the blue, my mother happened to mention them to me. 'Look here Anni', she said to me, 'there are still these letters you sent from the Berghof and all these photos from up there. Why don't you take them along with you?' You can well imagine how over the moon I was. After more than twenty years I felt as if I had stepped back in time, back to being in the Berghof. Don't forget, I had many lovely memories of the time I had spent there.

Even at the time the idea came to me that, what with all these documents, one should be writing a book. At the beginning, however, I didn't want to talk about this topic. Nobody beyond the borders of Loosdorf even knew about me having been employed at the Berghof. Additionally I actually couldn't really see a good reason for me to once again become involved with those times and so intensely, which would be the case when it comes to a book. This only fundamentally changed when I met and got to know you. Other than that I had also seen a television interview with Traudl Junge, Hitler's secretary.[23] André Heller's project with Traudl Junge impressed me so much that it made me decide that it would be a pity if my memories would simply become lost to the world once I died – and I am indeed getting on – being in my eighty-second year on this earth.

Did you get to meet Traudl Junge personally?

I myself didn't, but Gretel did. When I celebrated my seventy-fifth birthday I spent three days with Gretel and Willi in Munich. Of course there was much talk about our time together at the Berghof. Gretel then told me that she was still in contact with Traudl Junge. But of course, shortly after the Second World War had ended, I made a point of looking into the whole issue and I began to read an awful lot of relevant books on the subject.

Together with my husband Karl, who was a secondary teacher for German and history in Loosdorf, I travelled several times to the Berghof. Already back in the 1950s we owned a car, a beige-coloured Opel Rekord. At the time this was a day's excursion for us. During the first few years we were still able to see larger parts of the building's ruins – the Berghof having been bombed and burnt down.[24]

As the years passed, trees and bushes overshadowed my memories. At each visit I became melancholic.

Let's return to the Berghof. Were there any other topics that were subject to the obligation of strict secrecy? Besides the relationship between Eva Braun and Adolf Hitler? Subjects that you weren't allowed to mention, not even with so much as an oblique allusion?

Most certainly. Right at the beginning I somehow got involved with something else that had caused quite a stir on the Obersalzberg. I had been entrusted with the task of cleaning the room of Rudolf Hess. This room was referred to by staff simply by the name of Untersberg Room.

Hess was the Deputy Führer, and during his controversial secret mission to Scotland he crashed his plane. That was on 10 May 1941. He had, it was reported, hoped to arrange for peace talks with the British government with the help of the Duke of Hamilton. Later on Hitler declared him insane and stripped him of all of his Party and state offices. How was this incident reported on the Obersalzberg? Surely the Scotland trip had not been undertaken in accordance with Hitler's approval.

Of course, I myself also had no knowledge of the actual background of the Hess flight. I am also unaware if this was anything ever properly looked into. All I can tell you is that there was a huge upheaval at the Berghof about this whole event. I would say the term 'sheer disbelief' would, in my opinion, best describe the reactions that ensued. It deeply unsettled everyone. And they immediately had a response ready, which was that Hess was mentally ill. Every staff member was saying it.

And was he really sick? Of course, there are more than enough indications to suggest that. He attempted to commit suicide in autumn 1941 while a prisoner of war. Apparently even at the time he was supposed to have suffered from a neurological disease.

Having cleaned his room and having seen what I did, I am convinced that Hess was a sick man. The shelves in his bathroom were stacked with medications.

What kind of medications were they?

No idea. Little bottles. A huge number of little bottles. And tablets. There were quite a lot lying about. The only one who knew what these medications actually were was Dr Theodor Morell. At the time he was the Führer's private physician at the Berghof. Actually he was, in fact, more than just Hitler's doctor. What I mean is that Morell was a really close confidant of Hitler. That's at least what made the rounds among us employees. I can still remember Dr Morell very well. He occupied a certain room at the Berghof, which I was shown soon after my arrival: it was this room – the Untersberg Room – that Hess had lived in just shortly before. And as far as the medications were concerned, that was a topic constantly spoken about by the employees.

So was gossip quite common?

I wouldn't put it quite like that, because, in actual fact, one had to be extremely quiet throughout the day. This was terrible for me. One had to behave as if one was a shadow, you couldn't utter even one loud word. We virtually crept through the hallways. You could hear only whispering and murmuring.

As a rule the ladies and gentlemen slept in, usually till ten or eleven o'clock in the morning. And that is why there had to be complete silence until then. It was only at that time that we could go up to the rooms and start cleaning. On many evenings there were gatherings that lasted for a very long time. I sort of described things a bit differently in the letters to my parents: 'One had to be very quiet',

I had written, because the Führer works so hard. And that is why he needed his rest – above all, early in the morning.

Did you have a lot of respect for Hitler and his entourage?

Hitler was the source of a lot of fascination for most people. That was true for myself as well, but above all for Eva Braun. He was quite conscious of his charm, and he used it with full intent. Here is a small example, which I still remember, and which gives you a taste. What do you think he gave Eva Braun for her birthday?

No idea, jewellery perhaps?

No. A picture. A picture of himself. Eva Braun received from Hitler for her birthday a picture of himself. It was a portrait that he had commissioned from a painter in Bad Tölz. Sometime later I travelled with Eva Braun to Bad Tölz to visit that same painter, because, this time, she had wanted to commission a painting of herself. She posed for hours. And that is the painting she then presented to Hitler.

While telling this story I remember that, on the first floor at the Berghof, there was a separate room specifically designated for Hitler's presents. That was a room where all the junk of little value ended up, without Hitler ever even having seen it. These were presents coming from Hitler's followers from all corners of the Reich. The stuff that was piled up there was just unbelievable. Among the things was even a bird cage.

Once I opened one of the books lying around there. Then, suddenly, my eyes fell upon the name of the one who offered this book as a present: Family Lukesch from Loosdorf. How small the world is.

How had you been introduced to Eva Braun?

First Gretel had briefed me about Eva Braun's position. Soon this was to be followed by the next instruction – Eva Braun was the mistress of the house. And, as such, I was to address her as *gnädiges Fräulein*.

Eva Braun then was No. 2 at the Berghof? The First Lady at the Berghof, so to speak?

No. She definitely wasn't that. She simply was the mistress of the house. And she was particularly important during Hitler's residency. But she most certainly wasn't the First Lady on the Obersalzberg.

And besides that? Who was more important than Eva Braun when Hitler was not actually residing at the Berghof?

If Gerda Bormann, Martin Bormann's wife, came then it was she herself who was more important. The same was true for Emmy Göring, the wife of Hermann Göring. Frau Göring was, so to speak, the First Lady of the Reich. Eva Braun wasn't, of course, married to Adolf Hitler. For that reason, she wasn't either legitimately nor officially entitled to take front position. This was exemplified during a minor, at first glance inconspicuous, incident. Every day the gardener was to bring fresh flowers for the ladies. During the winter they mostly were white lilac. If Frau Göring was in residence, she received fresh flowers in her home. During that time Eva Braun received her fresh flowers only every second day.

What was your first personal encounter with Eva Braun like?

Before any encounter, it was just constantly having to listen to further instructions. Actually, instructions generally just seemed to carry enormous weight. Hardly a situation existed that did not come with a detailed list of guidelines as to how everything should be handled. Etiquette was of utmost importance.

'Listen, what do I do when the *gnädige Fräulein* has to sneeze? What is it that I have to say then?' I asked Gretel.

'Nothing' was her curt answer. 'Something like this, we tend to simply ignore.'

Then, as if on a fast track, I was told how to serve the different dishes, how I should handle the plates and how to pour. Without further ado, I was then already being sent to Hitler's living room, where Eva Braun was sitting. I was visibly anxious. Gretel first tried to soothe my nerves: 'She knows in any event that you are not trained. So just calm down and pull yourself together.'

I entered the room to pour Eva Braun a glass of red wine. I was extremely insecure and Eva Braun, noticing this immediately, turned to me.

'*Gnädiges Fräulein*', I said, 'I am just feeling somewhat insecure.'

'Well, I'll just have to send you to the Hotel Kaiser in Munich, so that you learn to be perfect', Eva Braun retorted. Of course, I had never seen the Hotel Kaiser from the inside.

It is possible that, in the course of time, I became proficient in the art of serving, and could do so to Eva Braun's satisfaction – in any event, at least, I hope that this was the case.

What was your relationship to Eva Braun? At the end of the day, you were only eight years younger than Hitler's lover?

She was a lady, and it was very important to her to keep a specific distance from others. There was never a telling off that came from her side or anything insulting. So she wasn't a typical 'boss' who might have had her colleagues feel that she held a special position.

In your letters you write only about a gnädiges Fräulein, *but you never ever mention the name Eva Braun. Why actually did you do that?*

Because we weren't allowed to do so. It was specifically explained to me that, when it comes to Eva Braun, I was not to write anything about her. That's why I referred to her in my letters as *gnädiges Fräulein*. My parents, in any event, already knew after my first visit home whom I was talking about.

This is perhaps a good time to read to you my second letter home, as by that time I had somewhat settled down at the Berghof:

Dear Parents,

I am sure that my last fat letter has arrived by now. I posted it at the Königsee. Yesterday I had my first afternoon off, from three o'clock in the afternoon until early morning the next day. Every fifth day I am off. On the other hand there is no sign of a Sunday. When I arrived in Salzburg, Gretel immediately told me that the Führer was in residence, as well as Göring and some others. I witnessed the reception of the Croatian man from very close up. It was totally fabulous. By the time all this is in the papers, it is already old news for us. I also saw the presents. Every day I feel more confident finding my way around the house. It certainly wasn't easy at the beginning.

Willi was really nice yesterday. He also had the day off. We drove in a fine car (with a radio) to Berchtesgaden and the Königsee. There were two other gentlemen who had come along. Then I spent time with Gretel in the apartment until twelve midnight, and there was champagne and pralines. The film projectionist from the Berghof was also there.

So I have already had the honour to make up the bed of the Führer several times (every day, in fact). Everything has to be put out smartly, just right. The nightshirt and the slippers – all has to be laid out precisely, as per instructions, 'in military fashion'. When I was cleaning the Führer's bathroom yesterday, the handle of his razor fell off. I simply put it into my apron pocket for the time being, but then forgot to take it out again. In the evening I look at it and ask myself: 'Where on earth did I get this from?' I then go from one gentleman's room to the next in order to find out where it is missing. Then I realise that it belonged to the Führer. By that time he hadn't yet noticed that it had gone missing. For several days, access to his study was not allowed. The Führer himself had locked the doors. He is constantly working and never allows himself a break.

According to his demands, the employees receive the same food as he and his guests do. Yesterday for dinner we had a large piece of pork Schnitzel (freshly fried), salad, cheese platters, beer, apple cider and fruit. Really lovely, right? I hope I won't become too fat. I weigh myself daily, in the Führer's bathroom. I have gained one kilo.

Warm wishes, Annerl

Three days later, on 11 June, I had already written my third letter home and I want to read to you only these sentences:

… You must have surely read about the visit of King Boris from Bulgaria with the Führer. The reception was simply marvellous. I was able to observe everything from very close up. It is a really great feeling to know that one may sleep under the same roof as the Führer. There were also other very high-ranking personalities. But, above all, I enjoy working in the Führer's quarters.

This afternoon we make up his bedroom. I will give the bathroom a thorough cleaning, as well as the large study. You wouldn't believe the number of books – this man must study and work an awful lot.

That would also probably explain why I had the impression ten days earlier that Hitler worked around the clock. And here is something else. On 25 June, so three days after the invasion of the Wehrmacht into Russia, I wrote to my parents yet another letter:

… What's your view on the new war? I myself got very scared at the beginning. Now, it is over. I have the feeling that there, as well, it will pass over quickly – just like it did in France …

I don't think there is much to add to this misconception of mine.

*In your letters you report on several excursions you made together with Eva
Braun. Do tell us a bit about them.*

I travelled several times with Eva Braun and her dogs to Munich. These were
official business trips. She owned a house there, on the Wasserburgstrasse.[25] While
it may not have been a villa, it was still a rather large, one-family home with a
garden. When I stayed overnight, I was put in a room on the first floor. She also
had a permanent member of staff living there; her name was Paula and she also
did the cooking. Eva Braun's main reason for going to Munich was to meet up
with old friends from her youth and her school years. But she also often went to
the theatre or the opera. Even though these visits were purely for work, they held
quite some excitement for me, and I immediately wrote to my parents to report
on them – this was in spite of the censorship as, in truth, nobody was supposed to
know who was Eva Braun nor, above all, what her special position was:

> ... You will now surely want to know what 'official business' this was in Munich. I
> am able to describe this to you in general, vague terms. A lady of highest standing
> had arrived in Munich to stay at her villa. As she is one of our customary guests
> back at the Berghof, she had to be received properly here as well, and we were
> called in to help. We unpacked her belongings and were at her service. Gretel is
> still there actually. So I was no longer needed and only had to assist during her
> arrival and was then allowed to return here. Names are of no importance.
>
> I am sure that there will be more ladies arriving next week. Once again, I
> will slip into the role of chambermaid. Lots of '*bitte sehr, gnädige Frau*' etc. It is
> certainly true that, with time, one seems to be able to display a more confident
> manner. How, for example, could a Frau Doktor from Loosdorf possibly live up
> to any of the gentry coming and going at this place?[26]
>
> To be honest, it really is the ideal career for somebody like me. I had always
> been interested in something like this. Yesterday, in the Führer's bedroom, I tried
> on his slippers. But they are too big for me. He wears shoe size 44 ...

Were you allowed to accompany Eva Braun to the Opera?

No, that was out of the question. But once she allowed me to use her own opera
ticket as a present. For me, this was really an exceptional experience, as I loved
the opera. I learnt how to play the piano as a child, and music always meant a
lot to me. In any event, that night, Paula the cook and I were sitting together

in the most elegant box. Imagine, a chambermaid and a cook sitting together in a box at the Munich Opera, which belonged to Reichsschatzmeister Franz Xaver Schwarz,[27] the Party's National Treasurer. All opera glasses were turned on us. What a strange feeling. On the programme that evening were *Cavalleria Rusticana* and *Der Bajazzo*.[28] Of course this was an evening that made a huge impression on me. But it also had its funny moments. After a while cook Paula turns to me and says in her heavy German accent, which I could not at first understand, something like 'them is fifty'. I eventually figured out that she was alluding to the orchestra consisting of fifty musicians. The sheer number seems to have overwhelmed her more than the music.

What did you have to do in Munich? Apart from visiting the Opera?

So, for example, Eva Braun's dogs had to be taken to the grooming parlour. That really did exist. The dogs were given a bath there and their fur was trimmed. Her first dog was called Negus. It was a black Scotch Terrier. Negus was male and named after the Ethiopian emperor[29] against whom Mussolini waged war. Maybe she chose that name because the dog was so black – I simply cannot recall it exactly. In any event Eva Braun must have thought at one point that Negus shouldn't be so lonely any more.

So we got a second dog, a little female called Stasi. Stasi was a typical Bavarian name. Stasi was also a full breed. It was, of course, extremely important that they were full breeds. I am reminded here of a funny incident that happened to Döhring. I caught Stasi and Negus right on the Berghof's staircase carpet just when they were about to part from each other. But obviously, after 'the act', they didn't quite succeed. So I ran up to Döhring, shouting 'Come quickly. The dogs … the dogs …'

Well, I wasn't very familiar with the intimate lives of dogs, so I called Döhring for help. Döhring came running down the corridor, clasping his head with both hands. 'What on earth should I be doing? I surely cannot be expected to throw cold water over them, what with this beautiful carpet.'

And what did he do then?

He said, 'Let's just leave and pretend we haven't seen anything.' So we left the dogs to themselves. But, indeed, what should Döhring have done?

There was yet another incident: very shortly after he had arrived at the Berghof, Stasi, the younger dog, swallowed one of Eva Braun's Leo tablets.[30] It was a laxative. On that very day I was just in the middle of writing a letter to my parents, which then ended with the sentence: 'Good Lord, this might really turn out nasty. I think I better take him outside.'

These excursions to Munich must have been an entertaining change of scenery for Eva Braun

I can remember quite clearly that I once had to spend the night 'away', so not in the house at the Wasserburgstrasse. Eva Braun must have had a visit – in any case, I was put up in some barrack, which was commonly referred to as the Führerbau. That's where the Begleitkommando usually stayed the night. I got a bedroom that had seven empty camp beds. The bedding was totally filthy and I reported that the next morning to Eva. She became quite annoyed when it came to things like that. She immediately called for the manageress of the house and voiced her displeasure. In situations such as these, she could really raise her voice. Nothing like this should ever happen again, she added.

But, overall, Munich for me involved work, just the same as at the Berghof. In actual fact, I did the same for Eva Braun in Munich as I did at the Berghof, with the only difference being that what I did in Munich was in a smaller and private environment. I served at the tables when there were visitors, mostly 'ordinary people', so not politicians or prominent figures, but old schoolmates or work colleagues or friends of the Braun family.

One day there was fried duck on the menu. While serving, I, of course, was able to listen in. They were discussing what position the Church held, and Eva Braun did not mince her words. She did not like it that the religion of some important Party members would simply be cast aside. With her comments she was referring to Bormann and the SS-Reichsführer Heinrich Himmler.[31] It wasn't right to deprive old women – who had lost their sons at the front – of their faith as well, she said, a support that would provide some solace to them. Why couldn't Himmler wait with his ideas about religion until the war had ended? And she thought exactly the same with regards to Bormann.

Was Eva Braun religious?

No, I don't think so. Not at all. Religion at the Berghof was an absolutely taboo subject. I grew up in a very religious home with my parents, but as soon as I had arrived at the Berghof I decided to let my religion temporarily fall by the wayside. This was a taboo subject.

In what way did the fact that religion was a taboo subject find expression at the Berghof?

Maybe Bormann best exemplifies this. He didn't think much of religion. He really pulled all kinds of tricks out of his pocket.

What exactly do you mean by tricks?

He would come frantically crashing into the waiting room. 'Does anyone have a prayer book? I urgently need a prayer book', he yelled. 'I need a prayer book this instant.' God help the individual who either had a prayer book on him or even made any attempt to look for one. Those were Bormann's favourite moments. Döhring would tell this story a hundred times. And if anyone had handed him a prayer book, he would be truly sorry, Döhring continued. That person was bound to have been sent packing the very same day. We were, therefore, forewarned.

But Bormann had other things up his sleeve as well. He always chose different routes to drive up to the Obersalzberg. And every *Marterl*[32] he would encounter on the way to the Berghof, he simply had it immediately removed. That seemed to be of great importance to him.

On 5 December 1941 I wrote to my parents: 'Today Saint Nicholas came to our children – it was Frau Döhring. I have never seen such a beautiful one.'

Back to Eva Braun. She had a sister, Gretl, didn't she, and she often came for a visit to the Obersalzberg. Did you also know Gretl Braun?

Of course I did. Gretl was a constant visitor. She was a very pretty and fun-loving lady. To be honest I think that, in actual fact, the Berghof really bored her. I suspect she would have preferred to have more male company. It was actually only us women up there – at least when Hitler wasn't around.

There was also a Frau Schneider, a friend of Eva Braun's from her youth, who often came for a visit. She spent several weeks at the Berghof, along with her nanny and her two children. Her daughter Uschi was some three years old at the time, and the second child only seven months. Something happened and I will never ever forget it: after the nanny had given the baby a warm bath, she showered him off with ice-cold water. Of course the baby cried his head off. I was appalled. But there, like a shot from a pistol, came the nanny's answer – the typical one for those times – that the child has to be toughened up. That was important, she said.

And then there was Frau Dreesen from Bad Godesberg on the Rhine. She was the owner of the Hotel Dreesen, a very elegant hotel where the Party bigwigs tended to stay.

It is a historically significant place, this Hotel Dreesen.[33] In 1938 British prime minister Neville Chamberlain stayed there overnight, when he discussed with Hitler the crisis around the Germans of the Sudetenland.[34]

Indeed, Frau Dreesen was accordingly well treated. Once, when during coffee Frau Dreesen was just visiting, she voiced her feeling that she, by rights, should receive the Blutorden.[35]

Why? Was it because Hitler loved to frequent her hotel or because of how much she did for the Nazis?

No, no. The reason is actually much more ridiculous than that. During a Party parade, somebody had stuck a needle in the posterior of the *gnädige Frau*. Ridiculous. While the women present, such as Gretl Braun and Frau Schneider, thought that this was very funny, obviously Frau Dreesen felt differently about it.

It obviously was quite pleasant, being part of these private gatherings of lady friends. There couldn't have been much on while Hitler wasn't present at the Berghof, could there?

In truth, during these times we were our own guests. There wasn't a lot to do, as there were no guest rooms to clean, there was no reason to serve anything and, apart from Eva Braun and Frau Schneider, there was nobody there whom we had to look after.

Who was this Frau Schneider you refer to, and who seemed to be such a frequent guest at the Berghof?

She was one of Eva's friends from her youth. Frau Schneider, for one, benefited a great deal from this friendship, if I might put it that way. But, on the other hand, I also saw Eva Braun's side of things. As, frankly, what on earth should she have done during all these days? She was glad that at least Frau Schneider and her children were there.

Already in the early 1930s Eva Braun had attempted suicide twice. Did you have the impression that she was depressed or that she was in pain in any way? That, to put it in different words, she was bored to death at the Berghof?

I was under the impression that she spoke to Hitler often on the phone. But, still, her friends and her sister were for her practically the only people who could help make her life just that little bit more bearable and pleasant because, in reality, there was hardly anything for her to do. She wasn't Hitler's wife and, therefore, she couldn't present herself publicly as such. And when Hitler was residing at the Berghof, she was expected to an even greater degree to recede into the background. This certainly couldn't have been easy for her.

But I suspect that she was prepared to take this sacrifice on herself based on her utter adoration of Hitler. Even to us chambermaids, it was clear why Hitler had not made her the First Lady of the Reich – most of the women in Germany admired and even worshipped Hitler. This, however, was precisely the reason why Hitler, of course, had to remain free and unattached. Eva Braun, as well, worshipped Hitler and was always gushing over his beautiful blue eyes. Frau Schneider did the same. And I, as well, was fascinated by Hitler's eyes. I would often stand in front of his portrait and have a good look at him. Today, thinking back, I sort of suspect that Eva Braun believed that one day Hitler would indeed marry her.

Then there was also the war going on. This meant that sacrifices had to be made. Many women had their husbands at the front, and many lost them there. In my opinion Eva Braun tried to see her situation as being somewhat similar to these wives', and made this comparison. She thus must have thought that the Führer was in demand and needed by the war and that she, therefore, obviously had to step back. When Hitler wasn't there, she would constantly be standing in front of his portrait – that painting made by the artist from Bad Tölz, and which she had received for her birthday. She thought that this portrait made his eyes look particularly beautiful. This picture took pride of place in her room. In her own way she made every effort to get on with her life as best she could. Financially she wanted for nothing really. Which other mistress gets the Berghof as a 'present'?

But that sounds more like a golden cage.

Indeed that's what it actually was – and definitely for Eva Braun. And even I, a mere employee, could empathise, as I felt much the same. Though it was true that one could hardly ever leave the Berghof, it was also the case that the residence offered everything in abundance, and there was no 'need' to leave.

The war with Russia started in June 1941 – shortly thereafter there was Stalingrad, and it came with everything a war brings in its wake. Above all this was true for the soldiers at the front. But it had not yet hit us. At the Berghof we still had everything we wanted.

Let's remain on the topic of the relationship between Hitler and Eva Braun. As an employee, how much of this state secret were you able to pick up during the times when Hitler was in residence at the Berghof? How did these two while away the time?

At about three o'clock in the afternoon both of them went to the teahouse together. But please make sure not to get this mixed up with the world-famous teahouse up at the Kehlstein that Hitler would use to impress state visitors. Hitler's dogs were always part of this outing – always his Alsatian called Blondi, as far as I can remember. And then there were also Eva Braun's dogs, Stasi and Negus. The dogs got along well and were allowed to run around freely. At this tea ceremony, the visitors who happened to stay at the Berghof at the time participated as well, and Hitler's servants waited at the tables. These servants even wore military uniforms, but were not armed. Very often Dr Morell, Hitler's private physician, would join, as well as his second private physician, Dr Brandt. Generally the whole party consisted of some ten people.

It took about ten minutes by foot to get from the main building to the teahouse. Hitler felt very secure in terms of his own safety because, when he set off to walk to the teahouse, he never requested that additional posts be set up. The guards were positioned at Haus zum Türken.[36] They stood outside, day and night. Just like tin soldiers. It is a curious fact, but during the entire period I never once exchanged a word with any of these guards. In any event, what I want to say is that Hitler was relatively unprotected on his walk to the teahouse. Most of the time there was cheesecake being served at the teahouse – Hitler's favourite pastry.

Lilli, our cook, made sure to bake it for him especially. He loved it so much that it was even sent to him when he was at the Führer headquarters in Berlin.

These visits to the teahouse became the one permanent feature in Eva Braun and Hitler's shared diary. Hitler spent all the rest of his time in his study, where he was not to be disturbed under any circumstance. This, I suspect, was equally true for Eva Braun.

The atmosphere in the teahouse was always extremely pleasant. Sometimes Eva tried to do something to make Hitler happy, so she would put on a *dirndl*, just for him. But in spite of all this friendliness between them, I really cannot remember a single time when Hitler and Eva Braun would ever hold hands, or even go as far as give each other a kiss, either at these tea gatherings or at any other semi-official events.

These tea gatherings normally lasted for about an hour – no longer than that. Afterwards Hitler immediately withdrew to his study. Alone. And that meant that there had to be absolute silence throughout the entire house, so that he was not disturbed in any way whatsoever. While he was at the tearoom, we were immensely busy. The three of us had to walk through the rooms of the Führer, Eva Braun and all the guests; the bathrooms would be cleaned, empty fruit bowls refilled, fresh towels had to be provided, beds prepared and a thousand other details needed to be checked.

That's why I can at least say this much: during the day Hitler never lay in his bed. Eva Braun's bed as well always remained untouched during the day. The reason I am mentioning this is because Döhring, the housekeeper, said in interviews that Hitler and Eva Braun did not have an intimate relationship. Well, indeed. Döhring later also called her a silly noodle. But then, back in 1941 and 1942, he still always addressed her as *gnädige Fräulein*.

As for an intimate relationship between Hitler and Eva Braun, I can only say that Gretel's descriptions fundamentally differ from what Döhring claims. After all, it was Gretel who had to buy Eva Braun's medications, so that she could defer her cycle for when Hitler was at the Berghof.

Let's talk about the pleasant 'creature comforts' available at the Berghof. Before you mentioned that it was entirely customary for these social evenings to last very long into the night. Were there, in other words, wild parties at the Berghof, while soldiers in Russia were freezing?
That's probably exaggerated but, yes, there were guests, of course, who wished to be entertained. And they were. In the cellar of the house, for example, there was a marvellous bowling alley. It could well happen that the ladies and gentlemen

would all of a sudden, at eleven o'clock at night, have the idea that they desperately wanted to go bowling. Something like that could easily last until two o'clock in the morning. And to round the evening off, I was requested to serve them turtle soup. I mean, let's think about this seriously, it was spring 1942, and it wasn't as if everything outside the Berghof was available in abundance. Quite the contrary. But what we were eating up here was turtle soup[37] that came, mind you, out of tins from abroad. And even us staff were living quite a good life.

This is what I wrote to my parents:

> ... Today, I am having a blue Tuesday.[38] The reason was that I was invited yesterday to Willi's and Gretel's and, of course, it was an occasion to empty several bottles of champagne and liqueur. Tonight I will go to the movies.

The cinema was very close to the estate, just below the Platterhof.[39] It was organised by Kraft durch Freude,[40] and they also provided the film they felt was suitable. This cinema was mainly used by those soldiers who were being housed in the barracks on the Obersalzberg.

One thing that interests me especially is who the people were who were ordering turtle soup at two o'clock in the morning.

The only thing I still remember is that Martin Bormann was part of that gathering. Guests, in general, could get quite boisterous, and on that evening the atmosphere was rather relaxed. I myself saw Reichsleiter Bormann dancing with Gretl Braun and holding his arms tightly around her. Then both lost their balance and fell on the floor. Immediately Bormann shot an angry look in my direction: 'Anni, you didn't see anything' is what he said. I mean, look, Bormann was a married man with children. His family also lived on the estate and owned their own house, a little way down from the Berghof. Besides, Eva Braun was also there on that night. By the way there were even some rules in place that restricted the dancing. Swing was strictly prohibited and only 'traditional' local stuff was permitted.

Was Gretl Braun at the time not already married or engaged to Hermann Fegelein, whom Hitler, by express order, was to have executed?

No, not at that time. I actually think she didn't even know him yet. Gretl Braun was a vibrant, pretty, young woman, and at the Berghof there was an immense shortage of men. It was so bad that once in a while the film projectionist had to be brought in when there was a bowling or opera event – and, truth be told, this man did not fit in that group of people at all.

The Berghof had its own cinema?

The Berghof had a cellar in which films were kept in storage. Every film that came out was immediately sent to the Berghof. There was something like an improvised private cinema set up in the Great Hall. That means that they pulled up the large Gobelin tapestry and behind it a wide screen had been installed. Just like in a real cinema. Every day a new film list was drawn up, which was submitted to Eva Braun, who could then select the film she wished to see that same evening after dinner.

How should one imagine this? Eva Braun is sitting all by herself in the Great Hall and watching films for hours at a time?

Well, Frau Schneider would also be there most of the time, as well as Gretl, of course. Sometimes Hitler's dentist, Dr Richter, would also join in. The Great Hall was known around the world. The weekly newsreel kept portraying it in their screenings. By the way we are talking about a gigantic room, in which also stood the famous globe, whom many people know from having watched Charlie Chaplin's *The Great Dictator*.

The back of the room was taken up by an absolutely huge window, which had a clear view of the Untersberg. Along one side of the room hung the expensive Gobelin tapestry, behind which was hidden the cinema screen. Discreetly installed on the opposite side wall was the projector. If you didn't know about the projector being there, you would never have noticed it. All the heavy sofas and chairs had to be turned around for the film viewings, so that the guests had a perfect view of the screen. That too was one of the duties that the chambermaids had to attend to. Champagne was set up and bowls of sweets were placed on the large marble table. Sometimes Eva didn't like one or the other of the films shown, and then she would simply interrupt and select a different film, and she was always observing what clothes the actress wore. In fact, one time, an actress wore the exact same dress as her, which Eva Braun had had her salon make up for her. I am not sure any more whether Eva Braun had copied the dress from a film, or whether it was the other way round.

There was great excitement among the ladies about this dress, whatever the situation might have been. 'You look much better in the dress,'

'With you wearing it, the dress seems much more beautiful.' This went on for ages.

Sometimes even the kitchen staff were allowed into the hall to watch a new film. I can still remember quite clearly that the guests would often leave a drop or two of their champagne, which we had served previously. As soon as the visitors had left, us chambermaids cleared everything away and drank up the remainder of the champagne. Nobody was even around who could have caught us.

Here is a letter from 14 July 1941 concerning the life these 'ladies' led at the Berghof. It also aptly describes the large dinner parties which took place, and the lifestyle favoured by these upper-class people:

> ... When the Führer is in residence, only servants may serve at the tables. But at the ladies' tables, us chambermaids have to do it. I had already mastered the art of laying the table and how to serve – from Gretel. A few days ago, I had to do it all on my own. I had, all in all, four people at the table: our three ladies (writing their names doesn't add anything but, suffice it to say, they were really big deals) and a Dr Richter, the Führer's dentist. It is unbelievable what has to be set out, if one follows all the rules. So, here I was, going from one person to another with my serving dishes, when Gretel pops in and announces the arrival of Herr and Frau Reichsleiter Bormann. Everything started tumbling around (I mean in my head). Afterwards both Gretel and I served at the tables.
>
> Later on a film was shown in the hall, and it fell upon me to pour the champagne. Mother, this is what's going on every day around here. You might certainly sit and wonder when I tell you about the lives of these great ladies.
>
> They wake up at about midday and immediately press the button. There comes Anni – that's me – flying down the hallway and knocking at the room. 'Good morning, *gnädige Frau*', she says and opens the windows. 'What does the *gnädige Frau* wish for breakfast?' Then, after a while, here comes Anni again, laden with a big silver platter upon which little plates and jugs are piled high, setting it all up artfully on a small trolley with wheels and rolling it to the bedside. Then she retreats without making a sound. It certainly isn't easy to juggle everything with one hand, what with such a heavy platter. At the beginning, I thought that I would just never ever be able to manage. At this point, I am feeling very secure doing it all. If this whole thing came crashing down, quite a bit of valuable stuff would be gone. You just have to understand that all this stuff was made from very precious porcelain and crystal.

The ladies then go to the bathroom before setting off for a walk. They don't eat anything during the day, nothing from breakfast till dinner. Dinner is usually at eight o'clock in the evening. Then usually comes the film . . .

And further on, in the same letter, I write that I, too, am doing really, really well:

. . . The day after tomorrow I'll go to Berchtesgaden and will have a haircut. I am planning on a nice, new hairstyle. I am attaching a little photo which is from my identity card. Unfortunately it is really awful. We are now getting a lot of lovely fruit: peaches, cherries, apricots, greengages, just about everything really. Mornings and evenings, I now drink dark brown ale. As for ice cream, we have a whole variety available here. No problem to just go and get one, if one wishes. I had so much of it yesterday that I thought, goodness, I am building up an entire glacier in my tummy.

Warm wishes, Annerl

Let it just be mentioned here that, at the time, nobody took confidentiality quite as seriously as they would do nowadays. So, on 21 August 1941, I wrote the following to my family:

. . . We now have to sign this piece of paper, promising to let nothing of any official nature slip out into the public, nor are we to speak about it among ourselves. But isn't that obvious? We haven't done so until now, in any case . . .

How else did Eva Braun spend her time at the Berghof when Hitler wasn't there?

When she was in her rooms, more often than not she would occupy herself with her dogs. That could take ages. She also had two bullfinches, which were allowed to fly freely around the room, even while we were cleaning it. One of them always got himself caught in the curtains, which was slightly unpleasant, as firstly we would not be allowed to open a window during the cleaning and, secondly, once finished we had to catch these birds and put them back into their cage. Sometimes this was nearly impossible. In those cases we just had to wait until they flew back into their cage by themselves.

Nevertheless I still have to tell you a bit more about our daily routine because I don't want people to get the wrong impression about what it was that was happening during the day at the Berghof.

Of great importance to the ladies, for example, was their afternoon coffee.[41] We had special coffee sets for these occasions, which were hand-painted with a flower design. Really pretty. It was my duty to lay out the coffee table meticulously.

These coffee afternoons often took place in Eva Braun's living room. Frau Schneider was usually there, but Frau Bormann and even Frau Göring certainly never joined in. I wouldn't quite say they felt that Eva Braun was inferior to them, but, from their perspective, they somehow didn't seem suitable.

I can remember Frau Bormann visiting Eva Braun only the one time – for us it came as a surprise, and seemed to be a very precious occurrence. Frau Göring never ever came for coffee.

In any event, at these coffee gatherings, Eva Braun and her companions played cards or Bridge. I still remember that, one time, a certain Professor Breker[42] and his wife, who was Greek, were guests at the Berghof. Breker was considered to be a sculptor par excellence. When it came to art, Hitler's ideals went back to antiquity, so no wonder that he liked Breker's work so much. We had gone to Munich even before that visit of Breker's to the Berghof in order to admire his sculptures at an exhibition.

After coffee, usually walks through the estate would be next on the programme. Of course the dogs joined. The property was huge, as all the farmers who had worked the land previously had been bought out and had moved away.[43] For example, if you walked out of Berchtesgaden and crossed the Salzach bridge, you would have already encountered the first guard of the Berghof to whom you needed to show your pass. On foot it took about twenty to thirty minutes to get from the Salzach bridge to the Berghof. I never managed to walk across the entire estate. The whole area was simply much too big. I did actually know a few houses, such as the guest house, the homes of Göring and Bormann, the Platterhof, which, as far as I know, existed before Hitler bought the Berghof.

And how did staff spend time while Hitler wasn't in residence at the Berghof? There can't have been too much to do.

It was us three chambermaids. My God, what was it we all chatted about? Resi, who was about my age, came from the Berchtesgaden region. And Elfriede was also our age. As time went on, we became rather good friends; having said that, none of us actually had a boyfriend at the Berghof. In this respect we were quite isolated even if we were allowed to go out sometimes, for example to the cinema. Apart from some telephone calls, our contact with the world outside was reduced to writing or receiving letters.

At the time I had a boyfriend called Ruprecht who wrote to me many precious letters. I am not sure whether Resi also had a suitor, but Elfi certainly didn't have one. Overall we spent, in my opinion, quite happy times together. Often we would dance around and sing, even during our work, which we tended to always do together, the three of us. I would often sing 'Mei Mutterl war a Weanerin' or 'Hü-hü, alter Schimmel'[44] and the other two listened to me. In what was called the staff room we would also put on records and dance to the music. Even today I still know the lyrics by heart.

And then I had also been given express permission to play the grand piano in the Great Hall – of course only when there were no guests around. As I had no sheet music with me, I mostly played 'Glühwürmchen'[45] or a different Viennese waltz – so only pieces which I knew by heart.

We really didn't want for anything. It even meant that, when I had to go with Eva Braun to Munich, I would feel homesick for the Berghof. And even beyond that, the time up there was quite eventful for me.

You mentioned your boyfriend Ruprecht before. Who was that?

I met Ruprecht in 1940 in Loosdorf. He was German and had visited friends in Loosdorf. He fell in love with me, but it wasn't the other way round. He had already joined the Wehrmacht when I met him. In any case he had been writing me letters from the front before I had even started my work at the Berghof. But our correspondence continued throughout my stay up there. We wrote to each other very often, but sadly I no longer have his letters.

Ruprecht loved me but I felt quite burdened by this, as I couldn't reciprocate his love. And I also didn't dare write this to him. This type of dishonesty weighed heavily on me. I still remember the poem I sent him for Christmas. It was part of a Christmas present I had sent – a magnificent leather bag containing an entire shaving set in it:

Imagine it were peacetime and you are close to those you hold dear
An opportunity you should not fear,
An opportunity you don't want to miss

but, oh, your beard could interfere with a kiss.
And, since war means fighting and being strong,
your beard will grow so very long.
Just shave it off and once again you'll feel free,
as it surely befits a soldier to be.

Rupp, as I called him, was with the Gebirgsjäger[46] in Russia, in the Caucasus. In one letter he also sent me some drawings he had made of the Russians, and sketches from the front. He wanted me to be able to better empathise with his situation.

That was winter 1941, which was an incredibly cold one. In the end, a short time after that, he was killed in Russia. So I was spared having to be honest with him. And he, in turn, was spared the knowledge that I was not able to return his love for me.

It was immensely sad that Ruprecht and other men had to suffer and die, but in the end it wasn't any of us who could have changed anything. Together with the lady visitors, we sat at the Berghof and our participation consisted only of knitting socks for the soldiers at the front. Saying that, these ladies weren't even capable of getting the heels right. But what else could we have done? Everyone had to fulfil their so-called duty. As for me, I considered it my duty to at least write letters to the soldiers at the front, as I thought it was the only possible way to support and help them. Everyone had to meet their obligations, regardless of what position they held.

My lot was certainly much better than that of many others. It was my destiny to be in Hitler's house. And, to be honest, I didn't feel guilty that my fortune turned out to be so much better. Every morning we eagerly expected the postman, who brought us the letters. We called him 'Zechi' because his name was Zechmeister. 'My God', he always said, 'you don't even know how good you have it here.'

Which event related to Eva Braun are you happy to remember?

Christmas 1941. Full of anticipation, I had written two days earlier to my parents. Reading this letter again, I recognise that already the good life had clearly coloured my thinking.

Just imagine if you will: in the middle of the war, here I am writing to my mother that what I really wish for are vases made out of lead crystal and a hand-painted coffee set. These were items that I held in my hands every single day and which I had obviously come to take for granted. Somehow, up there, I must have lost all connection to the harsh reality of what everyday life was beyond the Obersalzberg.

This Christmas celebration was, in any event, unforgettable. I was so impressed that I didn't even give a single thought to the fact that this would be my first Christmas without my family. It might be best if I read to you some parts of my letter of 27 December, as it probably conveys my impressions best:

… This lovely Christmas period has now passed without me having had the time to reflect that this would be my first time not being able to be at home. Let me describe the celebration: we had to work till four o'clock in the afternoon on Christmas Eve.[47] Then we got ready, dressed up, and at five o'clock the celebration with the guests started in the Hall.

'Silent Night' was sung under the beautiful tree and we all then looked for the spot where our presents were waiting for us. We wished each other and the guests 'Merry Christmas', and thanked them for everything.

This is what I received: a lovely new sewing kit – made out of leather – from the *gnädige Fräulein*. In it were two pairs of scissors and everything else you can imagine. I am sure it must have cost twenty Reichsmark.[48] I also received a travel kit made out of leather; in fact it was a kind of box that you could zip up and where one stores toiletries, such as a clothes brush, hairbrush, comb, a perfume bottle, a soap box, a manicure set, a powder compact and really just any toiletries you might need for travelling. It surely must have cost twenty to twenty-five Reichsmark. Everything is silver-plated.

A different lady, coincidentally, also presented me with a sewing kit. But I will exchange it. Then I also got an absolutely gorgeous silk scarf and a pair of pure silk stockings.

From the Führer I received a fabulous leather writing case, which you can lock. Gretel gave me a case full of beautiful writing paper. From the Führer also came a blue leather handbag and a Christmas and New Year's card, signed by him. This card really gives me the greatest pleasure.

Then I got another fifty Reichsmark. A little basket filled with biscuits and apples. Well, that's it. Isn't that lovely?

After the celebrations we had goose liver and desserts. Later on we celebrated all over again with our own tree. I simply cannot describe how beautifully everything was decorated. There was punch to drink, champagne, pastries, snacks and we danced throughout. At midnight we had canapés and at five o'clock in the morning we had some chicken soup. Yes, that's how long our Christmas Eve lasted. Christmas Day was just as beautiful and went on until one o'clock the next morning. In truth I didn't feel homesick for one minute, even though I did worry about this beforehand . . .

Unforgettable for me was the dress that Eva Braun wore that evening. It consisted of tiny glass pearls and weighed quite a lot. No fabric could be seen. The reason I still remember this so precisely is because it was my duty to get the dress ready for that evening and lay it out properly. On that same evening Eva Braun also presented me with a very beautiful, brown-leather handbag from Paris. I still have the leather handbag, as well as the silk scarf which Frau Schneider presented me with.

It sounds like a very lavish affair for Christmas. Many others didn't have it so good, not even close to it.

And after Christmas it got better still. The ladies and gentlemen left for Munich, meaning that we were at the Berghof on our own, which in this case meant Döhring, his wife, Willi, Gretel and us chambermaids. For us this was the most wonderful time. We had films screened for us, for example *Petersburger Nächte* and *Wunschkonzert*;[49] on top of that, there was no work that had to be done. In the mornings the only things that needed to be done were opening the windows for a bit and turning off all lights for the night. That was it. To be clear we actually didn't do a thing during that period.

But then came spring 1942 and the good life was virtually over.

Yes. Hitler had given the order that staff, as of immediately and like every other German citizen, needed to be provided with food stamps. Until then we really had it extremely good and had received the same food as our guests: tropical fruit and all such things, and everything we got was in abundance on top of that. But in spring 1942 this all stopped. Even the guests had to be provided with food stamps immediately.

I, of course, didn't like this one bit. Until then we had had sausages and cheese for breakfast, and then, suddenly, we just had to make do with whatever there was. We were constantly given orange marmalade, for example, which I really hated. During those times I longingly remembered the smoked meat we used to have at my parents' home. It is for that reason that I started saving up my days off so that I would be able to spend a few days with my parents in Loosdorf at Easter. Making phone calls turned out to be not so easy any more either. Towards the end of 1941 there was a short period during which making phone calls was forbidden. This as well is something I mentioned in one of my letters:

Dear Parents,

In the future I too will have to make more use of my pen. We now no longer have permission to make private phone calls. Apparently the demand on the connections has been too heavy. I myself am not too bothered about it as usually we had little to say to each other anyway. Right, Mother? So I'll just look forward again to your informative letters. We had these girls staying here who made phone calls to all corners of the world. One made daily calls to her boyfriend in Prague. I doubt that this prohibition on calls will last very long though. It just won't work here. If I, therefore, call you again, don't start worrying, as there will certainly be an opportunity which will present itself . . .

There were other cutbacks, and these even had an impact on the ladies of the house. It was, for example, deemed inappropriate to wear fur coats, while our soldiers froze to death in the Russian winter. That's why there was the call for everyone to donate their fur coats so that they could be sent to the front: that was quite a sensitive topic for the ladies and gave them real headaches. Of course the 'regular' people were requested to donate their fur coats to the soldiers at the front, but for the ladies at the Berghof it was a different matter. These coats, we overheard the ladies saying, were much too valuable for the front. For that reason they were simply deposited in the cellar of the house.

During those times, which just got increasingly worse, we still succeeded in making do. In this vein I wrote to my parents very proudly in February 1942 that we had such a lovely time the Sunday before:

. . . In the morning we had some very good coffee with *Gugelhupf*,[50] and for lunch, much to everyone's delight, we had a roast goose with potato dumplings. The cook made 120 such dumplings, and they were all gone by the end. Some actually took a bet as to who would be the one who could eat the most. They always go without having the meat and only eat the dumplings with the gravy, and that's the reason the record consumption of dumplings stands at eleven.[51] I myself can only manage about two and a half . . .

In 1942 you visited your parents in Loosdorf for Easter. What was your reaction?

Here is another story and it needs to be told first. Gretel and Willi knew, of course, that we weren't Nazis. And they were also aware that jealous feelings among certain Loosdorf citizens ran quite high, namely why would the daughter of the 'black' Mittlstrasser, of all people, be working at the Berghof, of all places.

This is also quite obvious in what I had written in one of my letters to my parents: 'Gretel said yesterday that when I go to Loosdorf I should put on make-up and really gloat once I am home. Just to spite those illegal ones.' Gretel, Willi and even Herr Döhring really laughed out loud when referring to how things were in Loosdorf.

Apart from their wheelwright workshop, my parents also owned a small farm in Loosdorf. That's why they actually didn't suffer any food shortage. Speaking about shortages, there was also no shortage whatsoever with respect to their spectacular preconceptions about what my role 'with Hitler' actually involved. To be precise, it all had to do with the son of my parents' maid, who had been killed on the Eastern Front. The maid felt, of course, that us Mittlstrassers were able to 'fix things'. She thought that because both my brothers were alive and I – well I – was 'with Hitler'. I had the impression that she wanted to hold us personally responsible for the death of her son. We could have prevented his death, but didn't do so, is what she must have felt. But even besides that, the Berghof certainly gave rise to quite a few discussions, as in the meantime I had grown accustomed to many things. Furthermore I had had sufficient opportunity at the Berghof to think about what, for example, could be done differently in my parents' household or, for that matter, what could be done better, just like at the Berghof. Why wouldn't I have wanted to have as nice a life as possible in my parents' home. And then people, of course, would comment, saying something like 'mark my words, at the Mittlstrassers' it'll soon look like up at the Berghof'. And they weren't even far wrong, as I pressured my parents into building their own bathroom, as well as a rustic living room, which I have to admit did resemble the one at the Berghof.

Back to Eva Braun. In one of your letters you describe an excursion you made together with Eva Braun and which took you to the Königsee.

The Königsee lies quite close to Berchtesgaden and was a favourite destination for our excursions on our days off. Once, I also went there with Eva Braun and her dogs. Eva was a very keen gymnast and sportswoman. But she also had another hobby, which was photography. In any event, quite a few photos exist showing Eva Braun performing her gymnastic exercises. But these photos probably displeased her, as back at the Berghof she cut them up and threw them into the wastepaper basket. But I picked them out and have kept them to this very day.

There were other pictures as well, which I decided to retrieve from the basket and preserve. These pictures were older, though, and obviously dated back to the time when she worked in the office of Hitler's personal photographer, Hoffmann. In one picture you see her sitting at a desk, and if you look closely you spot in the background written onto the shop window the words 'Photo Hoffmann'.

What was your first personal encounter with Hitler like? When did you stand in front of him, face to face, for the very first time?

Actually it was quite an unexpected moment, shortly after my arrival. I just happened to be in the hallway. Well, hallway might not really be the correct word, as in truth the hallway was actually a hall. A wide staircase led up to the first floor and to the hall, which in turn connected to Hitler's study, his bedroom, to Eva Braun's rooms and our staff room. I still remember every second of that encounter, every detail. The staircase was covered by a thick, heavy, woollen carpet and had a mixed colouring of red, brown and beige. The carpet was woven so tightly that if anybody walked on it you couldn't hear a thing. You actually only heard your own breathing and heartbeat.

I walk up the staircase and in front of me lies this long, wide hall. Opposite the top of the staircase are these massive windows, which spread a sort of unreal light throughout the entire space. On your left are the rooms of Hitler's servants. Doors are locked. I can't see anybody. I walk past the gigantic wooden doors. Rustic doors. They all have wood carvings. The entrance to Hitler's study is at the end of the hallway. I have no idea what I am actually doing here as I had finished my work quite a while beforehand. Suddenly his door opens. Hitler comes towards me. Alone. My heart nearly stopped. He walks straight up to me. What was it again that Gretel instructed us to do? What was it that I am supposed to say? What am I even doing here? I am totally lost for words.

He is about ten metres away from me, but is slowly coming closer. The carpet is so heavy. My footsteps can hardly be heard. The paintings on the wall, which I had previously admired so often, just simply fade past me. Rubens. All originals. Fat, naked women. Thick, golden picture frames. Dazzling splendour. He is wearing a pair of black uniform trousers and a beige–brown uniform jacket. No medals. No frills. A shirt. A tie. His clothing seemed severe, almost exaggerated in how correct it was. I continue walking without saying a word. What am I to say, if he addresses me? I move to the side, feeling embarrassed. Then I look straight at him. He looks at me at exactly the same moment. Totally friendly. What did Gretel say again? '*Heil, mein Führer*'.

'*Heil, Anni*', Hitler says. Calm and so friendly.

Everything moves quickly. I have the impression that he is examining me. At the time my hair was blond and slightly wavy. Somehow the Germanic type. Minutes later I realise that he had called me by my first name.

When I returned home for my first visit, this definitely was my top story. My encounter with Hitler. Full of enthusiasm I tell my parents the whole story, from beginning to end.

How come Hitler knew your name?

I suppose that he had been informed by Gretel or my cousin Willi as to my presence at the Berghof. The minute Hitler departed, I wrote to my parents:

> ... Yesterday, in the newsreel, you could see the Führer once again. That's really
> fun, as I, of course, now know everyone who is in his entourage really well. We are
> all just saying to each other, if only the Boss would return soon, and we all very
> much look forward to that day ...

What was Hitler's room like?

You could reach Hitler's study from the Hall. Next to his desk hung pictures of his parents. To the right was the father, his mother was to the left. You can see this picture clearly on the coloured photographs of the room.

In the middle stood a meeting table, and the back of the room was taken up by a small library. Of course we had to be especially careful when we cleaned Hitler's rooms. Because the Führer always got up late, we always cleaned the study first.

Was he a tidy man? Was he pedantic?

Tidy, yes, this he most definitely was, and maybe one could even call him pedantic. I can still remember being told that he once berated a certain general by the name of Dietl[52] – I think he belonged to the Gebirgsjäger. This general, who had just arrived in the hall, was told off by Hitler right then and there, because – that's how the story goes – the latter had not properly cleaned his boots before entering the Berghof.

But what is there really to clean in a room such as Hitler's study? Nothing. One was hardly able to vacuum, as he always slept in so late. So we just had to limit ourselves to making sure that the tables and telephone were properly dusted.

Was Hitler's desk untidy?

No, everything was kept completely tidy. Hitler had, of course, three servants, and that's why there was hardly anything for us to do. Certainly his bedroom was a different matter. Here we had to clean his bathroom and make his bed. But, hold on a minute*... there was something else in his study – just look. I still have some blotting paper that belonged to Hitler. He used it when he was signing documents. His signature is still clearly recognisable. When I tidied up his desk, it was just lying there. I simply thought to myself that, on some level, this too is a kind of a document, so I kept it. As it was my duty to keep his desk clean, I felt that clearing away an old piece of blotting paper was sensible.

I probably included it in a letter that I then sent to my parents, otherwise I would probablty not have it any more, seeing that more than sixty years have now passed.

And what was the state of Hitler's bedroom?

What I recall is a very simple bed. Realising that Hitler slept using only a simple quilt and not a duvet surprised me even at the time. Eva Braun, for example, slept with a heavy duvet. A book by Wilhelm Busch[53] lay on his night table.

In front of his bed stood his slippers, which I often happily tried on. I can't even quite figure out why I did this – it must have been that I just wanted to feel what it was like to be 'in the Führer's shoes'. I also tried on his caps, which of course were too big for me – as were the slippers. And then there was the

---

* author's note: Mrs Plaim leaves the room, walks onto her veranda and brings back a folder, from which she takes some documents. Proudly she lifts up some blotting paper.

bathroom with the bath, a washbasin and a set of weighing scales, which I also used practically every day. Despite letters being censored, I wrote home that I had gained one kilo. I wrote that I would have been quite sure about this, seeing that I weighed myself every day on the Führer's scales. And then, as well as these areas, there was the so-called suitcase chamber, a small room via which one reached the room of Eva Braun.

Did Hitler have a single bed or a double bed?

He had a simple single bed. A totally plain single bed.

And Eva Braun?

Her bed was larger. You could also turn her bed into a sofa, which then looked precisely like a sitting-room couch.

Did Hitler spend the night in Eva Braun's room or sleep in his own bed?

It is difficult to quite understand this. In fact nobody really ever knew where he slept. This subject has also been broached in a ZDF documentary. Gretel mentioned there that Hitler slept, of course, in Eva Braun's room or with Eva Braun, as she had herself been requested to go to the pharmacy and buy medications[54] that would delay Eva Braun's cycle.

Döhring, however, put this whole issue in a different light. But as mentioned before, he never really referred to Eva Braun in a very positive way. I never could actually understand that. And it was quite clear to Willi that the two of them 'had something going'.

Were you checked or observed while you cleaned Hitler's rooms?

When Hitler was in residence at the Berghof, we had to wait until he and his entourage had left to walk to the teahouse I referred to earlier, and which was within the boundaries of the grounds. So while he was away from the house, we had to tidy up his rooms. Usually it was the two of us – sometimes, though, it was only me. On his desk stood a very pretty box filled with inviting pralines, and I eyed them every day. One day I actually started [sic] to spoil myself and take one. That continued every day until I realised that I had actually tucked away nearly all the pralines and that the box was nearly empty. Suddenly it occurred to me that perhaps this was actually a trap – testing whether the staff were actually honest people. The house of the criminal police was situated right next to us and, besides, we actually weren't that busy. So I just stopped having these nibbles and simply left the box untouched. One day Döhring burst into the room when I was dusting the desk. He took the box which was nearly empty, examined it closely and looked me in the eyes. I got frightened, as I had thought that he had now caught me. Suddenly he said: 'Anni, just remove this stupid thing. It has been standing here for ages.' I was just so immensely relieved. Döhring was clueless. Later that day, with a completely clean conscience, I polished off the rest of the sweets. And I still have the box today.

The box, of course, now looks very tatty, as I had been using it for more than twenty years to store my sewing stuff. It is woven raffia. Sometime in the 1960s, it sort of dawned on me where I actually had this box from. Ever since I have kept my sewing stuff somewhere else. This of course doesn't change the sad look of this box.

Tell us more about your cousin Willi. Can you still remember some special incidents in which Willi was involved?

He once told me a story that I thought was totally believable. Hitler had given Willi the order that he was no longer to serve even a single bottle of champagne. Regardless of who might be requesting it.

A general approached Willi, as the story goes, who desired a bottle of champagne. Willi, however, refused to give him one, without thinking he had to tell him the reason. The general was quite furious and became aggressive. Only then did Willi explain to him that the Führer had ordered that no more champagne was to be served. Shortly thereafter the Führer called for Willi. Of course Willi was quite nervous and felt uncomfortable, as he thought that the general had complained about him and that he would now be told off. But something quite different took place. 'Mittlstrasser', said the Führer to him, 'one day you will hold a position where no general can ever give you orders.'

How should one understand that?

It was always said that Hitler had planned to embark on huge expansions at the Berghof after the expected victory had been achieved. Willi would have been one of those candidates who would have been given a suitably important position.

One might say though that your cousin was far from enthusiastic about the outbreak of the war. The Russian Campaign seemed to have bothered him in particular.

Everyone was very shocked at the Berghof when the information came in that the war was now going to start in Russia. 'They can get lost, as far as I am concerned', said Willi, 'this is all about money.' I suspect that he thought that he could lose everything he had built up for himself based on an inflation, which a Russian war might trigger. As soon as the Russian Campaign had started, the Berghof was plunged into depression.

In your hometown, much has happened as well. For many Hitler followers in Loosdorf, your occupation at the Berghof was a thorn in their side.

Ever since I started work at the Berghof there were constant reports against me being made to the Obersalzberg Kripo. The criminal police had their station right next to us. It was called Haus zum Türken. The Kripo had shown Willi these reports and he then told me later that once again the Loosdorf police had made a report against me. The reason they gave was always the same one: my family did not come from a National Socialist background. Or, more precisely, I came from a 'black' family. But Willi took care of all this. He must have explained to the Kripo that these reports were meaningless and they then simply threw them away.

One of these reports must have landed one day on Bormann's desk. Apparently your cousin Willi knew nothing about that.

I will never forget that day. Totally out of the blue I was suddenly called to see Reichsleiter Bormann. I had just been working in the wing with the guest rooms and had been making up beds. I neither had a bad conscience nor a bad feeling when I was told to see Bormann. Relaxed, I stood in front of him, but then it all of a sudden hit me that this was going to be serious. He was on his own, was wearing his uniform, and his eyes had a stony look. As per usual, I greeted him with '*Heil Hitler*', to which he responded with only a dry '*Heil*'. This was followed by a tense silence. Slowly he lifted his head and said: 'I have been informed that you come from a religious family. From a Catholic family. Your father is a church-goer.' I still hear the 'church-goer' ringing in my ears, as he pronounced the word with such a disparaging emphasis. 'We cannot tolerate this. You are to leave the Berghof immediately.'

I was appalled. I had felt so secure in my position. Shortly after having left Bormann's office, Eva Braun called for me. 'Anni, what was it that Reichsleiter Bormann wanted to see you about?'

'He ordered me to leave the Berghof immediately, because my father is not a Nazi and is a devout Catholic.'

There was no mistaking Eva Braun's reaction. 'I am calling the Führer headquarters immediately. You work for me, and I simply will not have someone behave like this towards me. You are my employee. Mine.'

And shortly thereafter Eva Braun called me to come to her yet again. 'The Führer has told me that I have to do as Bormann says. I am sorry.'

My work at the Berghof was terminated with immediate effect. The next morning I went about packing my suitcase and travelled by train to Vienna, where I stayed for a while with my uncle Josef Gruber. I was really embarrassed having to return to Loosdorf. Constantly my thoughts went back to the time of my arrival at the Berghof – to the time I had left Loosdorf with my pretty leather suitcase and my chic clothing. Back then I had packed my suitcase days earlier. More than just anxious, I was actually curious as to what was in store for me. That day I had gone to the railway station by foot, after having said my goodbyes at home, to my father, mother and my brother Hans. It was my mother who had cried most. I also had a really hard time saying farewell to our dog, a Scotch Terrier called Rolfi, whom I had loved dearly.

Now, leaving the Berghof, I packed that very same leather suitcase and put on the same chic dress I had worn on my arrival. First, I took my leave from Eva Braun in her room.

'I am so sorry, Anni. What will you do now?' she said. She stretched out her hand to me, sad and helpless.

After that I went to the small parlour where us chambermaids always sat together with the Döhrings. I said goodbye to Resi and Elfriede. Traudl Christek, my successor, had already arrived. Döhring, his wife Anni and their small children all said goodbye to me with tears in their eyes. I really had a hard time bidding farewell to Gretel.

Finally, it was time to say goodbye to the kitchen staff and . . . last but certainly not least to Eva Braun's dogs. Goodbye. This last goodbye is what I thought of when I left Loosdorf. The dog. That's what made it really difficult.

'Get in', Willi shouted.

Willi took me to Salzburg in exactly the same car as I had arrived in, and in which Döhring had his auspicious accident. We drove to the railway station.

How did your colleagues at the Berghof react to your dismissal at the Berghof?

Decades later Döhring vented his anger in a ZDF interview. He was so incensed that his voice actually cracked. What really infuriated him most was that I wasn't enough for Bormann, while my brothers were in the Wehrmacht and the Air Force, laying down their lives for Germany every single day. Döhring, of course, knew my brother Franz, who during the war had been an Air Force sergeant in Sicily. Franz was always so proud that his little sister was allowed to work in such close proximity to Hitler. He even came to visit me one time. He was the only one whom Döhring permitted to freely move around within the premises. My brother was even given permission to visit my room.

With that, was the chapter of the Berghof closed for you?

No. I still remained in constant contact with my relatives up there, and with the chambermaids as well. I continued writing letters to all of them. I even received the kind regards of Eva Braun. She wanted me to know that both her dogs had had puppies and that she would send me one. Soon afterwards I was informed that I should come to the railway station in Melk, where a wooden crate containing a dog had arrived – a small bitch. I still have the receipt in my possession. Staff at the station in Melk had already become quite friendly with the young dog and, at first, they didn't really even want to hand her over to me. But, of course, they knew who had sent her. The sender's details were clearly legible and it said 'Berghof Obersalzberg'.

I named the dog 'Stasi', after her mother. The minute I set eyes on the dog, my joy knew no bounds. She looked so incredibly adorable. My parents as well were really excited. I brushed and combed her daily, and looked after her really well. Just as I had done with her parents, up at the Berghof. It was part of my duties, to look after Eva Braun's dogs. Together with the dog, a small piece of the Berghof had come back to me. Many memories. My Stasi then had puppies herself. But they were not pure breds, as one day our neighbour's dog had jumped through the grids on the window of our house.

When I got married in 1948, I moved into a new flat with my husband. Stasi remained in my parents' house, as our flat was much too small to accommodate a dog. Although I visited Stasi often, it saddened me that I could not have her with me all the time.

In 1957, when she had become old and mangy, my husband and I decided to have our vet put her to sleep. I actually couldn't even think about this, and on the day it took place I put myself on a train to Vienna, just so that I would be far away from it all. The Loosdorf vet, Dr Heindl, gave Stasi an injection and buried her in the garden of the house where he had his clinic. It's exactly that house which my husband and I then bought from my aunt in 1960. This means that today I live in the house where my Stasi has been put to rest.

Why didn't you stay in Vienna after being dismissed from the Berghof, instead of returning so soon to Loosdorf?

I had actually intended to remain in Vienna and look for some work. But my parents felt that they needed me at home where there was plenty to do. Germany's situation in the war turned increasingly more worrying. Even ardent National Socialists at that time began losing their previously unshakeable belief in final victory. In fact people in Loosdorf became ever more friendly the closer the front moved towards our hometown. When in need, people seem to stick together. When the end of the war loomed, everyone helped each other – regardless of whether they had previously been 'black' or 'brown'. There was, for example, this man who had been my father's guard when he had been locked up in the pub just after the annexation. He had been a stringent Nazi. My father had known him many years before the annexation, but then politics came into the paths of human beings. In Loosdorf as well.

But when the Russians advanced towards us at the end of the war, the tide suddenly turned: my father's erstwhile guard came to him in order to find protection from the Russians. As my father had himself been locked up by the Nazis, there was this thought that my father had nothing to fear from the Russians. So my father just hired this previous guard in his wheelwright workshop. That's what happens when there is need – human beings become closer to each other. At the time there was widespread fear that horrendous things would happen once 'the Russians' arrived.

Weeks before the war ended, thousands of refugees would, on a daily basis, pass by the front of our house, which was right on the main road, along with their horses carrying their only belongings.

The refugees came from the Banat[55] and were incredibly poor. It was truly a disturbing sight. Once those endless throngs of refugees had passed, the next lot was just behind them. This time it was soldiers on retreat. There were Austrians among them too, those living in districts close to Vienna, who all were fleeing from the Russians. And finally it was the SS who were retreating. They were feared to the extreme, as they were hunting for deserters. Some people I knew were, in actual fact, shot by the SS.

In 1944, by the way, I saw for the first time with my own eyes inmates from the KZ. A canal was being dug behind our house. The workers assigned to the job were six or seven men, dressed in blue-and-white-striped rags; they were KZ inmates. They looked bad. One really had to pity them. I pinched some cooked potatoes and handed them to the inmates through the fence. At first I thought nothing of it, giving them something, but the guard who was on duty discovered and became quite angry with me.

In any event there was an underground munitions factory close by.[56] What exactly was produced there escapes my knowledge. But we had known since about 1940 that KZ inmates were being deployed[57] there. In Melk there even was a dedicated crematorium.

What are your thoughts today about the mass murder of Jews, minorities and political enemies of the Nazis?

Shortly after visits to Auschwitz were allowed, I travelled there with my husband Karl. Even today I see the enormous glass display cases in front of my eyes, where mounds of dentures were piled up high, masses of hair, mountains of glasses. One just cannot imagine what it means when human beings are robbed of everything – and I mean everything.

I saw the label on one suitcase and it was from a Jewish man from St Pölten, so he came from really close to where I was from. I was utterly devastated after this visit. I saw the barracks, the places where they burnt the bodies, and the gas chambers. During my time at the Berghof the people were euphoric, giddy with the sense of victory. Nobody could have imagined that this war would one day be lost.

Most people knew nothing about the extermination of Jews as it was brutally executed in Auschwitz. Of course nobody could fail to notice the extreme hounding of Jews that took place, of human beings in general, who had been distinguished and respected people before the war. Nobody can claim today that they didn't know. Many Jews, also from the Loosdorf area, had to leave their home. Many were chased from their homes.

But what actually happened to these people in their final hours, those facts were never ever known to me at the time. I also think that Eva Braun didn't realise what in truth was happening in the concentration camps. I am sure that she, as well as many others, must have seen that Jews and those who opposed the Nazis were mistreated. Pictures of how human beings were being crammed into freight trains like cattle we saw only after the war.

Today I cannot understand the fascination I had for Hitler at the time. His speeches, the enthusiasm which so many – me included – felt when he was screaming and barking, when he was smiling and gesticulating wildly. I don't know. I simply cannot understand why so many people were so enthralled.

What was your personal way of dealing with the impending doom of Hitler's Reich? As we know, the front kept drawing nearer to your hometown.

One of my friends, whose name was Lilli, was very worried and came to me. Her husband wanted her to flee at once because the Russians, so they were told, dealt with women most brutally – they were said to rape women.

'You can come with us', she said, 'we are going by car and we will bring meat and sausages along from our butcher's shop. Come with us. You worked for Hitler. Who knows what the Russians will do with you once they get wind of this.'

This was to be a difficult decision for me, but I decided not to leave. Lilli fled to Gmunden.[58]

Some days later another car arrived at our doorstep, with some soldiers and civilians. There, among them, sat Tilli, my favourite cousin, and she too tried to convince me to leave. All that was quite dramatic. I was standing next to my mother while the car was parked right outside our door with its engine still running. And once again I decided to stay. Maybe it had to do with the fact that I was extremely close to my parents. But, in any case, I ended up remaining in Loosdorf.

Then, finally, the SS left as well, but not before blowing up the two long bridges crossing the nearby river Pielach. This actually concluded the retreat of the army. And, as for us, we only waited to see what would come next – the invasion of the Russians.

And how did this Russian invasion turn out?

At first I heard only a dull, still rather soft rumbling that steadily grew louder. And then we saw the first tank. I immediately hid where I had always sought shelter even as a child: I crept into a gutter between two roofs. From there I could hear the tanks, but after a few hours I wanted to know more. So I moved forwards and carefully peered over the roof edge down to the main road – an endless column of tanks was right underneath me. Suddenly I noticed that a soldier in one of the tanks had been observing me. He stopped immediately and came into the house. That put an end to my secret hiding spot.

I ran away but still managed to see, from where I was on the main street, how one of my friend's fathers – a respectable businessman filled with desperation – took a gun and desperately shot at the Russian soldiers. I observed how the Russians overpowered him. They then killed him, by tying him to the tank and dragging him along for kilometres. I was still running for another fifty metres or so until I reached the house of another friend. We were three girls there and another girl from the neighbourhood then joined us. For the time being we were safe in that house.

But suddenly the Russians came bursting in and ordered all women in the house to walk to the bridge that had been blown up in Neuhofen.[59] So we all marched to this bridge. It must surely have been ten o'clock in the evening by the time we finally reached it. They told us that we had to rebuild the bridge. What nonsense. In the end we just stood around, frightened that this all was but a cheap pretext to round up the women.

After a while we all just started going home. For some reason, not a single Russian gave us a second thought. That's when the big hideout began.

And what was that like for you?

We spent the first night on the floorboards of this friend's place. It was a large factory with hiding possibilities that you would expect from such a building. We felt safe there initially. The following day this friend's mother even brought us breakfast. We just stayed up there. Nothing could possibly happen to us, we thought. Suddenly, however, we heard a big noise and cars – and Russian being spoken. This factory of all places was being confiscated and Russian soldiers would be moving in.

Obviously the problem was that we had nothing more to eat, as the mother of this friend could not look after us without risking our hiding place being discovered. As time went on, the whole situation became rather bizarre.

When my friend's mother had the time, she would always take the dog for a walk in the courtyard and pretend to have a conversation with it, which of course we could overhear. This is how it sort of went: 'Rolfi, can you imagine, they have now raped two women again.' This is how we were informed about these horror stories, via these 'dog-conversations'. The solution was that our food was wrapped into a bag, attached to a rope and then drawn up when the Russians weren't in the building. We must have been hiding there for about a week.

At my own house we already had Russian officers garrisoned, to whom my mother had already confided that we had hidden. These officers were, therefore, prepared that we would be returning in the foreseeable future and they assured our mothers that nothing untoward would happen to us. On some level they also meant some sort of protection for us. We nevertheless worried continuously about where we should be spending the night. Sleeping at home seemed to be too dangerous in everyone's eyes. Sometimes I stayed overnight with Frau Haselmayer, the widow of our cobbler. She was Czech and was therefore able to communicate with the Russians. After several weeks things calmed down and the situation was much safer, and there were no more rapes.

But for yourself things would be hotting up once more, as in the meantime the Russians had found out where you had been working previously.

For this I need to first tell you a short story. Our neighbour, a Social Democrat, became the new mayor of Loosdorf after the war. One evening he came to my father and told him that somebody had reported me to the Russian general, because I had 'worked for Hitler at the Berghof'. Later on I was told that the report had been made by the very same people who had reported me previously to Bormann on the Obersalzberg. Well, that's life.

So this would fit one of those rehearsed lines that 'We aren't big Nazis, but we have one who has worked at Hitler's'?

I don't even want to think about the reasons why people kept reporting me. The fact remains that, after the Russians came, most people just stuck together. Or let's just say that most of them did. The biggest Nazi of our town even came to my 'black' father and hoped that my family would protect him. These people were terrified. Some even committed suicide after the Russians had entered. One family I knew totally wiped itself out. Among the many who chose this particular option was the senior consultant of the Melk hospital.

What transpired after you were reported to the Russian general?

Our neighbour, the mayor, took care of it. He made an appointment with the general, explained to him in detail what this report was all about, and vouched for me. He told them that they could leave me in peace seeing as we actually weren't Nazis, and apparently this was sufficient. I never had to justify myself to the Russians with regards to this report.

One last question: what was your reaction when you heard that Eva Braun and Adolf Hitler did, in fact, get married at the end of the war? And, more importantly, what was your own take on their suicides?

I actually cannot remember how or where I was informed that Hitler and Eva Braun were dead. I suspect that I must have heard it on the radio. The news that both had died in the bunker didn't come as a big surprise to me, seeing that the Russians were already very close to Berlin. It was much more of a surprise to hear that Hitler did, in fact, marry Eva Braun – something that had been her deepest wish. That's what she dreamt about during her happy days, but of course she hadn't been able to make this a reality at the time. As far as I know, Hitler had not wanted her to come to Berlin at the end of the war. It was her wish to do so. Just as much as it had been her wish long ago to become Hitler's wife. I suppose that she must have known that the price she would have to pay to reach her goal was her life itself. She was prepared to die for and with Hitler.

And the Berghof? What information did you receive about the final days of the Obersalzberg?

Quite a lot. My cousin Willi told me all about it. Hitler had planned to take refuge at the Berghof at the end of the war. But at that point everything up there had been bombed to bits by the Americans. It was only the SS who stayed put. But, according to Willi, the situation even then was so dramatic that the SS men no longer trusted each other. And apparently this distrust grew so much that some simply started to defect. By the end, the rest of the SS men also departed.

Only Willi remained, along with Gretel and their son Klaus, who had been born in 1942. They were the only ones who actually witnessed the final days of the Berghof.

Were you sorry about the death of Hitler and Eva Braun?

No. The misery Hitler brought to this world makes me not regret his death for one second.

Endnotes

1   For the Kehlstein Haus, see endnote 39, p.147.

2   In Germany and Austria, *gnädig* (gracious) was a common way for staff to address their employer, but it would also be used between people addressing each other and belonging to the same, higher social class.

3   Situated within the Berchtesgaden Alps in the municipality of Schönau am Königsee, just south of Berchtesgaden and the Austrian city of Salzburg, the Königsee is Germany's third deepest lake.

4   Reichsleiter Martin Bormann took over a house owned by a local doctor named Seitz. This house site was ideal for Bormann, as it overlooked Hitler's Berghof and much of the rest of the Obersalzberg complex. From here, Bormann could keep an eye on everything, including the comings and goings at the Berghof. Bormann later enlarged and modernised the house, installing costly interior furnishings. He also had an extensive air-raid shelter and bunker system built into the hill behind the house, connecting it to the main air-raid control and communications centre underground. The April 1945 bombing attack substantially destroyed the house.

5   Kurt Kuch (10 August 1972 – 3 January 2015) was an Austrian investigative journalist who in 2011 received the 'Journalist of the Year' award from the industry magazine *Der Österreichische Journalist*. He was very well known for his investigative reports for the weekly magazine *NEWS* and for his books revealing secrets and scandals of public interest.

6   Loosdorf is a little town in the district of Melk in the Austrian state of Lower Austria.

7   Plaim uses the German expression *auf die Walz gehen*, which refers to the old tradition of an apprentice travelling for several years after completing his apprenticeship as a craftsman.

8   Stellmacherei is the workshop of a wheelwright, who makes wheels, carts and other agricultural equipment made of wood. The name of the profession differs regionally between Switzerland, Austria and Germany.

9   From 1868 to 1936 the Deutsche Turnen-Bund (DT; German Gymnastics Federation) was the umbrella organisation of the gymnastic clubs in Germany. Although it was based on the philosophy of educator Friedrich Ludwig Jahn (nicknamed Turnvater Jahn) (11 August 1778 – 15 October 1852), it never saw itself just as a sporting organisation, and always had a political national component.

10 The Christian Social Party of Austria (CS or CSP) was a party in Austria–Hungary and the First Austrian Republic. By using the name Christian it wanted to express opposition to Judaism, which it believed represented exploitative economic liberalism. Since conservatism came from the Christian milieu and was associated with priests who wore black, the movement's political 'colour' thus established itself.

11 Hans Georg Fritzsche (21 April 1900 – 27 September 1953) was a journalist who presented a weekly radio programme entitled *Hier spricht Hans Fritzsche* (Hans Fritzsche speaking) in 1923. In 1932 he was appointed Head of the Telegraphic News Service, a government agency. When in 1933 the Nazis incorporated this service into the Ministry for Propaganda, Fritzsche became a member of the National Socialist party and joined the Ministry. In 1938 he became Director of the Ministry press section, which had control

over some 2,300 daily newspapers. In November 1942 Fritzsche was promoted to Chief of the radio broadcasting service of the Ministry for Propaganda and was present at the daily briefings, which Goebbels held with his collaborators.

12   Döhring, as we read earlier in this book, was Hitler's housekeeper, but would sometimes take on other duties involving driving an official car.

13   Steyr was an Austrian car make, established in 1915 as a branch of the Österreichische Waffenfabriks-Gesellschaft (ÖWG) weapon manufacturing company. Renamed Steyr-Werke AG in 1926 and merged with Austro-Daimler and Puch into Steyr-Daimler-Puch AG, it continued manufacturing Steyr vehicles until 1959. During the Second World War this make, especially in a cabriolet version, was designed primarily for Nazi Germany's high-rank commanders and officers.

14   The official pass that Anna refers to was issued on Martin Bormann's order. All staff and guests allowed in the Führersperrgebiet were duty-bound to carry their identification pass on them at all times.

15   The *dirndl* is the name of a woman's dress worn in Austria, South Tyrol and Bavaria. It is based on the traditional clothing of Alpine peasants. It consists of a bodice, a low-cut blouse with short puffy sleeves, full skirt and apron. The colour, cut and pattern variations usually indicate a specific area in which that *dirndl* is worn.

16   Imi was from 1929 onwards a universal cleaning product made by the Henkel Works.

17   Part of the business of the propaganda machine at the time was to communicate as much as possible about Hitler and his life at the Berghof in an attempt to portray him as a modest man of the people, a lover of children, of nature and animals, as a man of good but modest and bourgeois taste, as a boss who was kind to his staff and as a hospitable and generous host to state visitors. Picture postcards, many produced by Heinrich Hoffmann, of Hitler and the Berghof abounded.

18   The *Arbeitsbuch* (workbook) was a document issued by state authorities, which was compulsorily handed over to an employer on recruitment. The aim was to control the occupational mobility of workers and make their new employment dependent on the approval of the former employer. After 1935, when it was introduced for all workers, the workbook was also an instrument of economic mobilisation for the preparation of the four-year plan by Göring. It comprised a thin booklet in A6 format with thirty-two pages.

19   German accents vary between regions, and sometimes they are so drastically different that people from one region don't understand those from another. As for Hochdeutsch (High German), generally, people of the higher social classes originating from Bavaria (e.g. from Munich) or larger Austrian cities (e.g. Vienna) speak what is referred to as the highest sociolinguistic variation, which is used in the media and for other formal situations. It does not have a specific accent and is now used in Germany, Austria and Switzerland. In less formal situations, Austrians tend to adopt forms closer to or identical with the Bavarian and Alemannic dialects. Thus, Schuschnigg would have spoken in Hochdeutsch, but his Begleitkommando would have probably used a dialect.

20   Kripo is short for Kriminalpolizei (criminal police).

21   This game 'Alles was Federn hat fliegt' is similar to the English children's game 'Simon says'. It is a game where the loser of a round has to pay a forfeit, such as standing on one leg for one minute.

22   Referring to black people as negroes was at the time common in Germany and Austria. It did not necessarily imply that Anna's comment was particularly racist. However, the situation of the black community at the time was precarious. The everyday life of blacks in Germany was characterised by exclusion and 'racial' persecution. In the regulations and commentaries on the Nuremberg Laws, it was stipulated that blacks were excluded from the Reichsbürgerschaft. From 1939 schools prohibited 'Mischlinge'. Some blacks were imprisoned in concentration camps because of 'racial hygiene'. When in 1943 all plans for the recovery of the former colonies in Africa were officially revoked, the situation of blacks in Germany deteriorated further.

23   *Im Toten Winkel* (Blind Spot) is a ninety-minute interview with Traudl Junge, the last personal secretary of the Third Reich dictator Adolf Hitler. Urged to tell her story by her friend, Austrian author Melissa Müller, Junge agreed to make a documentary with André Heller, an Austrian director and artist, some of whose Jewish family members died in Nazi death camps. Two excerpts from this interview, including the introduction and conclusion, are featured in the film *Der Untergang*, which itself is partly based on *Until the Final Hour*, Junge's memoirs about her experiences with Hitler, written in 1947, but not published until 2002.

24   The Obersalzberg was bombed by hundreds of British RAF Lancaster heavy bombers, which attacked the Berghof on 25 April 1945, five days before Hitler committed suicide in the Führerbunker and twelve days before the surrender of Nazi German military forces (to the Western Allied nations) on 7 May. At least two bombs successfully struck the Berghof and did considerable damage to the main building. On 4 May, four days after Hitler's suicide in Berlin, retreating SS troops set fire to the villa.

The Berghof's shell survived until 1952, when the Bavarian government demolished it with explosives on 30 April. The Berghof, the houses of Göring and Bormann, the SS barracks, the Kampfhäusl and the teahouse were all destroyed. This had been part of an agreement under which the Americans handed the area back to the Bavarian authorities. There was fear that the ruins would become a neo-Nazi shrine and tourist attraction.

25   Hitler provided Eva Braun and her sister with a three-bedroom apartment in Munich that August, and the following year the sisters were provided with a villa in Bogenhausen at Wasserburgerstrasse 12 (now Delpstrasse 12).

26   In Austria, there are several ways for women to obtain the title of doctor: (a) by achieving it based on university studies; (b) if a woman is married to a man who has a doctor-title, she automatically assumes the title as well; (c) Austrians tend to have their title or academic degree included in their passports and a master ('Magister') degree is often written before the name. Most titles are used instead of a name when referring to a person directly, either in person or in writing – for example 'Herr Magister' or 'Liebe Frau Doktor'.

27   Franz Xaver Schwarz (27 November 1875 – 2 December 1947) was an accountant who was appointed treasurer of the NSDAP in 1925. He overhauled the Party's finances and raised money for the publication of Hitler's book, *Mein Kampf*, that same year. In 1930 Schwarz negotiated the purchase of the Brown House, the Party's headquarters at Briennerstrasse 45, Munich.

28   Performed together, these two one-act operas – *Cavalleria Rusticana* by Pietro Mascagni and *Der Bajazzo* (aka *Pagliacci*) by Ruggero Leoncavallo – demonstrate how love of opera

thrives well beyond aristocratic circles.

29   Haile Selassie (23 July 1892 – 27 August 1975), born Tafari Makonnen Woldemikael, was a member of the Solomonic Dynasty. From 1916 to 1930 he was Ethiopia's regent, and then was crowned emperor. He westernised the institutions of his country and took it into the League of Nations. He played a crucial role in the establishment of the Organisation of African Unity; he was its Chairperson from 25 May 1963 to 17 July 1964 and again from 5 November 1966 to 11 September 1967.

30   The Leo pills, famous for their magical laxative effects at the time, were purely herbal and had no known negative side-effects. Numerous people consumed them daily – not to treat constipation but to lose weight.

31   Both Martin Bormann and Heinrich Himmler were fiercely anti-Christian, agreeing that National Socialism and Christianity are irreconcilable. Out of political expediency, Hitler intended to postpone the elimination of the Christian churches until after the war. However, his repeated hostile statements against the Church indicated to his subordinates that a continuation of the *Kirchenkampf* (Church struggle) would be tolerated and even encouraged. Bormann was one of the leading proponents of the ongoing persecution of the Christian churches, decreeing that members of the clergy should not be admitted to the NSDAP. As part of the campaign against the Catholic Church, hundreds of monasteries in Germany and Austria were confiscated by the Gestapo, and their occupants were expelled.

32   *Marterl* in Austria or southern Germany are wayside shrines each with a crucifix, usually as a memorial to an accident or as a place for travellers to pray for a successful journey. The word derives from *Marter* (torment), referring to the Passion of Christ.

33   Built in the Wilhelminian style, Hotel Dreesen was part of the Bad Godesberg development as a spa and tourist town for the rich. It is still run by the Dreesen family and has been an premier venue for VIPs from politicians to artists, such as Queen Silvia of Sweden, Dwight D. Eisenhower, Bruno Kreisky, Valéry Giscard d'Estaing, François Mitterrand, Javier Pérez de Cuéllar, Andreas Papandreou, Gustav Stresemann, Mikhail Gorbachev, Henry Kissinger, German Chancellors and many German ministers, Greta Garbo, Charlie Chaplin, Danny Kaye, Herbert von Karajan and Yehudi Menuhin.

34   After the First World War, the map of Europe was redrawn and several new countries were formed. However, when Adolf Hitler came to power, he wanted to unite all Germans into one nation. In September 1938 he turned his attention to the three million Germans living in the part of Czechoslovakia called the Sudetenland. Sudeten Germans had begun protests and provoked violence from the Czech police Hitler claimed that 300 Sudeten Germans had been killed. This was not actually the case, but Hitler used it as an excuse to place German troops along the Czech border. In an attempt to resolve the crisis, the British prime minister, Neville Chamberlain, flew to meet Hitler at his mountain retreat in Berchtesgaden.

35   Blutorden (Blood Order) was one of the most prestigious decorations in the Nazi Party. One side of the medal bore a depiction of an eagle with a wreath in its talons; on the reverse was a picture of the Munich Hall where the 1923 coup had ended in defeat, a swastika and the inscription: *UND IHR HABT DOCH GESIEGT* ('. . . and you were victorious after all'). The award was given to people who had (a) served time in prison for Nazi activities before 1933; (b) received a death sentence which was later commuted to life imprisonment

for Nazi activities before 1933; or (c) been severely wounded in the service of the Party before 1933. Subsequently, it was further extended to members of the Austrian Nazi Party who had participated in the 1934 February Uprising or July Putsch, or who had received a significant prison sentence or injuries for National Socialist activities. Obviously, Frau Dreesen felt that she had 'been severely wounded or received injuries in the service of the Party'.

36 The legend is that the 'Türkenhäusl' was named after a veteran returning from a war against the Turks in 1683. Local innkeeper Karl Schuster bought the Haus zum Türken in 1911 and converted it to a guest house. He was a somewhat outspoken critic of the Nazi takeover of the Obersalzberg, since this ruined his business, and he joined the majority of his neighbours who were forced to sell to the Nazis and leave the area in late 1933. The building was first used by the Führerbegleitkommando (FBK), Hitler's personal bodyguard. Bormann later assigned the building to the Reichssicherheitsdienst (RSD), the high-level Security Service responsible for Hitler's safety. In practice, the ex-hotel served as a headquarters for the round-the-clock SS guard detachment, and was also a telephone communications centre. Prisoner cells were maintained in the basement, above the bunker system, which was connected to Hitler's, Göring's and Bormann's private bunkers.

37 Turtle soup was invented in Great Britain in the eighteenth century and soon became a exotic delicacy for the upper middle classes in Europe.

38 Blue Tuesday is Anna's play on words and refers to Blauer Montag, or *blaumachen*. In small and artisan companies in German-speaking countries it was customary to 'only work with half the strength' on a Monday. To 'make blue' (*blaumachen*) is a common German term for idleness in general or absenteeism in professional life.

39 When Anna refers to the 'estate', she means the Führersperrgebiet, which was the area cordoned off around the homes of Hitler and the other SS leaders and which was guarded by SS posts. After the Nazis took over the Obersalzberg, the original Platterhof (a small hotel where Hitler had stayed in the early 1920s) was remodelled, and a larger multi-wing hotel erected around the original building; it was still known as the Platterhof. This was supposed to be a national people's hotel, where the common people of the Third Reich could stay when visiting their Führer, but in keeping with Martin Bormann's increased seclusion of the area around Hitler's Berghof, the Platterhof never served that purpose.

40 Kraft durch Freude (KdF; Strength through Joy) was a large state-operated leisure organisation in Nazi Germany. It was a part of the Deutsche Arbeitsfront (DAF; German Labour Front), the national German labour organisation at that time. Established as a tool to promote the advantages of National Socialism to the people, the KdF soon became the world's largest tourism operator of the 1930s. It was supposed to bridge the class divide by making middle-class leisure activities available to the masses.

41 The gatherings in the afternoon in German-speaking countries were mostly around coffee (cf. the British teatime).

42 Arno Breker (19 July 1900 – 13 February 1991) was a German architect and Nazi-supported sculptor who created public works endorsed by the authorities as the antithesis of degenerate art. In 1937 Breker joined the Nazi Party and was made 'official state sculptor' by Hitler. While nearly all of his sculptures survived the Second World War, almost all his public works were destroyed by the Allies after the war.

43 Whilst Anna is correct in remembering that the farmers were forced to move away, their property was bought up by Bormann and Hitler at the market price or above. However, if owners would not sell willingly, they were forced to do so.

44 'Mei Mutterl war a Weanerin' (My mother was a Viennese woman) is a song in Viennese dialect praising the mother, with a (waltz) three-four time, and 'Hü-hü, alter Schimmel' is another Austrian song with a happy tune.

45 Glühwürmchen (Firefly) from the operetta *Lysistrata* by Paul Lincke (7 November 1866 – 3 September 1946), who was a German composer and theatre conductor and considered the 'father' of the Berlin operetta. He has the same significance for Berlin as does Johann Strauss for Vienna and Jacques Offenbach for Paris. His well-known compositions include 'Berliner Luft' ('Berlin Air'), which became the unofficial anthem for Berlin.

46 The Gebirgsjäger (Mountain Forces) is the part of the German armed forces specially trained and equipped for battle in difficult terrain and under extreme weather conditions.

47 In German-speaking countries, Christmas celebrations start on 24 December.

48 With twenty Reichsmark in 1941 you would be able to purchase goods worth approximately €80 today.

49 *Petersburger Nächte* (Petersburgh Nights) is a 1935 film written and made by Jewish film-makers Grigori and Serafima Roshal whilst *Wunschkonzert* (Request Concert) is a 1940 German drama propaganda film by Eduard von Borsody. After *Die grosse Liebe*, it was the most popular film of wartime Germany, grossing the second highest box office receipts.

50 *Gugelhupf* is a light, yeasted marble cake, traditionally baked in a distinctive circular Bundt mould. It is popular in a wide area of central Europe, including southern Germany, Austria, Switzerland, Slovakia, Czech Republic, Poland and Alsace.

51 Dumplings in Austria and Germany are usually rather big, some 4–5 centimetres in diameter. They can be filled with vegetables (e.g. spinach) or minced meat – or with stewed plums or apricots.

52 Eduard Dietl (21 July 1890 – 23 June 1944) commanded the 20th Mountain Army on the northern Eastern Front. A convinced Nazi and one of Hitler's favourite generals, he was the first German soldier to receive, on 19 June 1940, the oak leaves cluster to the Knight's Cross of the Iron Cross. On 23 June 1944 Dietl was killed in an air crash in Austria.

53 Heinrich Christian Wilhelm Busch (15 April 1832 – 9 January 1908) was a German humorist, poet, illustrator and painter, often considered to be the 'Forefather of Comics' or 'first virtuoso of illustrated stories'. He published comic illustrated cautionary tales from 1859 onwards, and his most famous is *Max and Moritz* – a book mostly read to and by children even today. His work is replete with cruelties both to people and animals, couched in forthright verse, with taunts, derision, ironic twists, exaggeration, ambiguity and startling rhyme – as well as some anti-semitic references.

54 The 'medication' which Gretel must have purchase was a contraceptive pill. As well as promoting motherhood, the Nazis restricted abortion and contraception. During the 1920s Germany led the world in the development of contraceptive devices, including condoms, diaphragms and intra-uterine devices (IUDs). But the Nazis outlawed contraception – not only to increase the birth rate but also because many pioneers of contraceptive medicine were Jewish. Even publicising or discussing birth control was eventually banned in Nazi Germany. Propaganda described abortion as a 'crime against the body and against the state'.

Conversely, doctors would approve abortions – and, indeed, even encourage them – if the patient happened to be non-Aryan. In November 1938 a Nazi-run state court ruled that abortion should be legal and freely available for all Jewish women.

55   The Banat is a geographical and historical region in central Europe and was under Nazi occupation 1941–4. Nazi Germany had been intent on expanding into eastern Europe to incorporate what it called the Volksdeutsche (people of ethnic German descent). It established the political entity known as Banat in 1941. This included only the western part of the historical Banat region, which was formerly part of Yugoslavia. Following the ousting of Axis forces in 1944, this German-ruled region was dissolved.

56   The concentration camp at Mauthausen with its munition factories (e.g. in Gusen) was only one hour's drive away from Loosdorf.

57   Anna uses the word *einsetzen*, which can be translated as '. . . KZ inmates were being used, engaged, deployed, employed'; in fact, particularly in Mauthausen, the inmates were worked to death.

58   Gmunden in Austria is a 1½ hours' drive from Loosdorf. During the occupation, the US troops built a spy centre to watch over the Soviet Union. It also hired many former SS people, for their knowledge of the Soviet situation. At the beginning of May 1945, Gmunden was handed over to the Americans without a fight.

59   It is not quite clear which bridge Anna refers to.

Part 4

The Rise and Fall of
Adolf Hitler – In Brief

1918

The end of the First World War also means the end of imperial Germany and Austria. According to the peace treaties of Versailles and Saint-Germain-en-Laye (subsequently signed in September 1919), both countries have to cede territories to the victorious powers. The Danube area is split into a number of small countries. It is, above all, German-national factions who want to reverse these territorial losses. Many Austrians think that their future is to become part of Germany, but the peace treaties forbid an annexation.

1919

January: The Deutsche Arbeitspartei (DAP; German Workers' Party) is founded by Anton Drexler, a locksmith.
September: Adolf Hitler joins the DAP and becomes its fifty-fifth member.
16 October: Hitler's makes a memorable speech in the beer hall of the Münchner Hofbräuhaus.

1920

24 February: Hitler announces the twenty-five-point Party Programme in front of 2,000 people. On the same day, the Party is renamed the Nationalsozialistische Deutsche Arbeiterpartei (NSDAP; National Socialist German Workers' Party).

1921

3 February: Hitler's first speech at the Circus Krone, Munich's biggest venue. Entitled 'Future or Ruin', it denounces reparation payments to the Allies. Some 6,000 people attend. What follows are mass demonstrations; thus the NSDAP becomes a known entity throughout Germany.

1923

9 November: The Beer Hall Putsch, also known as the Munich Putsch, is a failed coup attempt by the new leader of the Nazi Party leader, Adolf Hitler. About 2,000 Nazis march to the centre of Munich, where they confront the police, resulting in the death of sixteen Nazis and four police officers. Hitler and his fellow conspirators are arrested.

1924

24 February: The trial for high treason against Hitler, Wilhelm Frick, Hermann Kriebel, Erich Ludendorff, Ernst Röhm, Rudolf Hess and three others begins.
1 April: Hitler and Hess are both sentenced to five years in *Festungshaft* (literally fortress confinement) in Landsberg am Lech. *Festungshaft* was the mildest of the three types of jail sentence available in German law at the time; it excluded forced labour, provided reasonably comfortable cells and allowed each prisoner to receive visitors almost daily, and for several hours. Here, Hitler writes the first part of *Mein Kampf*.
20 December: In the end Hitler served only a little over eight months of his sentence before his early release for good behaviour. During his internment, Hitler makes the decision to reach power via legal means.

1928

20 May: Federal elections held in Germany. The NSDAP wins 2.8 per cent of the votes and twelve seats in the Reichstag.

1930

14 September: In the Reichstag elections, the NSDAP succeeds in gaining 18.3 per cent of the votes and 107 seats.

1932

The Sturmabteilung (SA; the NSDAP's paramilitary wing) and the Schutzstaffel (SS) are banned for their radical nature. The NSDAP finds success in state elections in Prussia, Bavaria, Württemberg and Hamburg. In Mecklenburg, Oldenburg, Anhalt and Thüringen the National Socialist state governments now come into power.

4 June: German President Paul von Hindenburg dissolves the Reichstag and calls for a Presidential Cabinet to be formed.

31 July: Federal elections are held, following the premature dissolution of the Reichstag. Great gains by the NSDAP, which for the first time becomes the largest party in Parliament. Reich President Hindenburg rejects Hitler as Reich Chancellor.

6 November: In the federal election, the Nazis lose many seats, with the NSDAP having its number of seats reduced to 196.

1933

4 January: As a result of negotiations, Franz von Papen supports Hitler's nomination as the new Chancellor of Germany by the end of the month.

22 January: President Hindenberg is persuaded to appoint Adolf Hitler as Chancellor.

30 January: Hitler is sworn in as Reich Chancellor.

27 February: Fire at the Reichstag. Decree of the Reich President for the Protection of People and State issued by German President Hindenburg on the advice of Chancellor Adolf Hitler.

24 March: With the Enabling Act, Parliament grants the government extraordinary powers, violating the principle of the separation of powers.

1 April: Boycott against Jewish shops and businesses. This is the first time the regime moves against Jewish citizens in an organised fashion. A little bit later all Jewish civil servants are dismissed from government positions.

17 May: Unions and parties are dissolved and prohibited. Germany becomes a one-party state.

19 June: Prohibition of the NSDAP in Austria.

1 December: The Law for Securing the Unity of Party and State establishes an insoluble bond between the state and the NSDAP.

1934

January to April: Based on several laws, *Reichsstatthalter* are established in order to gain direct control over all states. Their independent state governments and parliaments are successively abolished, and the Reich government takes over direct control in a process called *Gleichschaltung* (coordination).

June to July: Fear of a socialist revolution, unification of the Reichswehr and the SA leads to the murder of the SA leadership, including the SA chief Ernst Röhm, followed by the liquidation of other political enemies. Concerned with presenting the massacre as legally sanctioned, Hitler has the cabinet approve a measure on 3 July declaring that 'the measures taken on June 30, July 1 and 2 to suppress treasonous assaults are legal as acts of self-defence by the state'. This will later be known as the Night of the Long Knives.

25 July: The July Putsch is a failed coup d'état against the Austrofascist regime by Austrian Nazis, which takes place 25–30 July. SS men disguised as Bundesheer soldiers and policemen push into the Austrian Chancellery. Chancellor Dollfuss is killed by two bullets. The assassins Otto Planetta and Franz Holzweber along with five of their conspirators are executed following a rushed court hearing.

2 August: A referendum on merging the posts of chancellor and president led to the approval of Adolf Hitler's assumption of supreme power.

1935

15 September: The Nuremberg Laws introduced by the Reichstag at a special meeting convened at the annual Nuremberg Rally refer to the Law for the Protection of German Blood and German Honour, which forbids marriages and extramarital intercourse between Jews and Germans, and the employment of German females under forty-five in Jewish households; the Reich Citizenship Law is also introduced, which declares that only those of German or related blood are eligible to be citizens of the Reich. Furthermore, Jews are prohibited to work in certain professions.

1936

7 March: In violation of the Treaty of Versailles, Germany reoccupies the Rhineland.

11 July: July Agreement between Germany and Austria to rebuild friendly relationships.

1937

November: Primary goal of the National Socialists is to gain *Lebensraum*, so Hitler reveals his plans for war.

1938

12 February: Austrian Chancellor Dr Kurt Schuschnigg meets Hitler in his Berghof residence in an attempt to smooth the worsening relations between their two countries. Hitler presents him with a set of demands which, in manner and in terms, amounts to an ultimatum, effectively demanding the handing over of power to the Austrian Nazis. The terms of the agreement, presented to Schuschnigg for immediate endorsement, stipulate the appointment of Nazi sympathiser Arthur Seyss-Inquart as Minister of Security, who controls the police. Another pro-Nazi, Dr Hans Fischböck, is named as Minister of Finance to prepare for economic union between Germany and Austria.

11 March: Schuschnigg holds talks with the leaders of the Social Democrats, and agrees to legalise their party and their trade unions in return for their support of the referendum. To no avail. Hitler first insists the plebiscite be cancelled. Hitler demands Schuschnigg's resignation, and for Seyss-Inquart to be appointed his successor. Schuschnigg resigns.

12 March: German troops march into Austria.

15 March: Hitler appears at the Heldenplatz in Vienna.

29 September: The Munich Agreement permits Nazi Germany's annexation of portions of Czechoslovakia along the country's borders mainly inhabited by German speaker.

9 November: Polish–German Jew Herschel Grynszpan mortally wounds German diplomat Ernst vom Rath. A pogrom against Jews throughout Nazi Germany follows as retaliation is carried out by SA paramilitary forces and German civilians. The name *Kristallnacht* comes from the shards of broken glass that littered the streets after the windows of Jewish-owned stores, buildings and synagogues were smashed. Some 100 Jews are murdered. Jews are forced to pay a fine of one billion Reichsmark. Jewish lawyers and doctors are barred from working for non-Jewish clients.

1939

16 March: The Protectorate of Bohemia and Moravia is established, following the German occupation of the remainder of Czechoslovakia.

22 May: The Pact of Steel specifies a military and political alliance between the Kingdom of Italy and Nazi Germany, known formally as the Pact of Friendship and Alliance between Germany and Italy.

23 August: Germany and the Soviet Union sign the German–Soviet Non-aggression Pact, in which the two countries agree to take no military action against each other for the next ten years. The Pact was a crucial precondition to the subsequent invasion and destruction of Poland, by German and Soviet forces.

1 September: German troops invade Poland, which has concluded an agreement with the United Kingdom. Britain and France declare war on Germany two days later.

21 October: Agreement between Hitler and Mussolini to resettle the German population of South Tyrol.

1940

The Tripartite Pact, a treaty of the German Reich on the initiative of Hitler with the Empire of Japan and the Kingdom of Italy (27 September), redefines the new order of Europe and East Asia and secures military cooperation. Hungary, Romania, Slovakia, Denmark, Finland, the Reorganized Republic of China (referred to as Nanjing), Bulgaria and Croatia join the Pact later on.

May–June: The Western campaign sees the occupation of Belgium, the Netherlands and large parts of France, including Paris.

22 June: Ceasefire of Compiègne: France is divided into an occupied zone and an unoccupied zone.

1941

22 June: Start of the Russian Campaign: Romania, Slovakia and Hungary join the war.

1942

20 January: At the Wannsee Conference the mass murder of Jews, as already tested in Poland since the end of 1941, is decided. To this end, a number of concentration camps are turned into extermination camps, or newly built. Jews from all parts of the Nazi-occupied territories are brought there in Sondertransporte. Names

such as Bełzec, Sobibór, Treblinka and Auschwitz illustrate the mass murder of millions of Jews.

1943

2 February: German troops capitulate in Stalingrad.

18 April – 16 May: The SS put a brutal end to the Warsaw Ghetto Uprising. It is the first time Jews rise up against what is certain death in the extermination camps.

13 May: German and Italian troops capitulate in northern Africa.

25 July: Mussolini, 'Il Duce', is deposed and arrested, but liberated two months later by the Germans.

1944

20 July: Claus von Stauffenberg and other conspirators attempt to assassinate Adolf Hitler inside his Wolf's Lair field headquarters near Rastenburg, East Prussia. Approximately 200 conspirators are arrested and, under Himmler's new *Sippenhaft* (blood guilt) laws, all the relatives of the principal plotters are also arrested.

1945

4–11 February: The Yalta Conference with Stalin, Winston Churchill and Franklin D. Roosevelt takes place, with the intention of discussing Europe's post-war reorganisation.

28 April: German army capitulates in Italy. Mussolini attempts to flee to Switzerland and is shot by partisans.

30 April: Shortly after Hitler and Eva Braun marry, they both commit suicide in the Berlin Bunker. In his political testament, Hitler assigns Admiral Karl Dönitz to the position of Reich Chancellor.

9 May: German Wehrmacht capitulates.

23 May: Dönitz government is dissolved. Dönitz is arrested.

Brief Biographies

Rudolf Hess

Hess was born on 26 April 1894 in Alexandria, Egypt. After attending schools in Egypt, Switzerland and Germany, and after an apprenticeship in a trading company, he enlisted in an artillery regiment. After the First World War, and during his studies in Munich, Hess joined the Thule Society, an anti-Semitic, right-wing group, one of many such organisations active in Germany at the time. He made the acquaintance of Adolf Hitler in 1920 and immediately joined the NSDAP (Membership No. 16). After the failed Munich Putsch in 1923, both men were incarcerated in Landsberg Prison, where Hitler soon began work on his memoir, *Mein Kampf* (My Struggle), which he dictated to fellow prisoner Hess. Hess then became one of Hitler's closest confidants, and his private secretary. During the Party crisis of 1932, Hess took over from Gregor Strasser, who had been defeated by Hitler in the earlier elections, and was responsible for several departments, including foreign affairs, finance, health, education and law. All legislation passed through his office for approval, except that concerning the army, the police and foreign policy. His biggest career jump turned out to be his appointment by Hitler as the Führer's deputy.

Hess above all was completely devoted to Hitler and thus became an important part in establishing the unrestricted ruling power of the Führer. Additionally, as of 1933, Hess was a member of the Reichstag and was appointed to the cabinet with the post of Reich Minister without Portfolio. At the outbreak of the Second World War, he had reached the pinnacle of his career. Hitler then appointed him as his second deputy, after Hermann Göring.

In spite of undeniably holding huge power, Hess receded into the background as the Nazi regime increasingly consolidated its power. It was Martin Bormann who was partially responsible for sidelining Hess from the affairs of the nation and from Hitler's attention; Bormann had successfully supplanted Hess in many of his duties and usurped his position at Hitler's side. Bormann did so entirely conscious of the power this would yield him. Already, by 1939, the role Hess played within the National Socialist state was reduced to one of being a mere representative. Then on 10 May 1941 a spectacular event took place that for ever placed Hess in the annals of history. Seemingly without any official order or authority from Hitler, Hess – a licensed pilot – flew to Scotland and parachuted down into enemy territory in order to hold peace talks with the United Kingdom. Hess was subsequently declared by the National Socialist regime to be mentally ill. He was held as a prisoner of war until the end of the war, first in the Tower of London, then at Mytchett Place in Surrey and eventually in the Berlin-Spandau prison. During his imprisonment, Hess, who was considered mentally unstable, with tendencies towards hypochondria and paranoia, attempted to commit suicide.

Hess was tried in Nuremberg in 1946 and was found guilty on two counts: crimes against peace (planning and preparing a war of aggression), and conspiracy with other German leaders to commit crimes. He was sentenced to life imprisonment, even though Winston Churchill expressed his doubts with respect to his sanity.

From 1966 onwards Hess became the only prisoner in the Berlin-Spandau prison, which was guarded by the four occupying powers. Even after Stalin's death, the Soviet Union rejected the possibility of Hess being pardoned. This, in turn, allowed him to become a 'martyr' in radical right-wing circles. After spending so long in solitary confinement at Spandau, the ninety-three year old finally committed suicide on 17 August 1987.

Theodor Morell

Theodor Morell was born on 22 July 1886 in the small village of Trais-Münzenberg in Upper Hesse. Being a son of a teacher, he at first began a teaching career but then changed to start his medical studies in 1907. In 1914 he settled in the vicinity of Offenbach and worked as a general practitioner, but was drafted the following year into the army. However, being considered unfit for service, he was dismissed, so began to establish himself in Berlin as a reputable specialist in urology. He was very quickly able to count among his patients some prominent members of Germany's capital city. His first appointment with Adolf Hitler was in 1936, and the latter was so enthralled that he nominated Morell as his private physician. Even though Morell owned his own clinic, he nevertheless accompanied the dictator everywhere between 1939 and April 1945. His therapy for Hitler was determined by bacteria of the intestines, hormones and vitamins. During the last three years of attending Hitler, Morell must have prescribed at least ninety-two different medications and gave Hitler more than 1,000 injections. Morell also devised Hitler's dietary regimes. For his mushroom diet, a special mushroom cultivar was planted on the Obersalzberg.

Just shortly before Hitler's suicide, Morell left Berlin to travel to Bavaria, where he was captured by American forces. In 1947 he was deemed not sufficiently fit to be imprisoned, and he died on 26 May 1948 in Tegernsee. Morell, who was not considered to be politically motivated, was extremely successful in using his position as Hitler's personal physician to his own advantage. As of 1943, he had built up a pharmaceutical empire, which began spreading across the entire German Reich. He was also a partner in the Nordmark pharmaceutical company based in Hamburg and in a private research lab in Bayerisch Gmain, which Hitler had given him as a present.

Martin Bormann

Martin Bormann was born on 17 June 1900 in Halberstadt and was the son of a post-office employee. After dropping out of formal school education, he went to work on a farm in Mecklenburg. Bormann joined the *Freikorps* organisation and was sentenced to a year in prison as an accomplice in a murder case.

After joining the NSDAP in 1927 Bormann quickly rose to the top. He began duties as regional press officer, and soon put his organisational skills to use as business manager for the Gau (region). After the NSDAP seizure of power, he was appointed chief of staff in the office of Rudolf Hess, the Deputy Führer, on 1 July 1933. Bormann also served as personal secretary to Hess from 4 July 1933 until May 1941. Hess's department was responsible for settling disputes within the Party and acted as an intermediary between the Party and the state regarding policy decisions and legislation. While Hitler was in residence at the Berghof, Bormann was constantly in attendance and acted as Hitler's personal secretary. In this capacity he began to control the flow of information and access to Hitler. During this period Hitler gave Bormann, who also oversaw the finances of all the Gau- and Reichsleiter, control of his personal finances. After the flight of Rudolf Hess in 1941 to Scotland, Bormann became his successor as Head of the *Parteikanzlei* (Party Chancellery). In this position he was responsible for all NSDAP appointments, and was answerable only to Hitler. He was continuously eager to solidify the Party's position vis-à-vis the Wehrmacht and the SS.

Bormann, an atheist, waged a particularly fanatical fight against the Christian Church. Nobody among the staff at the Chancellery on the Obersalzberg was permitted to belong to any religious group. Bormann was invariably the advocate of extremely harsh, radical measures when it came to the treatment of Jews, the conquered eastern peoples and prisoners of war. He signed the decree of 31 May 1941 extending the 1935 Nuremberg Laws to the annexed territories of the east. Thereafter he signed the decree of 9 October 1942 prescribing that the permanent Final Solution in Greater Germany could no longer be solved by emigration, but instead only by the use of 'ruthless force in the special camps of the east', that is, extermination in Nazi death camps.

Bormann was extremely savvy in knowing how to strengthen his position within the Party, and he did so by always being kept informed (even about departments which were not under him) as well as being at Hitler's every beck and call. Clinching his career was management of the construction on the Obersalzberg. He was literally given free rein and he ruled with an iron fist, affording him the nickname the 'Lord of the Obersalzberg'. Even his family felt his thirst for power. He and his wife had ten children and he didn't shrink from whipping them with his riding whip.

As 'Secretary' to Hitler, Bormann's power and effective reach broadened considerably during the war. Nearly every document addressed to Hitler went across his desk. It was he who decided what Hitler would see with his own eyes. He had already pre-typed rejection letters for unwelcome requests.

Thanks to his sense for intrigue, he knew fully well how to eliminate those who competed with him for the Führer's favour and became, above all during the last years, Hitler's closest confidant. When Hermann Göring made moves, just before the war ended, to take over power in case Hitler was taken prisoner or died, Bormann accused Göring of high treason and tried to convince the Führer to believe this. After Hitler's suicide, Bormann left the bunker complex to fly to the Obersalzberg. He and several others had been ordered by Hitler to leave Berlin, 'and to put the interests of the nation above their own feelings'. On 2 May 1945, during his escape from Berlin, Bormann was killed.

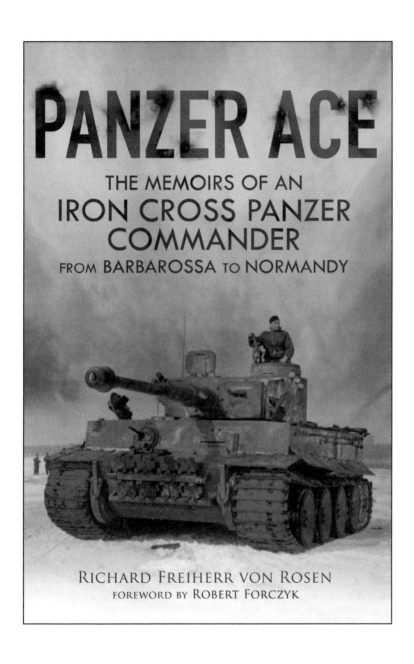

PANZER ACE

THE MEMOIRS OF AN
IRON CROSS PANZER
COMMANDER
FROM BARBAROSSA TO NORMANDY

RICHARD FREIHERR VON ROSEN
FOREWORD BY ROBERT FORCZYK

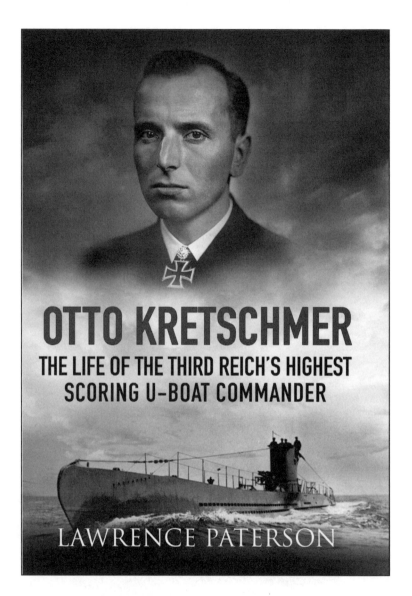

OTTO KRETSCHMER
THE LIFE OF THE THIRD REICH'S HIGHEST
SCORING U-BOAT COMMANDER

LAWRENCE PATERSON

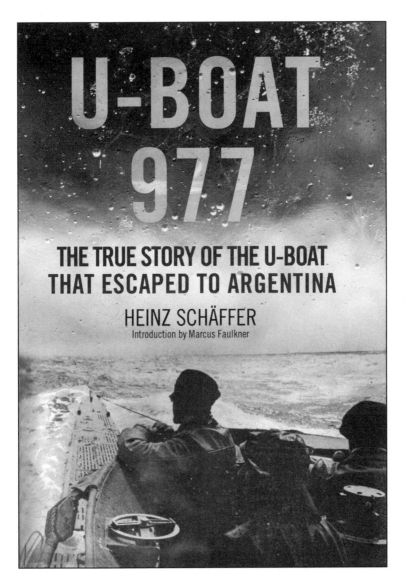

U-BOAT 977

THE TRUE STORY OF THE U-BOAT
THAT ESCAPED TO ARGENTINA

HEINZ SCHÄFFER

Introduction by Marcus Faulkner

DUEL
UNDER
THE
STARS

THE MEMOIR OF A
LUFTWAFFE NIGHT PILOT
IN WORLD WAR II

WILHELM
JOHNEN

Foreword by JAMES HOLLAND

Archibald McIndoe and the RAF in World War II

The

GUINEA PIG
CLUB

Emily Mayhew

Forewords by
HRH The Duke of Edinburgh _&_ HRH Prince Harry

HITLER'S
BRANDENBURGERS

THE
THIRD REICH'S
ELITE SPECIAL FORCES

LAWRENCE PATERSON

FOREWORD BY DAVID R. HIGGINS

LADY DEATH

THE MEMOIRS
OF STALIN'S SNIPER

LYUDMILA PAVLICHENKO

Foreword by Martin Pegler

GLADIATORIA

MEDIEVAL ARMOURED COMBAT

Dierk Hagedorn & Bartłomiej Walczak

Foreword by Sydney Anglo

THE
SECRET
SOUTH

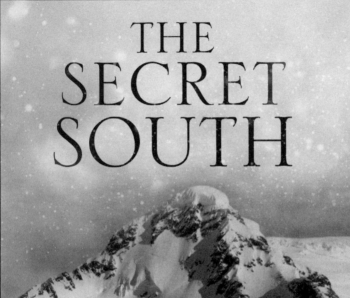

A TALE OF
OPERATION TABARIN
1943-46

IVAN MACKENZIE LAMB
EDITED BY
STEPHEN HADDELSEY AND RONALD LEWIS-SMITH

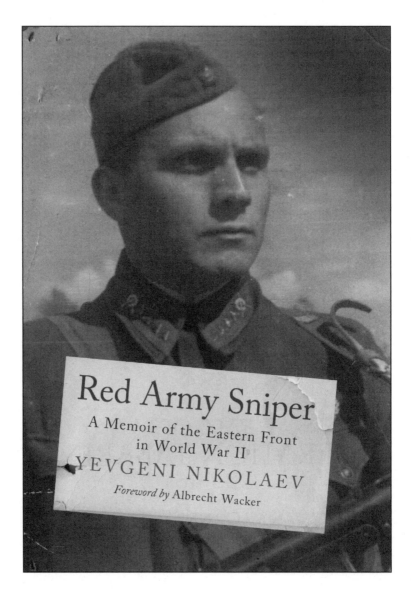

Red Army Sniper

A Memoir of the Eastern Front in World War II

YEVGENI NIKOLAEV

Foreword by Albrecht Wacker